THE ARCHITECT
OF THE
ROMAN EMPIRE

THE ARCHITECT
OF THE
ROMAN EMPIRE
27 B.C. – A.D. 14

BY

T. RICE HOLMES
HON. LITT.D. (DUBLIN); HON. D.LITT. (OXON.); F.B.A.

OXFORD
AT THE CLARENDON PRESS
1931

OXFORD UNIVERSITY PRESS
AMEN HOUSE, E.C. 4
LONDON EDINBURGH GLASGOW
LEIPZIG NEW YORK TORONTO
MELBOURNE CAPETOWN BOMBAY
CALCUTTA MADRAS SHANGHAI
HUMPHREY MILFORD
PUBLISHER TO THE
UNIVERSITY

PRINTED IN GREAT BRITAIN

PREFACE

THIS volume, a continuation of one published in 1928 with the same title, but dealing only with the period 44–27 B.C., is the writer's final historical work. Though I had already collected much material, it could not have been written without help; for since 1927 I have been too crippled to go to the British Museum, and many books which it was necessary to consult are not in the library of the Hellenic and Roman Societies. Miss Margaret Alford, whose generous offer I gratefully acknowledged in the preceding volume, has amply fulfilled her promise, not only checking innumerable references and, when it seemed to her necessary, supplying the words or the substance of what was referred to, but also spontaneously making extracts from books which she thought that I might find useful, never complaining if they were not required, and reading again passages which I suspected that she might have partly misunderstood or transcribed without the necessary context. Her help was especially valuable for the legislation of Augustus relating to marriage and for the appendices which I have written on the *ludi saeculares*, the site of Aliso, and the site of the Varian disaster. The use that has been made of it might have been less unworthy of such devotion if this book had not been written by an invalid who had just recovered from an illness, and whose sleep has often been broken by discomfort or pain.

Let me thank another helper. After the manuscript was sent to Oxford it was read by Mr. Hugh Last. Besides pointing out a few mistakes and omissions which had escaped my revision, he directed my attention to various articles which I had not read, because, being a cripple, I was unable to consult Bursian's *Jahresbericht*, and which are referred to on pages 76 n. 1, 89 n. 1, 129 n. 1, 178.

Mr. George E. Buckle[1] has observed that readers are 'divisible into those who welcome foot-notes as a necessary convenience and those who detest them as an irritating

[1] *The Times*, Nov. 29, 1930, p. 15, col. 5.

distraction'; and though there is perhaps a small third class—those who placidly ignore them—a writer anxious at any cost to achieve popularity might be influenced by the maxim of Macaulay: 'It is not by his own taste, but by the taste of the fish that the angler is determined in his choice of bait'. But since readers whom I have been so fortunate as to attract know that it is possible to combine foot-notes and even appendices with vivid narrative, I have adhered to the practice which I believe that they approve; for, though I agree with Professor Trevelyan that 'the same book should make its appeal both to the general reader and the historical student', I would add, holding that questions of evidence ought generally to be excluded from narrative, 'not always the same pages'. Even in writing the history of the Indian Mutiny, the evidence for which is as complete and credible as there is for any history, I was obliged to devote appendices to proving the truth of certain statements; and, as I remarked in *Caesar's Conquest of Gaul* (2nd edition, p. xiv), a writer who deals with ancient history is at a disadvantage compared with one whose period falls within more recent times.

I may repeat a note subjoined to the Preface of the preceding volume: 'General readers, who have no use for mere citations of authorities, will not, I hope, neglect those foot-notes which contain more. I suggest, however, that the best plan would be to read the narrative first from beginning to end without looking at foot-notes, which might be reserved for later reading. To the few who not only desire truth, but wish to satisfy themselves that it has been discovered, they and the appendices may be useful; to others, I trust, inoffensive.'

1 AKEHURST STREET,
    ROEHAMPTON, S.W.15.
        February 14, 1931.

CONTENTS

PART I

CHAPTER I

CHAPTER III

CONTENTS

PART II

LIST OF MAPS

[The maps of Gaul (in *Caesar's Conquest of Gaul*, my edition of Caesar *De bello Gallico*, and *The Roman Republic*, vol. ii), of Italy (in *The Roman Republic*, vols. i and iii), and of Asia Minor (in *The Roman Republic*, vol. i) might be useful to readers who possess or have access to any of those books.]

THE ARCHITECT OF THE ROMAN EMPIRE

CHAPTER I

'AUGUSTE', says Camille Jullian,[1] 'est l'homme du passé qui échappe le plus à notre analyse.' Perhaps the eminent historian, without laying stress upon the idea of analysis, meant simply that we could not hope to understand Augustus as we understand Cicero, who could hardly write or speak without self-revelation, and that the personality of Augustus is more enigmatical than any other that belongs to history. That is perhaps true; but a measure of useful knowledge may be attainable. What is the secret of re-creating an historical character? If it is of minor importance, a brief statement by a trustworthy observer may suffice. 'Inglis', said an officer [2] who had served under him throughout a critical period of Indian history, 'Inglis was a dense, stupid, ignorant man: still he *was* a man.' A vivid piece of characterization, which sums up all that the historian needs to know about the personality of a soldier who did not deserve oblivion. But some may object to such judgements that they are disputable, and may think that surer results are to be obtained from statement of facts, selected and arranged by an historical artist, whose object would not be to analyse, not to impose upon the reader his own conception, but so to present the characters with which he is concerned that they might reveal themselves as far as they were worth revealing. What a man did, what he thought, if one can ascertain it, what he wrote or, as a statesman or a legislator, caused to be written, what were his aims, what he said— learn all this, present it artistically, rejecting the unimportant, and the character will live. Sometimes even what was said to him may be helpful: 'You never forget anything', said Cicero [3] to Caesar, 'except injuries'. A noble trait revealed in a brief sentence by the witness who, avowing that he had watched with delight the assassination

---

[1] *Hist. de la Gaule*, iv, 1913, p. 53.
[2] The late Lieut.-General McLeod Innes, R.E., V.C., in conversation with the writer.   [3] *Pro Ligario*, 12, 35. Cp. *The Roman Republic*, iii, 292.

B

of the Dictator, lamented that he had not himself been one of the assassins.[1]

How far can a student of the Augustan Age attain these requisites ? It is true that, as a scholar [2] who has done much to make up for the shortcomings of the ancient historians observes, they often failed to record details about the improvements whereby Augustus so reformed the administration of the provinces as to make their inhabitants contented; but their failure does not affect our conception of his character. Nor does the lack of military history, properly so called, which forces us to be content with a bare outline of the important operations in Dalmatia, Pannonia, the Alpine region, and Germany, and with the knowledge that Tiberius, if he was not a great general, was a great organizer of commissariat. Materials of the kind that has made it possible to describe the relations between Caesar and Cicero so vividly that both are recognizable as really human beings are, indeed, wanting. Still, the student will find that information is tolerably abundant, even including letters which were obviously sincere; and if at the end of his researches he agrees with Jullian, he will probably conclude that in the nature of Augustus there was something inscrutable, and that, even if the lost autobiography should come to light, it might appear that the writer would not let himself be intimately known.

His historical significance may be fully appreciated. But if the personality of Augustus baffles psychological inquiry, one may still hope to estimate his historical significance. The initial difficulty is to find a pathway through the incomplete and disjointed historical materials. Studying the thirteen years in which Octavian was struggling to establish his position, one found the events grouped naturally as the outline of a drama. But, passing to the forty years during which, after he was called Augustus, he was designing the imperial structure, a student intent upon writing history may at first despair of being able to construct even a coherent narrative. Little by little, however, after mental digressions and retrogressions,

[1] *Att.*, xiv, 14, 4; *Fam.*, x, 28, 1. Cp. *The Roman Republic*, iii, 343, 351–2.
[2] Sir W. M. Ramsay (*Expositor*, Nov., 1912, p. 387).

he finds a way for himself through the maze, and ventures
to hope that others will consent to follow him.

The records of the Emperor's career show that, as might
have been divined, he had much work in contemplation at
the time of his settlement with the Senate.[1] Measures
which his adoptive father had been prevented by the
assassins from attempting—the development that must
follow the conquest of Gaul, the safeguarding of the
frontiers on the Danube and the Rhine, the exaction of
atonement from the Parthians for the humiliation they had
inflicted upon Roman pride—these demanded accomplish-
ment. How was Augustus to reconcile with them the
reduction to manageable proportions of his army, for
which eventually the pensions that had been lacking under
the Republic must somehow be provided ? By what precautions could the efficiency of the reduced force be combined with its obedience ? Much forethought would be
required to secure the just government of the provinces.
Egypt, which must ever be the principal source from
which Rome should be fed, presented problems inherited
from the Ptolemaic dynasty. Irregularities, which demanded correction, had crept, under the exigencies of the
civil wars, into the administration of the coinage. The
reform of provincial government would involve the
creation of an imperial civil service. The establishment
of regular postal communication, which Tiberius Gracchus
had begun,[2] must be completed; and to that end it was
essential to keep the Italian and the provincial roads in
constant repair. It was to this aim that Augustus first
applied himself after the foundation of the Principate.
Observing that, outside Rome, the Italian roads had been
neglected, he had the Flaminian Way, of which, on account
of its military importance, he took charge himself, repaired,
and requested various senators to repair others at their
own expense.[3] Statues were erected in his honour on the
bridge by which the Flaminian crossed the Tiber and at its
terminus, Ariminum. The bridge by which it crossed the

Marginal notes:
Measures which he contemplated at the beginning of the Principate. 27 B.C.

Repair of the Flaminian Way.

---

[1] See *The Architect of the Roman Empire* (44–27 B.C.), pp. 175–86.
[2] Dessau, *Inscr. Lat.*, 23. Cp. p. 35, n. 7, *infra*.
[3] Dio, liii, 22, 1–2.

[Nar.] Nera was famous in antiquity,[1] and is still almost un-rivalled in Italy. An arch, through which the road entered Ariminum, erected by the Senate and the Roman people in honour of Augustus, bore an inscription recording that on his initiative and at his cost this road and the other most Colonies frequented roads in Italy had been made good.[2] Colonies founded which he founded secured its safety and could always be in Italy. relied upon to support his government.[3]

After the repair of the Flaminian Way Augustus pur-posed, if we may believe Dio,[4] to invade Britain, but, find-ing that the Britons were likely to make terms, remained in Gaul. It is evident, however, that if such an enterprise had been seriously contemplated, extensive preparations would already have been made; and one may reasonably suppose that Dio or his authorities drew a hasty inference from the odes [5] in which Horace, perhaps with the approval or even under the influence of Augustus, announced an undertaking which would appease Roman desire for glory, but which it would certainly be wise to postpone for the more urgent needs of Gaul and Spain. It will be clear to all who know the history of the conquest of Gaul that Augustus, even before he set foot in the province, must have seen that important changes were needed for its security. He began by convening an assembly of notables,[6] to whom he doubtless explained the principal measures that he contemplated. The confederacies that had been formed under the domination of the Aedui and the The settle- Arverni must no longer be permitted to exist. It was per-ment of haps at this time, perhaps in later years, when he was able Gaul begun. to devote himself without interruption to the settlement of the country,[7] that he divided it into four administrative districts: the truth would seem to be that in his first year the division was foreshadowed, though much remained to

---

[1] Mart., vii, 93, 8.

[2] *J.R.S.*, xi, 169–70; Dessau, *Inscr. Lat.*, 84; Suet., *Aug.*, 30, 1; T. Ashby, *The Roman Campagna*, 1927, pp. 28–9.

[3] *Mon. Ancyr.*, v, 36–8; G. McN. Rushforth, *Lat. Hist. Inscr.*[2], 1930, pp. 33–4.   [4] liii, 22, 5.

[5] i, 21, 15; 35, 29–30; iii, 5, 3–4.   [6] Livy, *Epit.*, 134.

[7] Dio, liii, 12, 5. Cp. C. Jullian, *Hist. de la Gaule*, iv, 68 n. 1, 69 n. 2, and p. 56, *infra*.

SPAIN AND AFRICA

Kilometres

English Miles

be done. The districts were Narbonensis, virtually identical with the 'Province', which Caesar often mentioned,[1] and which, long before the conquest, had been a Roman possession; Aquitania, which, in his time mainly inhabited by Iberians and extending only from the Western Pyrenees to the Garonne, was now enlarged by the addition of the Celtican tribes—Santoni, Pictones, and Arverni—between the Garonne and the Loire, the administration of which, however, was to be distinct from that of the Aquitanians properly so called; Celtica, comprehending the other Celtican tribes, except the Helvetii, the Sequani, and the Lingones; and Belgica, including those three as well as the Belgae. Their exclusion from Celtica was perhaps intended to lessen the danger of a Celtican revolt.[2] Various tribes which Caesar omitted to mention, and which in his time had apparently no independent existence, appeared as separate communities, for example, the Silvanectes, who had been dependants of, or included among, the Suessiones.[3]

The very moderate tribute fixed by Caesar [4] was doubtless increased. In order to obtain an equitable basis for taxation, Augustus carried out the plan which his adoptive father had contemplated, of holding a census, in which the acreage and the nature of the land were accurately recorded and property was definitely registered. This was rendered possible by a survey which Agrippa, superintending the preparation of a map afterwards used by the elder Pliny, had already made.[5] Twelve years before, when he was in charge of the lately conquered country, he had rendered great service both to his fellow-citizens and to the natives by setting his troops to construct four trunk

---

[1] The Ruteni, who inhabited it (Pliny, *Nat. hist.*, iv, 19, 109), may have been united under Augustus with their kinsmen belonging to the group which Caesar called Celtae. See Jullian, *op. cit.*, p. 69, n. 3.

[2] Strabo, iv, 1, 1; Pliny, *Nat hist.*, iv, 17 (31), 105–7. Jullian (iv, 135, n. 1) holds that the Sequani, Helvetii, and Lingones were assigned definitively to Belgica when the armies of Upper and Lower Germany were formed. See p. 87, *infra.*

[3] Pliny, *Nat. hist.*, iv, 17 (31), 106; *Caesar's Conquest of Gaul*[2], 1911, p. 397.

[4] *The Roman Republic*, iii, 232. Cp. Fr. Kritz's note in his edition of Velleius (ii, 39, 2).

[5] *The Roman Republic*, iii, 325; Pliny, iii, 3, 17.

roads, which, extending from the Channel, the Atlantic coast, the Province, and the Rhine, converged upon [Lyons.] Lugudunum;[1] and perhaps it was on his suggestion that his chief cantoned the available legions along the valley of the Rhine,[2] where they not only served to deter Germans who might intend invasion, but also inspired such respect in Gaul that a cohort of twelve hundred men, stationed at Lugudunum, was deemed sufficient to hold the interior.[3]

Prelimin-   While Augustus was engaged in the work which, as he
ary work   doubtless foresaw, would have to be completed in later
of Augus-
tus in   years, he received alarming news from the adjoining penin-
Spain.   sula.[4] He had already determined to separate the southern and more civilized part (thenceforward called Baetica [Guadal- after the Baetis, which watered it) of Further Spain from quivir.] the northern, and to create a new province, Lusitania, the scene of Caesar's first military enterprise, roughly corresponding to Portugal and extending from the Guadiana to the Douro. Nearer Spain, thereafter called Tarraco- [Tarra- nensis from its newly-established capital, Tarraco, and gona.] Lusitania were imperial provinces; Baetica was one of those administered by the Senate.[5] Even under the Republic many Italians had settled in Spain for trade; and Caesar had done much to promote the prosperity of the country, especially of Baetica, in which he won the decisive victory of his last campaign.[6] During the past ten years six triumphs had been awarded to Roman generals for achievements in Spain;[7] but the Cantabri and the Astures, who inhabited the north-western territory, were so far from acknowledging Roman rule that they invaded adjacent districts,[8] and Augustus was forced to undertake a punitive expedition. It was probably in view of this campaign that Further Spain was divided; for it would be imprudent to leave Baetica and the more recently conquered country of the Lusitani, the Cantabri, and the

---

[1] Strabo, iv, 6, 11.   [2] See pp. 145–6.
[3] Jos., Bell., ii, 16, 4. Cp. Tac., Ann., iii, 41, 2.
[4] Dio, liii, 25, 2.
[5] Ib., 12, 4–5. Livy, Epit., 134; Class Rev., xxxviii, 134; E. Albertini, Les divisions administratives de l'Espagne rom., 1923, p. 32.
[6] The Roman Republic, i, 302–3; iii, 76–7, 310, 312.
[7] C.I.L., i², pp. 180–1.   [8] Flor., ii, 33, 47

Astures under the same administration.[1] Those who read in Dio's history [2] that the outbreak of the rebellious tribes and of the Alpine Salassi frustrated an intended invasion of Britain, which had refused to 'come to terms', will see that the historian was misled by rumour or by writers who felt that the abandonment of an enterprise upon which patriotic Romans had set their hearts needed some excuse.

The punishment inflicted upon the Salassi, who inhabited the valley of Aosta, by Valerius Messalla [3] had not been sufficiently drastic. They continued to make raids upon the farmers of Cisalpine Gaul, and until they should be completely subjugated the roads that crossed the Graian and the Pennine Alps, leading respectively to Lugudunum and the valley of the Rhone, would not be secure. While Augustus was busy in Spain he entrusted the task to Terentius Varro Murena, who accomplished it by invading their country simultaneously at several points. To secure the fruits of the victory thirty-six thousand men —all who were of military age—were sold into slavery in the market-place of Eporedia, and, to ensure the efficacy of this punishment, the purchasers were bound not to grant freedom to any before the expiration of twenty years.[4]

Varro Murena subjugates the Salassi.

[Ivrea.]

Before the end of the year in which he left Gaul Augustus reached Tarraco, where on the following New Year's Day he entered upon his eighth consulship.[5] His nephew, Marcellus,[6] and his stepson, Tiberius,[7] were with him, or joined him before he quitted the seat of war. The troops destined for the campaign—the last which he was to conduct in person, the first in which Tiberius served—were, it would seem, assembled near Segisamo,[8] on the road leading from Tarraco to the country of the Astures. Three

Jan. 1, 26 B.C.

[Sasamon.]

---

[1] Albertini, *op. cit.*, pp. 29–30.   [2] liii, 25, 2.
[3] See *The Architect of the Roman Empire* (44–27 B.C.), p. 134, n. 2.
[4] Strabo, iv, 6, 7; Pliny, *Nat. hist.*, xviii, 20 (49), 182; Dio, liii, 25, 3–4. Dessau (*Gesch. d. röm. Kaiserzeit*, i, 1924, p. 411, n. 2), citing *Notizie d. scavi*, 1899, p. 108, remarks that Mommsen (*Röm. Gesch.*, v, 18 [Eng. tr., i, 20]) was wrong in saying that Augusta Pretoria (Aosta) originally had only gates leading east and west, and therefore was only intended to secure the Little St. Bernard.
[5] *C.I.L.*, i², p. 58; Suet., *Aug.*, 26, 2.   [6] Dio, liii, 26, 1.
[7] Suet., *Tib.*, 9, 1.   [8] Ptol., ii, 6, 51.

Campaign of Augustus against the Cantabri and Astures.

columns marched successively northward, the first forcing the Cantabrians to retreat to the range called Mons Vindius (the Sierra Covadongo, in which the Ebro has its source), and starving them into surrender, the third, which crossed the plateau of Leon and Old Castile, blockading the Astures in Mons Medullus at a point which cannot be identified. Augustus, perhaps dissatisfied with the result of the campaign, and certainly ill from overwork and anxiety, retired to Tarraco, and doubtless it was during

His correspondence with Virgil.

his sojourn there that he corresponded with Virgil, who was living at Sorrento, near Naples,[1] begging him to send a specimen of the *Aeneid*. Virgil replied: 'With respect to my *Aeneas*, if I had it in a fit state for your reading, I would gladly send it; but the thing is only just begun, and indeed it seems almost folly to have undertaken so great a

Gradual subjection of the Cantabri and Astures.
[Cerro de Lancia.]
24 B.C.

work'.[2] Undaunted by defeat, the Astures again descended into the plain; but a lieutenant of Augustus, Carisius, the hero of the year's campaign,[3] captured their principal stronghold, Lancia, and thus, for the time, ended the war.[4] The temple of Janus was again closed;[5] but in the following year both the Astures and the Cantabri rose again, and, although the Governor, Lucius Lamia,[6] punished them with the ruthless ferocity with which the Romans treated obstinate enemies, not only devastating their country, but also cutting off the hands of all who were caught and then turning them loose to exist as they best could, one of his

[1] See *Class. Philol.*, xvii, 1922, p. 106.

[2] Macrob., i, 24, 11; Donatus, *Vita Verg.*, ed. Brummer, 104–8. Dessau (*Gesch. d. röm. Kaiserzeit*, i, 1924, p. 494, n.) thinks that Servius's words in his introduction to *Aeneis—postea ab Augusto Aeneidem propositam*—must not be taken literally. Why?

[3] E. Babelon, *Monn. de la rép. rom.*, i, 318–23, nos. 14–30.

[4] Vell., ii, 90, 4; Flor., ii, 33; Suet., *Aug.*, 20; 29, 3; Dio, liii, 22, 5; 25, 2. 5–8; 26, 1; Oros., vi, 21, 1–11. Prof. D. Magie (*Class. Philol.*, xv, 1920, pp. 323–39) has made a meritorious attempt to describe the war in detail, using epigraphical sources, and I have no criticism to make, except that, owing to textual uncertainties in Florus and Orosius and blunders in the former, the result is necessarily unsatisfactory. Magie, indeed, wisely forbears to attempt to describe the campaign of 25 B.C. According to Florus, Agrippa was one of the Roman officers, a mistake which Dio (liii, 23, 1–2; 27, 1) enables us to correct.

[5] Dio, liii, 26, 5; *Mon. Ancyr.*, ii, 24–5 (cp. Mommsen, *Res gestae*[2], &c., p. 50).

[6] Dio (liii, 29, 1), who omits the name Lamia, wrongly calls him Aemilius instead of Aelius.

successors was obliged, two years later, to cope with another revolt. For two years the tribes remained inactive; but in the next Agrippa, then Governor of Gaul, was forced to contend with the Cantabri, many of whom, though they had been sold into slavery after their last outbreak, had killed their owners and induced some of their compatriots to join them in rebellion. Agrippa, though he had to deal with a mutiny started by some of his own soldiers, who were demoralized by prolonged warfare, succeeded, despite many reverses, after he had degraded one legion and regained the obedience of the rest, in overcoming his enemy, destroying nearly all who were of military age, disarming the survivors, and compelling them to abandon their fastnesses, for which success he declined with wonted self-abnegation to accept a triumph, though Augustus had himself urged the Senate to grant it. Yet another rising, three years later, was merely an ebullition of despair.[1] Thenceforward until the time of Nero [2] the country remained virtually pacified. The Cantabri were placed under the Governor of Tarraconensis, the Astures under the Governor of Lusitania. The headquarters of the force which Augustus detailed to keep both tribes in subjection were between Lancia and Asturia Augusta, which was connected by roads, doubtless made by soldiers, with other towns,[3] while the great coastal road that linked the peninsula with Italy, extending from Tarraco to Carthago Nova, was prolonged from Tarraco to Valentia and called the Augustan Way.[4] At a later time the boundaries of the country were modified,[5] a disturbed strip of Baetica, comprising the mountainous region that bordered the upper valley of the Guadalquivir and the ridges, haunted by brigands,[6] between it and the sea, being placed under the Governor of Tarraconensis, who commanded the military force.

22 B.C.

19 B.C.

16 B.C.

[Carta-gena.]

3 B.C.
2 B.C.

[1] Dio, liii, 29, 1–2; liv, 5, 1–3; 11, 3–6; 20, 3; 23, 7; 25, 1; Mommsen, *Chron. min.*, ii, 135, 569.

[2] See Dessau, *Inscr. Lat.*, 103, 2648. Cp. Rushforth, *Lat. Hist. Inscr.*[2], p. 10.   [3] Albertini, *op. cit.*, p. 33. Cp. Rushforth, *op. cit.*, pp. 9–10.

[4] Strabo, iii, 4, 9; *C.I.L.*, ii, 4949–54; Dessau, *Inscr. Lat.*, 102. Cp. Rushforth, p. 11.

[5] Albertini, *op. cit.*, pp. 35–6.   [6] Cic., *Fam.*, x, 31, 1.

Notwithstanding the pacification of the Cantabri and the Astures, the Government was forced to acquiesce in their reluctance, as in that of the restless Celtiberians, to abandon their clannish habits for urban life.[1] But in the rest of the peninsula and especially in Baetica, which still, as in Republican times,[2] exported oil, wine, corn, salt, fish, esparto grass, and other products to Italy, though the Spanish cantons were not, like the Gallic, political commonwealths, Roman dress was so commonly worn, Latin so widely spoken, that the land which gave birth to the poets, Lucan and Martial, the philosopher, Seneca, the geographer, Mela, the librarian, Hyginus, and Quintilian, the literary critic, might fairly be called another Italy. Many communities obtained Roman citizenship and many others Latin rights.[3]

Augustus, after his own campaign, had discharged many of his veteran soldiers and encouraged them to settle in a newly founded Lusitanian colony on the site of the modern Merida, which was called Augusta Emerita.[4] As he was suffering from rheumatism, he spent some time at the watering-place which received the name of Aquae Augustae, now Dax, near the Western Pyrenees.[5] Prevented by this illness from attending the marriage of Marcellus and his daughter Julia, whose mother he had divorced before he married Livia,[6] he commissioned Agrippa to preside at the festivities.[7] It was not until the following year that he had recovered sufficiently to return to Rome.[8]

It was apparently in this year that Augustus made a bargain with Juba, whose father had fought so persistently against Caesar, and who had himself been exhibited to the Roman populace in Caesar's triumph, giving him in exchange for his hereditary domain, most of the inhabitants of which had become Roman subjects, the dominions of

Side notes: Romanization of Spain completed. Marriage of Augustus's daughter, Julia. 25 B.C. His settlement of Africa.

[1] Strabo, iii, 3, 7–8; 4, 19. Cp. C. Jullian, *Hist. de la Gaule*, iv, 318, 320.
[2] See *The Roman Republic*, i, 138–9.
[3] Pliny, *Nat. hist.*, iii, 1 (3), 7; 3 (4), 18.   [4] Dio, liii, 26, 1.
[5] Suet., *Aug.*, 81, 1; 82, 2; *Anth. Pal.*, 9, 419. Cp. C. Jullian, *Hist. de la Gaule*, iv, 64.
[6] See *The Architect of the Roman Empire* (44–27 B.C.), p. 109.
[7] Dio, liii, 27, 5; Hor., *Carm.*, 1, 12, 45–8; Vell., ii, 93, 2; Suet., *Aug.*, 63, 1.
[8] Dio, liii, 28, 1; 29, 1.

the Mauretanian kings, Bocchus and Bogud, and parts of
the adjoining region, Gaetulia.[1] Those who have studied
the history of the war with Jugurtha and of Caesar's
African campaign will understand in what relation the
main divisions of Northern Africa stood to Rome when the
Principate began. West of the old province of Africa was
Numidia, west of Numidia, embracing Morocco and extending to the Atlantic, Mauretania. Bogud and Bocchus,
who had sided with Caesar against Scipio and the elder
Juba, were left in possession of their domains, which were
indeed enlarged. During the Perusine war Bogud had
invaded Spain on behalf of Antony, while Bocchus acted
for Octavian. When, later, Antony forsook Bogud,
Octavian gave the greater part of his territory to Bocchus,
after whose death his kingdom was obtained by the 33 B.C.
younger Juba, who became known as a diligent collector
of historical and geographical records.

Though Africa was one of the provinces assigned on the
foundation of the Principate to the Senate, Augustus
stationed a legion, the commander of which was responsible to him, to protect its southern frontier,[2] which was
exposed to attack from the tribes of the desert; while in
Mauretania he founded eleven colonies,[3] independent of
Juba, which, though they doubtless tended to civilize the
country, were in fact fortresses, designed to accommodate
not only Italians whose lands he had confiscated, but also
the veteran soldiers who garrisoned them.[4] In connexion
with one of them, Rusazu or Rusagus, a fact should be
noted which illustrates the way in which the literary
material for the history of the empire is supplemented by
epigraphical evidence. Its geographical position, near
Cape Sigli, is indicated by an inscription on a watch-tower,
dominating a hill called the Tamgout, from which we learn
that the tower was repaired by the colonists, of whom the

---

[1] *Ib.*, 26, 2; li, 15, 6; Strabo, xvii, 3, 7.   [2] See p. 12.
[3] Zilis, Babba, Benasa, Cartenna, Gunugu, Igilgili, Rusguniae, Rusagus,
Saldae, Tupusuctu, Zuccabar (*Paulys Real-Ency.*, iv, 559; *C.I.L.*, viii, 8337,
8931, 8933, 20683).
[4] M. Rostovtzeff, *Social and Econ. Hist. of the Roman Empire*, 1927, pp.
280–1, 580, n. 58; J. Carcopino (*Bull. arch. du Com. des travaux hist.*, 1919,
pp. 170–7).

earliest, as it appears from an inscribed milestone hard by, were veterans of the 7th legion. So also were the men who garrisoned the neighbouring foundations,[1] linked by roads with Rusazu, Saldae and Tupusuctu. While the Mauretanian colonies, like others which Caesar and Augustus founded in the region near Sicily, tended to civilize the Berbers, they must have created the expectation, which was afterwards fulfilled, that Mauretania would ultimately be annexed to the Roman empire. When Octavian, before the foundation of the Principate, sent fresh settlers to Carthage, they were, as in his later colonies, Thuburbo and probably also Hadrumetum and Hippo Diarrhytus, time-expired soldiers, with whom, however, were associated natives who chose their own magistrates; for Augustus granted them not only autonomy, but also the privilege of coining their money. Certain coins have been found, evidently belonging to a Punic community which had been established in Carthage just before the foundation of the Principate, and which afterwards received Roman citizenship.[2] Gradually the communities, partly Punic, partly Berber, of Africa and Numidia, with Roman emigrants who had settled among them, recovered from the civil wars, the Roman settlers having their own territory and their own communal organization. The legion intended to keep at bay the tribes of the desert was quartered on the [Tebessa.] plateau east of the Aurasian range, at Theveste, which was 20 B.C. connected by roads with Carthage; and thus in the seventh year of the Principate the proconsul Lucius Cornelius Balbus was enabled to chastise the turbulent Garamantes, who, however, not long afterwards provoked further punishment.[3]

Roman Africa, which Augustus never visited, was not much less the creation of Caesar than Roman Gaul. But, as Mommsen[4] remarked, 'the toga suited . . . the new Roman of the Rhone and the Garonne better than the

---

[1] Carcopino, op. cit., pp. 171–2, 174–5.

[2] W. Barthel, Zur Gesch. d. röm. Staates in Africa, 1904, pp. 19–23. Cp. Klio, viii, 1908, pp. 459–60.

[3] Virg., Aen., vi, 794; Pliny, Nat. hist., v, 5, 36–7. Cp. Paulys Real-Ency., vii, 731, and Rushforth, Lat. Hist. Inscr.², p. 128. See p. 88, infra.

[4] Röm. Gesch., v, 655 (Eng. tr., ii, 339, 341).

"Seminumidians and Semigaetulians"', for, like the recal-
citrant Spanish tribes, Moors and Numidians retained their
primitive habits. Phoenician, which ceased to be used in
official documents soon after the death of Augustus, remained for many years the language of private intercourse.
The great aqueducts, of which the remains move the ad-
miration of tourists, made it possible to cultivate a country
which was then as dry and waterless as it is to-day,[1] so that
under Augustus, as under his adoptive father, Africa continued to supply Rome with corn[2] and, to some slight
extent, with olive oil. It may be doubted whether in his
time schools, such as those in which Augustine[3] received
his early education, had yet been founded. Indeed, despite
the use of Latin in official documents, the organized cult of
the emperors, and the ambition of some native families,
who aimed at social advancement, the Romans, although
they gave Africa peace and prosperity, never made her
Roman.

But knowledge of the ancient historians and even of
inscriptions is not sufficient to enable the reader to appreciate the civilizing work of Rome: he must travel through
the country. The aqueducts near Tunis will set him thinking. Then let him explore the wonders of Lambaesis and [Lam-
Thamugadi. Above all let him visit the little town El bèse.]
Djem, where, hard by the desert, he will see that amphi- [Timgad.]
theatre, not much smaller and less mutilated than the
Colosseum, which I have ventured to call 'the noblest ruin
in the world',[4] and which, since it was built for the enter-
tainment of the myriads who thronged it, still bears its
lonely witness to the Roman Peace.

Occupied as he was with the settlement of the West,
Augustus did not forget the East, the Hellenic civilization Polemo,
of which, without attempting to Latinize it, he was careful King of
to protect.[5] Polemo, the Greek King of Pontus, who, honoured.

---

[1] Cp. *The Roman Republic*, iii, 423, n. 5.   [2] Hor., *Carm.*, i, 1, 9–10.
[3] *Conf.*, I, ix, 14–5; II, iii, 5. Cp. *Paulys Real-Ency.*, ii, 2363.
    See, besides the authorities already cited, *Class. Rev.*, xl, 15, and T. R. S.
Broughton, *The Romanization of Africa proconsularis*, 1929, especially pp. 57,
78, 86, 226–8.
[4] *The Roman Republic*, iii, 237.
[5] Cp. Rushforth, *Lat. Hist. Inscr.*[2], p. 23.

though he assisted Antony in the Parthian war, had been loyal to his conqueror,[1] was rewarded soon after the

26 B.C. foundation of the Principate by enrolment among the Friends and Allies of the Roman People.[2] In the following year Amyntas, King of Galatia, who had named Augustus his heir, was killed by the Homonadenses, a tribe of predatory mountaineers, who inhabited the northern slopes of

Annexation of Galatia. the lofty plateau called Mount Taurus: his territory was of course annexed by Augustus, who placed it with the adjacent western and southern regions, comprising Southern Phrygia, Pisidia, and Lycaonia, under a Roman governor, while certain parts of Pamphylia, which had been given by Antony to Amyntas, were restored.[3] So long as the Spanish war lasted it was impossible to punish the Homo-

Augustus provides for its security. nadenses; but Augustus did what he could to secure the Phrygian plain by founding at Antioch the colony Caesarea. While the colonists, veterans of the 5th legion, which had won fame in the civil wars, guarded the fertile plain against the mountaineers, the Greek-speaking inhabitants, profiting by the peace thus secured, acquired wealth, which, as they were gradually admitted to Roman citizenship, gave them influence, though the colonists remained the dominant power.[4]

Settlement of Egypt. Let us now see how Augustus dealt with the province, if it may be so called, which, as he declared,[5] he had added to the empire, but which, never consulting the Senate about its government, he nevertheless treated as an estate belonging to himself.[6] Autocracy, indeed, was indispensable, for in Alexandria perennial feuds between Greeks and Jews broke out from time to time in street fighting,[7] while in the country petty disputes led to battles between villages;[8] and in such cases order could be restored only by instant action.

The main objects which Augustus kept in view, apart from the preservation of order and the promotion of

---

[1] *The Architect of the Roman Empire* (44–27 B.C.), pp. 125, 147, 159.
[2] Dio, liii, 25, 1.   [3] *Ib.*, 26, 3.   [4] *J.R.S.*, xv, 172–3.
[5] *Mon. Ancyr.*, v, 24. Cp. Macrob., i, 12, 35, and Dessau, *Inscr. Lat.*, 91.
[6] B. A. van Groningen (*Aegyptus*, vii, 1926, pp. 195–7). J. G. Milne, *Hist. of Egypt under Roman Rule*[3], 1924, p. 120.
[7] Cp. *The Roman Republic*, iii, 183.   [8] Milne, *op. cit.*, p. 122.

commerce, were to increase the depleted revenues of Rome
and, since the Ptolemaic court, for whose benefit a tribute of
corn had been levied, no longer existed, to secure as much
as might be obtainable for feeding the Roman population
in addition to what they received from Sardinia, Sicily, and
Africa. It was with this aim that he had ordered the
clearing of the canals in the Delta,[1] which was completed
so effectively a few years later by Aelius Gallus that a rise
in the Nile of twelve cubits, or about eighteen feet, was as
beneficial as a rise of fourteen had been before[2]—in other
words, that extensive tracts bordering the valley were restored to cultivation—and Egypt was able to supply
annually to Italy twenty millions of Roman bushels[3]—one-
third of the required total.[4]

While Augustus allowed much of the existing administrative system to remain, he found it advisable not only to
suppress bribery and illicit profiteering,[5] but also to introduce divers innovations. Monopolies, which had enriched
the Ptolemies, were abolished. They had been maintained
by levying duties on imports, which were now abandoned
in the interest of Roman merchants with the substitution
of monthly licences to trade.[6] A new impost, the poll-tax,
was levied at varying rates on males between the ages of
14 and 60, except Roman citizens and burgesses of the
three Greek cities—Alexandria, Ptolemais, and Naucratis.[7]
Forced labour, on five days annually, was still required, as
it had been from time immemorial, for the maintenance of
irrigation, but might be commuted by a fixed payment.[8]
The revenue was collected on a new principle. Under the
Ptolemies the collectors, as well as most of the other
officials, were the paid agents of the king; under the Empire
only those whose duties were purely clerical and the few
Romans selected for the higher posts received salaries; the

[1] See *The Architect of the Roman Empire* (44–27 B.C.), pp. 170, 260.
[2] Strabo, xvii, 1, 3.
[3] About 1,900,000 pecks.
[4] Ps. Victor, *Epit. de Caes.*, i, 6. See *The Roman Republic*, i, 362.
[5] Rostovtzeff, *Social and Econ. Hist.*, &c., p. 264.
[6] *J.R.S.*, xvii, 3.
[7] The earliest evidence for the poll-tax is in receipts of 18 B.C. (*J.R.S.*, xvii, 2). [8] *Ib.*

collectors were Greeks, who, while they were exempt from
the manual labour required from the lower orders, were
obliged to serve without remuneration, and were, moreover, held liable for shortage in the quota of corn fixed for
their respective districts. Under Augustus, however, the
old system continued for some years side by side with the
new.[1] Lands which had belonged to Ptolemaic soldiers
were confiscated, to provide for Roman veterans,[2] and
a large part of that belonging to one village came into the
possession of relatives of Augustus.[3] Indeed there are so
many allusions in papyri to estates which had passed into
the ownership of the State that it has been suggested[4] that
'a persistent though unobtrusive course of policy had been
pursued to this end'. The priests were allowed to choose
between surrendering the temple lands in return for a fixed
payment and retaining the income accruing from a limited
area.[5] This secularization of property, the motive of which
may be supposed to have been the desire to paralyse a
focus of anti-Roman sentiment,[6] occurred under the
19 B.C. Governor Petronius in the eighth year of the Principate.[7]

The rules drawn up by order of Augustus for the guidance
of the official known as the idiologus,[8] whose business was
to maintain the gradation of classes which still characterized
Egypt as it had done under Ptolemaic rule, have been aptly
called an instrument of fiscal oppression.[9] The highest
class naturally consisted of Roman citizens—officials,
traders, ex-soldiers, who had acquired citizenship on their
discharge, and freedmen.[10] Immediately below them ranked

---

[1] *J.R.S.*, xvii, pp. 4–5. See also xvi, p. 132.
[2] M. Rostovtzeff, *A large Estate in Egypt*, &c., 1922, p. 13, n. 27.
[3] *Ib.*, p. 12. Cp. Rostovtzeff's *Social and Econ. Hist.*, pp. 267–8, 572–5.
As Stuart Jones (*Fresh Light on Roman Bureaucracy*, 1920, p. 14) observes,
'many of the most important [estates], such as those of Maecenas, were
acquired by inheritance, and not by confiscation.'   [4] *J.R.S.*, xvii, 4.
[5] Milne, *op. cit.*, p. 287. Cp. Rostovtzeff, pp. 264–5, 572, n. 40.
[6] Milne, *op. cit.*, p. 10.   [7] *J.R.S.*, xvii, 2, 4.   [8] Strabo, xvii, 1, 12.
[9] Stuart Jones, *op. cit.*, pp. 8, 12, 15–7, 23–4. Milne (*op. cit.*, pp. 125, 302
§ 7, 308 § 3), affirms that the idiologus was 'titular high priest of all Egypt',
but Stuart Jones (cp. *Journ. Egypt. Archaeol.*, xii, 318) has given sound
reasons for believing that he did not acquire the priestly office before the
period of the Severi.
[10] Some freedmen resident in Egypt had only Latin rights. Cp. *The Roman
Republic*, i, 5–6, 47; iii, 322.

the burgesses of Alexandria, next to whom were classed
successively the members of the other Greek communities
and Hellenized individuals who, determined to rise, had
taken advantage of Greek education. Lowest of all were
the forefathers of the modern fellahin, who, poverty notwithstanding, were forced to pay the newly established
poll-tax, and, just above them, a class permitted to pay it at
a reduced rate. It was the duty of the idiologus to keep
these classes distinct by registering persons and property,
closely scrutinizing the credentials of any one who claimed
a privileged status, and enforcing the penalties to which all
who disregarded rules relating to intermarriage and inheritance were liable. If any Egyptian found it prudent to
adopt a Greek name, he was obliged to apply to the idiologus
for permission. Fines exacted from the personnel of the
temples for breach of regulations yielded a considerable
sum: for instance, a priest who wore woollen clothes and
neglected to have his hair cut was fined a thousand
drachmae,[1] or about forty pounds.

Augustus made military arrangements for the preservation of internal order as well as for external warfare. At
Nicopolis, which, it will be remembered, he had himself
founded,[2] a legion was quartered, to overawe the Alexandrian populace.[3] South of the Delta the inhabitants had
long been in chronic rebellion. Even before the beginning   29 B.C.
of the Principate Cornelius Galbus, the first governor of the
province, was obliged to crush a revolt at Heroonpolis, on
the line of a canal which Augustus afterwards made to link
the Nile with the Red Sea; and a fortnight later he had to
deal with an outbreak, provoked by the arrival of the tax-
collectors,[4] in the Thebaid, a tract extending from Antinoë,
on the site of the modern Scheck-Abadé, to the first
cataract of the Nile. Besides the Alexandrian legion there
were two others, one of which was stationed at Babylon,
near the entrance of the Delta, nine cohorts of auxiliary
infantry, and three squadrons of cavalry;[5] but when it

---

[1] Stuart Jones, *Fresh Light*, &c., p. 24. Cp. *The Roman Republic*, i, 344–5.
[2] *The Architect of the Roman Empire* (44–27 B.C.), p. 170.
[3] Milne, *op. cit.*, p. 2.   [4] *Ib.*, p. 5.
[5] Strabo, xvii, 1, 12. 30. Cp. Milne, *op. cit.*, p. 171

became evident that serious disturbances were not to be dreaded, except in Alexandria, where Petronius quelled a riot, it was found safe to withdraw one legion from the province.[1]

The preservation of order naturally promoted prosperity. The historian of the social and economic conditions of the empire learned from study of the archaeology of Southern Russia that industrial life in Alexandria was never so prosperous as after the civil wars. The manufacturers of the city supplied the entire Roman world with certain kinds of linen, perfumes, silver plate, jewellery of a special type, and various articles of glass and ivory. Alexandrian traders were glad to invest their money in the purchase of Egyptian land, capitalists came from Italy to try their luck in so promising a sphere, and officials who had served Cleopatra took advantage of settled conditions to acquire landed property and to exploit the opening markets for Egyptian products.[2]

Plans for promoting commerce with India.

But the troops stationed in Egypt were not destined only for the work of military police: Augustus determined to gain access to commercial routes which had hitherto been almost entirely closed to Roman enterprise. Foreseeing that the peace which he had given to the world, besides promoting trade in general, would encourage wealthy citizens to purchase those luxuries which India produced, he resolved to remove the obstacles that hampered that branch of commerce. Merchants had not yet penetrated to India by land:[3] the cost of buying from the native traders who used the Arabian routes was prohibitive; and, if the Red Sea was to be opened to navigation, it would be necessary to deal with the Sabaeans who controlled the eastern, and with the Ethiopian Axomites of the western coast.[4] Since the Sabaeans were known to have acquired wealth by trafficking in precious stones, cosmetics, spices, and other Indian wares (for caravans

---

[1] Strabo, xvii, 1, 53; Tac., *Ann.*, iv, 5, 3. Cp. Milne, *op. cit.*, pp. 171–2, and J. Lesquier, *L'armée rom. d'Égypte*, 1918, pp. 15, 101–4.

[2] Rostovtzeff, *Social and Econ. Hist.*, &c., pp. 73, 507 n. 35, 266, 572 n. 42.

[3] E. H. Warmington, *The Commerce between the Roman Empire and India.* 1927, p. 22.

[4] *Ib.*, pp. 14–15.

came from their country to the coastal towns of Palestine),
Augustus abandoned for once his non-aggressive policy
and, in the third year of the Principate, sent Aelius Gallus
to subdue them if conciliation should fail. But, if he ever
appraised the Governor's military capacity, he overrated it.
Gallus, who might easily have obtained the necessary
geographical information from merchants, neglected to
make inquiries, and, telling the story of his campaign to his
credulous friend, the geographer Strabo, glozed over his
errors of judgement, invented a victory, and exaggerated
his difficulties. Augustus himself or his advisers may, indeed, have been partly to blame. One hundred and thirty
transports, specially built for the conveyance of half the
army, were ill-suited for navigation off the Arabian coast,
of which, moreover, their pilots had no experience. Eighty
ships of war caused needless expense and delay, for the
Sabaeans had no fleet to oppose them. The expedition was
planned with almost incredible folly. A glance at the map
is enough to show that the troops should have been embarked at Berenice, the southernmost Egyptian port, and
that the transports should have sailed thence across the
Red Sea to Arabia Felix. In fact they started from
Arsinoë (near Suez), the northernmost harbour, and, after
several had been wrecked, disembarked the army, already
weakened by sickness, at Leuce Come, where it was forced
to winter, and whence it was obliged in the following spring
to make a long march southward past a desolate coast.
The legionaries easily routed the Sabaeans whom they
encountered; but disease made havoc in their ranks, and
when at last, after a six months' march, they reached the
massive walks of Mariaba,[1] the Sabaean capital, Gallus,
after wasting six days, retreated, being short of water, in
despair. From the port of Egra the remnant of the army
crossed the Red Sea to Myos Hormos, near the entrance of
the Gulf of Suez, and made its way across the desert southward to Coptos, whence it returned down the valley of
the Nile to Alexandria. Gallus unjustly laid the blame of his
failure on the Nabataean vizier, Syllaeus, who had accompanied him in command of a thousand men, and who

Margin notes: 25 B.C. Expedition of Aelius Gallus. [Marib.] [Kunft.]

---

[1] See *Journ. Asiat.*, 7ᵉ sér., iii, 1874, pp. 3–4.

was executed some years later at the instigation of Herod;
but he was himself dismissed from his post.[1]

The Sabaeans, despite the failure of the expedition, must
have been impressed by the fame of Augustus, for they
stamped his effigy on their coins;[2] and he made good use of
the information that had been obtained. A camp was
established at Coptos; the routes leading thence to the
Egyptian harbours were placed under military supervision; the soldiers who occupied the camp were set to
repair the cisterns on the roads to Myos Hormos and
Berenice, so that water should not thenceforth be wanting;
and, to defray the expense of the military stations, duties
were levied at Coptos.[3] Aelius Gallus told Strabo[4] that
a hundred and twenty ships sailed annually from Myos
Hormos to India. Receipts relating to the customs duties
of the villages in the Fayum and of Syene (now Assouan)
testify to trade with the oases.[5] Thenceforward Alexandrian merchants acquired great wealth from the commerce
with the East; for, besides the sea-borne trade, Augustus
encouraged that of the overland routes, suppressing
brigandage in the neighbourhood of Damascus and
securing the valley of the Euphrates.[6] It was a sign of
growing commercial activity as well as of the world-wide
fame of Augustus that embassies from India waited upon
him, seeking for the first time the countenance of a Roman
ruler.[7]

Growth of trade with the East.

Ethiopian relations with Rome.

With the Arabian expedition was perhaps connected an
Ethiopian invasion of Egypt, which occurred while it was
still in progress. Cornelius Gallus, after suppressing the

---

[1] *Mon. Ancyr.*, v, 23; Strabo, xvi, 4, 22–4; xvii, 1, 53; Jos., *Ant.*, xvi, 10,
8–9; Dio, liii, 29, 3–8. Cp. Mommsen, *Röm. Gesch.*, v, 608, n. 2 (Eng. tr., ii,
291, n. 2), and Milne, *op. cit.*, pp. 277–9. [In case any learned reader should
ask why I have ignored the theory that Aelius Gallus was not Governor of
Egypt at the time of the Arabian expedition, I may say that it seemed to
me certain, in view of the statements of Strabo and Dio, that he was, and that
the theory has been sufficiently refuted by Hardy (*Mon. Ancyr.*, pp. 122–3)
and Milne (*l.c.*).]

[2] B. V. Head, *Hist. num.*[2], 1911, p. 813. Cp. Warmington, *op. cit.*, p. 15.

[3] C. Dittenberger, *Orientis Graeci inscr. sel.*, ii. 1905, no. 674.   [4] ii, 5, 12.

[5] *J.R.S.*, xv, 269.

[6] Strabo, xvi, 2, 20. Cp. Warmington, *op. cit.*, p. 33.

[7] *Mon. Ancyr.*, v, 50–1; Hor., *Carm. Saec.*, 55–6; Suet., *Aug.*, 21, 3;
Flor., ii, 34, 62; Oros., vi, 21, 19. Cp. Warmington, pp. 35–6.

revolt in the Thebaid,[1] marched southward to Syene, and
on the island of Philae, just north of the first cataract, met
envoys from the Ethiopian region, Meroë, with whom he
made an agreement, by which the country above the
cataract known as the 'Thirty-mile land',[2] though it was
recognized as an Ethiopian possession, was constituted a
Roman protectorate.[3] While Aelius Gallus was retreating
from Mariaba an Ethiopian force, complaining of Roman
aggression, but perhaps taking advantage of the absence of
his troops, seized Syene and Philae, despite the agreement,
and defeated the auxiliary cohorts in the district. Petronius, the governor who succeeded Gallus,[4] severely
punished them, storming their chief town, Napata, and   [Meraoui.]
others, whereupon their queen, whose titular name,
Candace, is known to readers of the *Acts of the Apostles*,[5]
sued for peace. Petronius, who returned to Alexandria,
was recalled two years later by the news that four hundred
men, whom he had left to hold the Ethiopian town, Premis,   [Ibrim.]
were besieged by the queen. He forced her to raise the
siege and, when she desired to reopen negotiations, ordered
her to apply to Augustus. Her envoys, who met him in
Samos, were favourably received. The result of their
negotiations was that the Roman troops were withdrawn
from the southern part of the protectorate, the Roman
advanced post was established at Hiera Sycaminos, and   [Maharra-
the 'Twelve-mile land'[6] between it and Syene was made a   kah.]
military frontier.[7] Thenceforward, it would seem, Ethiopian relations with Rome were generally peaceful. Corne-   Disgrace
lius Gallus, to whose forward policy they were originally   of
due, is said to have erected many statues of himself in   Cornelius
Egypt[8] and to have inscribed upon the Pyramids records   Gallus.
of his achievements. Accused by Valerius Largus, a
former friend, he was recalled by Augustus and forbidden

---

[1] See p. 17, *supra*.   [2] Triakontaschoinos.   [3] Strabo, xvii, 1, 53.
[4] *Ib.*, 1, 54. Cp. Milne, *op. cit.*, pp. 277–9.
[5] viii, 27.   [6] Dodekaschoinos.
[7] *Mon. Ancyr.*, v, 22; Strabo, xvi, 4, 22; Pliny, *Nat. hist.*; vi, 29 (35),
181; Dio, liv, 5, 4–6. Cp. p. 37, n. 5.
[8] A few Anglo-Indians may remember having seen the monument which
that vainglorious hero of the Indian Mutiny, T. H. Kavanagh, erected in
Lucknow.

to enter the imperial provinces. In consequence of the charges brought against him the Senate decreed that he should be banished and his estate confiscated; but before the decrees could take effect he committed suicide. Augustus, on hearing of his death, shed tears. Proculeius whose interview with Cleopatra will be remembered, felt such contempt for Largus that, when he happened to meet him, he covered his nose and mouth with his hand, hinting to bystanders that in the presence of such a treacherous friend it was unsafe to breathe.[1]

Details of Roman trade with India.

The trade with India, which Augustus had done so much to promote, was mainly in luxuries, and was stimulated by the craving for the pleasures of the table, for personal adornment, and for domestic display. From writers of the Augustan Age[2] we learn that epicures (to whom perhaps the medicines of the East may have been occasionally beneficial) were fond of dishes seasoned with pepper, while rice, which, like all other oriental wares, was very costly, served not only for food but also for beautifying the complexion, the arms, and the hands of Roman ladies.[3] Wealthy connoisseurs delighted in pointing to the ivory which adorned their tables, couches, and bedsteads.[4] Moralists complained that silk was worn not only by women, but also by effeminate men.[5] A small box, made of onyx and containing spikenard, was obtained by Horace[6] in exchange for wine amounting to the equivalent of three dozen bottles. Diamonds, sapphires, rubies, turquoises, amethysts, opals were lavishly displayed by women whose lovers could afford to pay for them.[7] Children were doubtless amused by listening to parrots which had been

---

[1] Dio, liii, 24, 2–3; Suet., *Aug.*, 66, 2; *The Architect of the Roman Empire* (44–27 B.C.), pp. 164–5. Milne (*op. cit.*, p. 5) remarks that the one known example of Gallus's vainglorious inscriptions—on the island Philae (Dessau, *Inscr. Lat.*, 8995) 'does not suggest any suspicion of his loyalty'.

[2] E.g. Hor., *Ep.*, ii, 1, 270; *Sat.*, ii, 4, 73–4; Ovid, *Ars amat.*, ii, 417.

[3] Hor., *Sat.*, ii, 3, 155; Pliny, *Nat. hist.*, xviii, 5 (6), 71; xv, 7, 28; Mart., iii, 42, 1. Cp. Warmington, *op. cit.*, pp. 218–19.

[4] Hor., *Carm.*, ii, 18, 1; *Sat.*, ii, 6, 103. Cp. Warmington, p. 163.

[5] Ovid, *Amores*, i, 14, 5–6; Virg., *Georg.*, ii, 121; Hor., *Epod.*, viii, 15–6. Cp. Warmington, p. 175.

[6] *Carm.*, ii, 11, 16; iv, 12, 17; *Epod.*, v, 59; xiii, 8–9. Cp. Warmington, p. 195.　　[7] *Ib.*, pp. 40–1. Cp. p. 235, and *The Roman Republic*, i, 94, 98.

taught to speak.[1] Italy exported no products of her own in exchange for these luxuries: they were paid for in cash; and since many of the coins found in India were plated with base metal, a German commentator has suggested that they were struck especially for trade with natives who could not at first distinguish good Roman coins from bad.[2] One may hesitate to believe that the controller of an imperial mint lent himself to a deception which would not only have injured Roman credit, but must soon have been found out.[3]

A well-informed student has argued[4] that although, as he himself recently affirmed,[5] 'All the evidence points to a general improvement in the condition of Egypt during the first century of its government by the Romans', it was eventually ruined by 'Roman mismanagement', and there is 'ground for believing that the condition . . . steadily deteriorated from the very beginning of Roman rule and that this was the inevitable result of the mistakes . . . in the organization adopted by Augustus'. The point which he emphasizes is that 'the revival of agriculture and commerce did not mean a corresponding increase in the wealth of Egypt', for, 'though more corn was produced, a great part was immediately shipped to Rome . . . and the carrying trade was largely in the hands of Roman companies and Jews. The pressure was naturally felt first by the Greek merchants of Alexandria . . . as they dared not defy Rome openly, they tried to annoy it by attacking the Jews, who had obtained special privileges from Augustus, and so were regarded as not only successful competitors in business but favourites of the foreign despot.'

Was Augustus responsible for the eventual ruin of Egypt?

The general conclusion of this critic is that the 'ruin to which Egypt was reduced after four centuries of Roman

---

[1] Warmington, pp. 153, 361 n. 27.   [2] *Ib.*, pp. 39, 292.

[3] When Mr. Warmington says (p. 292) that, 'At first the Romans sent out under Augustus and Tiberius very fine pure gold and silver coins, but at the same time tried the effect of bad coins', is he writing loosely? I can hardly believe that the importers who sent gold and silver should have simultaneously experimented with 'duds'. Mr. R. H. Barrow, however, (*Slavery in the Roman Empire*, 1928, p. 145), thinks that 'the *fourre* denarii of the first century—copper . . . coated with a film of silver—may owe their existence . . . to calculated frauds of the Mint officials'

[4] *J.R.S.*, xvii, 1927, pp. 1–13.   [5] Milne, *Hist. of Egypt*[3], p. 24.

rule' was mainly due to the tribute of corn, which 'was wasted . . . by being used to pauperize the inhabitants of Rome'. It 'had to be supplied whether the harvest was good or bad—unless, as occasionally happened, a prudent Emperor remitted part when the Nile flood was poor—and the evidence suggests that it was fixed at the amount which could be paid in a good year'. If the harvest was insufficient, this amount 'had to be made up by drawing either on the seed-corn or on the food supply of the fellahin. . . . This drain of capital . . . was initiated by Augustus, and it is to him in the first instance that the ruin of Egypt must be ascribed.'

Now, whatever may be thought of the conclusion, the statement of facts must be treated with respect, for the critic's authorities are good—papyri found 'in the rubbish heaps of Egypt', which 'have brought us more closely into touch with the conditions of the lower classes . . . than was possible so long as our knowledge was derived from Roman historians, who got their information from official records'. But he has not enabled us to study the particular papyri upon which his conclusion was based—for instance, to consider whether 'the evidence suggests' what it suggested to him; unless he changed his mind within the two years that immediately preceded the publication of his criticism, we are puzzled how to reconcile it with his statement [1] that 'during the greater part of the second century of Roman rule'—that is, for more than a century after the death of Augustus—the prosperity of Egypt was 'fairly well maintained'; and since he tells us [2] that it was not until 'the middle of this period' that 'signs that the prosperity was on the wane' began to appear, we may reasonably ask for proof that Augustus, and not successors who may have disregarded his example, caused the decline. Moreover, we are bound to consider whether Augustus, to whose reforms the excellence of the administration that in the imperial period so greatly benefited the other provinces was due, can fairly be held responsible for the ruin of Egypt. Did he not habitually act upon the principle which Cavour in boyhood defined—'Pour être un homme d'État utile il faut

[1] *Hist. of Egypt*[3], pp. 55–6.   [2] *Ib.*, p. 57.

avant tout avoir le *tact* des choses possibles'?[1] Was it possible for him, since he could hardly be expected to sacrifice Rome for Egypt, to avoid the expedients to which he had recourse? It may be true that, as the critic has suggested,[2] the strain of payments to Rome was probably increased by alterations made by Augustus in the Egyptian currency, one result of which was that a fourfold increase in wages was counterbalanced by an equal depreciation in the value of the coins with which the wages were paid.[3] But while Augustus, not less than his critic, deplored the pauperization of the Roman populace by doles of corn, his clear vision discerned that that long-standing practice could hardly be abolished;[4] even if it had been, the amount of corn required to feed the populace would have remained the same; and to transfer the carrying trade from Roman companies and Jews to Greek merchants was obviously impracticable. The critic may be reminded that he affirmed lately, with perfect truth, that without the revenues derived from the valley of the Nile Augustus would 'hardly have been in a position to relieve the over-burdened fiscus at Rome'[5]—a duty which no prudent ruler could shirk. Augustus may have made an error of judgement when, perhaps following too closely the example of his adoptive father,[6] he renewed to the Jews, despite Greek protests, all the privileges which they had enjoyed under the Ptolemies;[7] but it could hardly be maintained that this policy or even that 'fiscal oppression' which his regulations encouraged the idiologus to practise,[8] contributed to the ruin of Egypt.

Before Augustus left Spain, on the day when he entered upon his tenth consulship, the Senate, which during his absence had authorized him to do whatever he might think right, confirmed all his acts by oath. On his homeward journey, which was delayed by illness, he promised to give every citizen four hundred sesterces (the equivalent of

Jan. 1, 24 B.C. Gratitude of the Senate for the return of Augustus from Spain.

---

[1] See *The Architect of the Roman Empire* (44–27 B.C.), pp. 141, 176.

[2] *J.R.S.*, xvii, 5.   [3] T. Frank, *Econ. Hist. of Rome*², 1927, p. 399.

[4] Suet., *Aug.*, 42, 3.   [5] *Hist. of Egypt*², p. 121.

[6] See *The Roman Republic*, iii, 210, 507–9.

[7] Jos., *Ant.*, xiv, 7, 2; xix, 5, 2; Philo, *leg. ad Gaium*, 10. Cp. *Edinburgh Rev.*, July, 1925, pp. 39–40, 44.   [8] See p. 16.

four pounds sterling), but with characteristic caution forbade the promise to be announced by edict until the Senate should have signified its approval. The complaisant assembly released him from the obligation; and, on his arrival, by way of thanksgiving for his safe return, honoured Marcellus and Tiberius, who had served under him in Spain, permitting Marcellus to sit in the House among the members of praetorian rank and to stand for the consulship (which he was not destined to hold) ten years before the legal age, and granting Tiberius the right of premature candidature for every office.[1] 'The whole body of citizens', we read in the Ancyran Monument,[2] 'privately and as municipalities, sacrificed continually on behalf of my health at all the shrines'. It has been truly said that innumerable inscriptions bear out this boast of the First Citizen, and 'show how real and personal was the regard felt for him throughout the Roman world.[3]'

Rejoicing over the recovery of Augustus was shortlived. In the following year serious illness led him to provide for the contingency of his death, and he summoned the magistrates with the foremost senators and knights to consult with him on public affairs. Without appointing a successor, though they expected that he would choose Marcellus, he handed to his brother consul, Gnaeus Calpurnius Piso, a statement relating to the troops, legionary and auxiliary, and to the revenue, and to Agrippa his signet ring. A physician, Antonius Musa, who, like most of his professional colleagues, was a freedman, treated him so successfully that he was able to go down to the Senate, intending to read aloud his will, with the object, it is said, of showing that he had not taken upon himself to appoint a successor; but the members, doubtless wishing to assure him that they had absolute confidence in his determination to respect their constitutional rights, would not suffer him to proceed.[4] Then occurred an event of which the

23 B.C. Illness leads him to summon the magistrates to consult on public affairs.

---

[1] Dio, liii, 28, 1–3.   [2] ii, 18–20. Cp. *Klio*, Beih., xix, 1927, pp. 67–8.
[3] Hardy, *The Mon. Ancyr.*, pp. 62–3.
[4] Dio, liii, 30, 1–3; 31, 1. Ferrero (*Grandezza*, &c., iv, 164 [Eng. tr., iv, 235]), citing Suet., *Aug.*, 38, 1, but drawing upon his own imagination, says, 'Augustus declared that in consequence of his illness . . . he felt obliged to retire into private life'.

traditional accounts are uncertain. Dio[1] relates that while Augustus would not commit the power which he felt that he might not himself live long to exercise to a youth whose judgement he could not yet trust, he shrank from appearing to commit it to Agrippa on his own responsibility,[2] and, wishing to avoid the risk of friction between his nephew and Agrippa, to whom the lad was unfriendly, sent Agrippa to Syria: Agrippa, Dio adds, acting with even more than his usual self-effacement,[3] sent his lieutenants to Syria, and remained himself in Lesbos. Suetonius gives two inconsistent accounts: in his life of Augustus[4] he says that Agrippa, piqued by the preference of Augustus for Marcellus,[5] went off in high dudgeon to Mytilene—evidently on his own initiative; in his life of Tiberius[6] that Agrippa's motive was to avoid the appearance of opposing Marcellus or belittling him by remaining in Rome.

Why did Agrippa go to the East?

Now in the latter part of the year, either before or very soon after Agrippa departed, Marcellus, despite the efforts which the physician who had cured his uncle made to save him, died,[7] and thus the alleged reasons for Agrippa's

---

[1] liii, 31, 32, 1.

[2] This is perfectly credible. The attitude of Augustus will be understood by those who have watched the career of Marshal Pilsudski, the present Dictator of Poland. 'The Marshal', says *The Times* (April 16, 1929, p. 17, col. 3), 'has always preferred the reality of power to its appearance . . . from the first he showed the greatest anxiety to set up a Government he could control, rather than govern in his own name. He also showed an unexpected desire to respect constitutional forms as much as the circumstances would permit . . . he refused to govern unconstitutionally without [Parliament] . . . he was . . . hampered by his hankering after Parliamentary approval for his acts'.   [3] ἔτι καὶ μᾶλλον μετριάζων.   [4] 66, 3.

[5] This is to my mind incredible, being unlike what we know of Agrippa.

[6] 10, 1. Pliny (*Nat. hist.*, vii, 46, 149) regarded the retirement of Agrippa as discreditable to Augustus.

[7] Between the 1st of August (Pliny, *Nat. hist.*, xix, 2 (6), 24) and the end of December (Dio, liii, 30, 4). Cp. Vell., ii, 93, 1. According to Servius (*ad Verg., Aen.*, vi, 861), Marcellus was in his eighteenth year. Propertius (*Eleg.*, iii, 18, 15), who gives him two more years (*misero steterat vicesimus annus*), may have been compelled by metrical reasons to adopt a round number and is perhaps less trustworthy than the commentator. On the other hand, it seems hardly probable that Augustus would have given his daughter Julia in marriage to a boy of 15 (Dio, liii, 27, 5). But readers who cannot decide between the authorities will doubtless reflect that the question at issue is unimportant.

Ferrero (*Grandezza*, &c., iv, 190, n. 1 [Eng. tr., iv, 249, n. *]) insists that 'Marcellus must have died in 22, not in 23', for 'Velleius . . . says . . . *ante*

retirement vanished. Yet he remained in the East for
more than a year, returned to undertake important public
duties, and was then highly honoured by his chief.[1] Is it
not probable that the reasons which Dio and Suetonius
give for his departure were based upon rumour, occasioned
by the fact that neither he nor Marcellus had been
appointed as a successor to Augustus ? Dio himself bears
witness to the gossip of those days when he relates[2] that
Livia was accused [probably by conservative opponents
of the government] of having caused the death of Marcellus,
because her husband had preferred him to Tiberius, her son.
An American scholar,[3] who remarks that Agrippa's
reception on his return would have been very different if
the alleged reasons for his departure had been real, in-
geniously conjectures that he was sent on a diplomatic
mission to induce the Parthian king, Phraates, to restore
the captured Roman standards[4] in return for the restoration of his son, who had long been in the power of Augustus.[5]
This exchange was, in fact, carried out.[6] The offer to effect
it 'could not,' says the critic, 'come from Rome, lest
national vanity should be wounded,' nor could Augustus
reveal without loss of dignity that he was ready to purchase
it. Some one must suggest to Phraates that by an acceptable offer he could get back his son,[7] and 'the man best
qualified to negotiate the bargain was he who stood next to
the Princeps.' My readers will perhaps ponder this conjecture: for myself, I would accept it if it did not seem more
probable that Tiberius, who, as we shall see, actually
recovered the standards, conducted the negotiations which
were an essential preliminary. May we not suppose that
Agrippa, himself suggested, or accepted from his chief the

triennium fere quam Egnatianum scelus erumperet, and the *Egnatianum scelus*
is of the year 19'. But Velleius, when he wrote *fere*, was careful not to commit himself to a precise date, and Dio says that Marcellus died soon after
Augustus was cured by Musa, that is, in 23.

[1] Dio, liv, 6, 4–5.   [2] liii, 33, 4.

[3] Prof. David Magie (*Class. Philol.*, iii, 1908, pp. 145–52).

[4] See p. 3, *supra.*

[5] See Dio, li, 18, 3, and *The Architect of the Roman Empire* (44–27 B.C.),
pp. 260–1.   [6] Dio, liii, 33, 2.

[7] As Magie remarks (p. 151, n. 5), Justin (xlii, 5, 9) says that Augustus
sent back Phraates's son gratis; but, he adds with evident truth, 'the terms
of the bargain were undoubtedly kept secret'.

suggestion, that it would be well for him to absent himself
for the time being from Rome ?

But what made this a specially memorable year was that
in it the constitutional powers of Augustus were increased
and formally defined. The Senate, which, if we may trust
Dio,[1] had already made his power virtually absolute, now,
confirming an enactment that followed the battle of
Actium,[2] decreed that he should be invested with the
tribunician power, which gave him the semblance of a
democratic magistrate, for life; that, although he had
just resigned his eleventh consulship,[3] nominating as his
successor with judicious magnanimity one Lucius Sestius,
who, as one of the proscribed, had fought against him
under Brutus, and still openly honoured the memory of
the Republican leader, he should have the privilege of
proposing at every session any one measure that he approved; that he should hold for life the proconsular power
for the control of provincial administration; and that in
every province he should have greater authority than the
governor himself.[4]

The
constitu-
tional
position of
Augustus
defined.

[1] liii, 28, 1–2.

[2] See *The Architect of the Roman Empire* (44–27 B.C.), pp. 172, 180, 222.

[3] *C.I.L.*, i, p. 472. Cp. Dessau, *Inscr. Lat.*, 86, and Rushforth, *Lat. Hist. Inscr.*[2], p. 6. According to Mommsen (*Röm. Staatsr.*, ii[3], 797, n. 3), the resignation occurred on July 1; for, remarking that Augustus seems to have made the consulship half-yearly from this time, he considers it probable that the new consuls entered office on that day. In *Röm. Staatsr.*, ii[3], p. 87, n. 4, he says that the change of *fasces* on July 1 is attested for the years A.D. 1–6, 8–12, and is probable for the rest of the non-annual consulships of the second half of Augustus's reign.

[4] Dio, liii, 32, 3–6; 33, 1; *C.I.L.*, i, pp. 441, 450, 466. Dio says that these privileges were given to Augustus because he was truly honoured (ἐπ' ἀληθείας τιμηθείς), for he generally treated the Romans as free citizens. No doubt; but may we not reasonably presume that in resigning the consulship he counted on receiving, or stipulated that he should receive, a *quid pro quo?* Dio (liii, 37, 3) says that Augustus resigned the consulship, which he had held conjointly with a colleague since the foundation of the Principate, 'in order that as many as possible might become consuls'; Pelham (Essays, pp. 79–80) that 'a stronger reason must have been' his 'anxiety to lessen the danger . . . . from the wounded pride and jealous ambition of the leading nobles, who keenly resented the loss of the official career which they had been taught to regard as their birthright'.

Ferrero (*Grandezza*, &c., iv, 177, n. 1 [Eng. tr., iv, 242, n. †]) argues that modern historians have erred in laying stress upon the grant of the tribunician power. Augustus, he says, 'already enjoyed the inviolability of a tribune [see *The Architect of the Roman Empire* (44–27 B.C.), pp. 120, 221–2]: he never

But, it may be asked, did not the tribunician power itself confer the right of convening the Senate and of introducing public business ? Why, then, did the Senate deem it necessary to empower Augustus to propose any one measure, and why was he restricted to one ? The answer is that by resigning the consulship he had lost the prior right of reference that belonged to it; though he could still introduce business, he could only do so, until the extraordinary power was conferred upon him, after the higher magistrates. That power restored the consular power which he had lost; but it was limited by the proviso that 22 B.C. he might introduce one measure only.[1] In the following year his right to convene the Senate was presumably made independent of the standing order which gave it first to the consuls and praetors and only after them to the tribunes.[2] Probably it was in the earlier or the later year that he was given authority to issue senatorial decrees, although he was no longer a consul.[3] He had now regained every privilege that belonged to the consular office, by resigning which he provided an outlet for ambition that might otherwise be dangerous.

One feature in the character of Augustus was too strong and too constantly evident to need analytical skill. He was a mighty worker, and he worked with whole-hearted devotion for the public weal. Preoccupied with the settlement of Gaul and Spain and Africa, of Galatia, and of Egypt, contending against ill health, he had found time

---

used the veto or . . . the power of proposing laws until the year 18, and these two rights were the most important parts of a tribune's power. Hence it certainly follows that the life tribuneship was merely an honorary gift'. No. Augustus (*Mon. Ancyr.*, i, 28–30; 3, 11–21; ii, 21–3) understood its importance better than Ferrero.

[1] Pelham (*Essays*, 1911, pp. 74–7), who argues, conclusively, I think, that this proviso, which Dio defines by the words χρηματίζειν περὶ ἑνός τινος καθ' ἑκάστην βουλήν, was identical with that described in the well-known *lex de imperio* of Vespasian (see Dessau, *Inscr. Lat.*, 244) as *relationem facere*, and controverts Mommsen (*Staatsr.*, ii, 837, n. 3 [cp. the 3rd edition, p. 899, where Mommsen, as Haverfield observes, 'slightly altered his view, though still explaining χρηματίζειν . . . of the written proposal']), who held that the right conferred in 23 B.C. 'empowered Augustus to submit to the Senate a proposal in writing through the medium of a third party, and even when absent himself'. Cp. Rushforth, *Lat. Hist. Inscr.*², p. 35.

[2] Gell, xiv, 7, 4.   [3] Pelham, *op. cit.*, p. 77.

to regulate the disordered administration of the coinage. After the death of Caesar the Senate had for a short time exercised the right of coining, which had always theoretically belonged to them; but in the subsequent struggle the Triumvirs and their opponents alike issued coins, each on his own account. Octavian, after he became supreme, continued until the settlement in which he was recognized as *Princeps* to issue gold and silver coins, not in Rome but in the East, not as Triumvir (for he had resigned his triumviral office), but as Imperator. After that settlement this coinage ceased and was succeeded by local issues of silver and copper in Asia Minor. At the period which this narrative has reached the newly defined power of Augustus enabled him to take a decisive step: as Imperator (in the extended sense which the word had recently acquired)[1] he intended to issue the gold and the silver coins; as holder of that tribunician power which was now definitively acknowledged, he represented the Roman People and intended, in conjunction with the Senate, to supply the needed token money.[2] With what tact and caution he contrived ultimately to keep in his own hands the sole power of coining the precious metals without questioning the authority of the Senate will appear in the next chapter.

Administration of the coinage regulated.

[1] See *The Architect of the Roman Empire* (44–27 B.C.), pp. 178 n. 6, 268.

[2] *J.R.S.*, vii, 61; H. Mattingly, *Coins of the Roman Empire*, &c., i, 1923, pp. xiii–xv. Cp. Hill, *Historical Roman Coins*, pp. 162–3.

CHAPTER II

Floods in Rome and pestilence in Italy.

23–22 B.C.

THE years in which the constitutional position of Augustus was defined were long remembered as calamitous. The measures that Caesar had planned for preventing floods in Rome[1] had not been carried out. Augustus, indeed, in the years 7 and 6 B.C. provided for the security of the Field of Mars;[2] but it was not until the reign of Tiberius that a permanent commission for embanking the Tiber was appointed;[3] and an inundation, which destroyed the wooden bridge, was followed by a pestilence which caused serious mortality and an almost complete cessation of agriculture, resulting in scarcity.[4] The Roman populace, who are said to have attributed these evils to the First Citizen's resignation of the consulship, took advantage of his absence to blockade the Senate House, and, threatening to set fire to it, forced the Senate to decree that, notwithstanding the abolition of the dictatorship,[5] he should be appointed to that office, which

[1] See *The Roman Republic*, iii, 324.

[2] Rushforth, *Lat. Hist. Inscr.*², pp. 26–30.

[3] Dio, lvii, 14, 7–8. Suetonius (*Aug.*, 37) wrongly attributes the appointment to Augustus.

[4] Dio, liii, 33, 4–5; liv, 1, 1. Cp. Hor., *Carm.*, i, 2. Ferrero (*Grandezza*, &c., iv, 159 [Eng. tr., iv, 232]), remarking that 'a modern writer' regards the pestilence as 'an epidemic of typhus', adds that 'Augustus was attacked by it'. Perhaps; but we only know that in 23 B.C., before the outbreak of the pestilence, he was seriously ill.

[5] See *The Architect of the Roman Empire* (44–27 B.C.), pp. 5, 187–8. Ferrero (*Grandezza*, &c., iv, 185, n. 2 [Eng. tr., iv, 247, n. *]) insists that Dio was wrong in referring the pestilence, the consequent famine, and the popular belief that they were due to Augustus's resignation of the consulship to 22 B.C., and that they really belonged to 23. For, he argues, Velleius (ii, 94, 3) tells us that Tiberius was quaestor at the age of 19 [No; 'in his nineteenth year' (*undevicesimum annum agens*)], when, in obedience to Augustus, he provided for a supply of grain, and Augustus could not have given this commission to Tiberius until [in 22] he had himself become superintendent of the corn supply: Tiberius was quaestor in 23, and 'on matters concerning his life Velleius is a more credible historian than Dio'. Ferrero would have done well to consult Mommsen (*Res gestae*², &c., p. 24), who points out that the violence of the populace in blockading the Senate House and threatening to burn it could only have occurred while Augustus was absent, that is, in 22. It is true that there had been scarcity in 23 and that Augustus had remedied it through the agency of Tiberius; but, as we learn from the Monument of Ancyra (ii, 11–2), this was not an official act: Augustus paid for the corn with his own money.

a deputation soon afterwards begged him to accept.[1] He of course refused, declining also to be elected censor (though he performed duties belonging to the office), but consented to accept the office of superintendent of the corn supply,[2] which Pompey had held thirty-five years before, and which imposed upon him the duty not only of maintaining the doles of grain that were given monthly to Roman citizens, but also—what was far more difficult—of ensuring that a supply should be available at a moderate price for the whole population of the city.[3] In the previous year he had distributed special allowances at his own expense,[4] and he was afterwards able to record that the power now conferred enabled him, with the state funds, to relieve the populace from panic.[5] After he declined the dictatorship he was offered the consulship for life, to be held in conjunction with an ordinarily elected colleague, but refused to accept it.[6]

Augustus consents to superintend the supply of corn.

But no public services could conciliate the nobles who from political or personal motives were inimical to Augustus. Lampoons were scattered in the Senate House, which he took the trouble to refute, though he used his tribunician power to veto a bill for preventing testators from making scurrilous remarks in their wills.[7] A Greek historian, Timagenes, had the audacity to circulate libels about Augustus and Livia; and when Augustus, after warning him repeatedly in vain, forbade him to enter his house, he was welcomed by Asinius Pollio and other nobles, whose conduct Augustus judiciously ignored.[8] Soon after the battle of Actium the younger Lepidus, whose father he expelled from the Triumvirate,[9] had been capitally punished for conspiracy;[10] and a plot was now formed by one Fannius

Plots against his life.

[1] Vell., ii, 89, 5; Suet., *Aug.*, 52; Dio, liv, 1, 2–3. See also *Mon. Ancyr.*, i, 31–2, with which cp. *Klio*, Beih. xix, 1927, Tab. 1, following p. 36.

[2] Vell., ii, 95, 3; Dio, liv, 1, 4–5; 2, 1. 3; *Mon. Ancyr.*, i, 31–4. Cp. *Philol.*, xxix, 1870, p. 39, and O. Hirschfeld, *Kaiserl. Verwaltungsbeamten²*, pp. 330–46. Dio (liv, i, 5) remarks that Augustus 'already had more power than the dictators.' [3] See *The Roman Republic*, ii, 61–2.

[4] *Mon. Ancyr.*, iii, 11–12. Cp. Vell., ii, 94, 3. [5] *Mon. Ancyr.*, i, 34–5.

[6] *Ib.*, i, 35–6. Cp. Mommsen, *Res gestae²*, &c., p. 27.

[7] Suet., *Aug.*, 55; 56, 1. [8] Seneca, *De ira*, iii, 33, 4–8.

[9] *The Architect of the Roman Empire* (44–27 B.C.), p. 117.

[10] Vell., ii, 88.

Caepio, who was joined by Licinius Varro Murena, a brother-in-law of Maecenas.[1] It happened that Marcus Primus, an ex-governor of Macedonia, who was charged with having made war upon a neighbouring tribe, declared that he had done so with the approval of the Emperor. Augustus, who had come voluntarily to give evidence, replied to a question of the praetor that the plea was false. 'What are you doing here?' asked Murena, who was defending Primus. 'Who summoned you?' 'The public weal,' Augustus replied. The reply delighted those whom Dio called 'people of good sense'.[2] The execution of Caepio and Murena, whose conspiracy followed, and who had been tried in the court that adjudicated on charges of treason,[3] did not deter others; but while Gaius Furnius was contending with the Cantabri,[4] and Petronius with the Ethiopians,[5] Augustus was able to start on an administrative tour,[6] which, beginning in Sicily, was prolonged through Greece and the province of Asia as far as Syria. While he was still in Sicily, riots broke out in Rome about the election of the consuls who were to hold office in 21 B.C., and the turmoil was so alarming that Augustus was implored to return. This he refused to do, but he summoned Agrippa, whom he had appointed to represent him in the East, to leave his sphere of government and return to Rome, at the same time requesting him to divorce his wife and, that his authority might be enhanced by an alliance with a member of the imperial family, to marry Julia,[7] the widow of Marcellus. Agrippa had already embellished public buildings in Rome, and now, again at his own expense, constructed an aqueduct, which he named Augusta,[8]

He starts for the East on an administrative tour.

Why he summoned Agrippa to return to Rome and to marry Julia.

[Aqua Virgo.]

---

[1] *Ib.*, 91, 2; Suet., *Aug.*, 19, 1; Dio, liv, 3, 4–7.

[2] One may doubt whether Dio had good authority for saying that it was in consequence of this reply that Augustus was 'given the right to convene the Senate as often as he pleased. Cp. p. 30.

[3] See *The Roman Republic*, i, 63.

[4] See p. 9.   [5] See p. 21.

[6] According to Ferrero (*Grandezza*, &c., iv, 199 [Eng. tr., iv, 255]), he was 'reduced to flight, lest the dictatorship . . . should be forced upon him'.

[7] Dio, liv, 6, 1–5; Jos., *Ant.*, xv, 10, 2. ' It is certain', says Hardy (*Mon. Ancyr.*, p. 73), 'that Augustus hoped to secure from the marriage . . . a settlement of the succession.'

[8] Dio, liii, 23, 1–2; 27, 1–2; liv, 11, 7.

the part within the city being carried on arches, remains of which are to be seen in the Via del Nazzareno. He governed Rome till 19, when he was transferred to Gaul and soon afterwards to Spain,[1] where, it will be remembered, he finally subdued the Cantabri.[2] Augustus, after founding colonies in Sicily and Greece and settling affairs in both, sailed to Samos, where he passed the winter and received the Ethiopian envoys,[3] crossed thence to Asia, the province to which Samos belonged, punished Cyzicus, although it belonged to a senatorial province, by deprivation of autonomy for an outrage committed against Roman citizens, and, proceeding thence to Syria, inflicted the same penalty for riot upon Tyre and Sidon.[4]

If Dio's chronology is correct, it was in 20 B.C., during his absence, that Augustus was chosen as 'Commissioner of the Roads near Rome'.[5] Discharging the duty by appointing a curator for each trunk-road, he erected at the north end of the Forum the so-called 'golden milestone', a column covered with gilded bronze, on which were engraved the names of the chief cities of the empire with their distances from the capital.[6] Perhaps he had already planned the imperial postal service, which, originally modelled on that of Republican times[7] and carried out by couriers stationed along the main roads, was developed before the end of his reign by the organization under which one courier, who could answer questions relating to the dispatches that he carried, performed the whole journey, with changes of horses, in the same carriage.[8] Though the service was designed solely for imperial purposes, not for the benefit of the public, who, when they wrote letters, were still obliged, as in the days of Cicero, to entrust them to

He provides for the repair of roads.

The postal service.

---

[1] *Ib.*, 6, 6; ii, 1–2.   [2] See p. 9.
[3] See p. 21.
[4] Dio, liv, 7. Dio says that Augustus 'enslaved' (ἐδουλεύσατο) the citizens of Cyzicus, Tyre, and Sidon. Evidently he means 'deprived them of political freedom'. Cp. liv, 23, 7.
[5] *Ib.*, 8, 4. Cp. O. Hirschfeld, *Kaiserl. Verwaltungsbeamten*[2], p. 205, and *C.I.L.*, ix, 2845.
[6] Dio, liv, 8, 4. Cp. T. Ashby, *The Roman Campagna*, &c., pp. 38–9.
[7] See *The Roman Republic*, i, 114, and *J.R.S.*, x, 83–4.
[8] Suet., *Aug.*, 49, 3; *J.R.S.*, x, 85; xv, 60–1, 73; Rushforth, *Lat. Hist. Inscr.*[2], pp. 32, 35.

private or commercial couriers, the roads by which it was carried on helped to diffuse civilization.[1]

But the most noteworthy event that occurred in the absence of Augustus was the restoration of the standards that had been captured by Parthian armies. Although Augustus had not the gratification of receiving them in person, Tiberius was able to take his place. Four years before
the battle of Actium, Artavasdes, the King of Armenia, whose advice Antony followed in his Parthian campaign, but who failed to help him in his retreat, had fallen into the power of Octavian, and had been sent with his sons, Artaxes and Tigranes, to Alexandria, where he was put to death by Cleopatra. Artaxes, who contrived to escape, succeeded after a temporary reverse in securing his father's throne with the help of certain Armenian notables; and Octavian, who found it prudent to acquiesce in this arrangement, sent Tigranes to Rome. Soon after he left Samos he was invited by the Armenian nobles friendly to Rome to raise him to the throne, and entrusted this duty to Tiberius, who entered Armenia with an army, and himself placed the crown on the prince's head.[2] Armenia was thus made into a client kingdom, a course which, since the country was intimately connected with Parthia, was destined to lead to trouble. A representative of the Parthian king delivered the Roman prisoners and the standards to Tiberius, whose troops exultantly saluted the absent Emperor as Imperator.[3] Ignoring the negotiations that had led to such success,

[1] *The Legacy of Rome* (Oxford), pp. 144, 161. See *The Roman Republic*, i, 114.

[2] *The Architect of the Roman Empire* (44–27 B.C.), pp. 127, 136, 161, 169; *Mon. Ancyr.*, v, 24–8; Vell., ii, 94, 4; Tac., *Ann.*, ii, 3, 4; Suet., *Tib.*, 9, 1. Before Tiberius arrived in Armenia Artaxes was slain.

Ferrero, who asserts (*Grandezza*, &c., iv, 184, n. 1 [Eng. tr., iv, 246, n. *]) that the cession of Armenia 'must have been included in the negotiations', might have done well to read the relevant passage in *Monumentum Ancyranum*.

[3] Livy, *Epit.*, 141; Vell., ii, 91, 1; Flor., ii, 34, 63; Suet., *Aug.* 21, 3; *Tib.*, 9, 1; Justin., xlii, 5, 11; Dio, liv, 8, 1. M. Gelzer (*Paulys Real-Ency.*, x, 481) thinks that Suetonius (*Tib.*, 9, 1) was wrong in saying that Tiberius recovered the standards, for, he says, Dio does not confirm this statement, and Velleius would not have been silent on the point. The criticism seems to me frivolous. Neither Velleius nor Dio cared to do more than record the recovery. Mommsen (*Res gestae*[2], &c., p. 126) accepts Suetonius's statement.

Augustus recorded that he had compelled the Parthians to restore the standards and to implore the friendship of the Roman People.[1] The standards, on being taken to Rome, were deposited in a small temple, dedicated to Mars the Avenger, on the Capitol, whence eighteen years later they were transferred to the greater temple which Octavian in the campaign of Philippi had vowed to build, to avenge his adoptive father's murder.   A triumphal arch was erected in the Forum; Roman coins depicted suppliant Parthians; on the statue of Augustus in the villa of Livia at Prima Porta Mars was portrayed on the emperor's corslet in the act of receiving the standard of a legion;[2] and Horace,[3] celebrating the happy event, which he had anticipated eight years before,[4] satisfied national pride with little more than legitimate poetical licence.

The tour of Augustus was drawing to its close. Before he left Syria to spend the winter in Samos, to which, in celebration of his visit, he granted autonomy, and in which he received one of the embassies that reached him from India,[5] he restored to Tarcondimotus the Second, in accordance with his policy of refraining from territorial aggrandizement, the greater part of Cilicia, of which that monarch's father, Philopator, had been deprived after the battle of Actium. The part that was not restored comprised maritime districts, doubtless retained in order to cripple the naval power of the dynasty, which had been used by Pompey against Caesar.[6]

Augustus might have remained longer in the East if the Senate, alarmed by riots and murders which occurred at 19 B.C.

---

[1] *Mon. Ancyr.*, v, 40–2.

[2] *Ib.*, iv, 3; Vell., ii, 100, 2; Suet., *Aug.*, 29; Dio, liv, 8, 2–3; lx, 5; Servius *ad Aen.*, vii, 606; Mommsen, *Res gestae*[2], &c., pp. 124–6; Rushforth, *Lat. Hist. Inscr.*[2], pp. 20–2; A. von Domaszewski, *Abhandl. zur röm. Religion*, 1909, pp. 53–7; G. F. Hill, *Historical Roman Coins*, 1909, pp. 138–43.

[3] *Carm.*, iv, 15, 4–8; *Epist.*, i, 12, 27–8.   [4] *Carm.*, iii, 5, 3–12.

[5] Dio, liv, 9, 7–8; *Mon. Ancyr.*, v, 50–1; Mommsen, *Res gestae*[2], &c., pp. 132–3. See p. 20, *supra*. It has been suggested (see Dessau, *Gesch. d. röm. Kaiserzeit*, i, 1924, p. 387 and n. 1) that the embassies from India and elsewhere which Augustus chronicled (*Mon. Ancyr.*, v, 50–3) were not political, and that the envoys may have been impostors! Nonsense. What object could impostors have had in making long and costly journeys?

[6] Dio, xli, 63, 1; li, 2, 2; liv, 9, 2. Cp. *J.R.S.*, ii, 105, and *The Roman Republic*, iii, 113.

the time of the consular election, when he refused to be nominated himself, had not sent envoys to urge him to return;[1] but on the voyage he halted at Athens, where Virgil met him. They travelled together to Megara, and then crossed the Adriatic; but on the 21st of September,[2] soon after they landed at Brundisium, the poet, whose declining health succumbed to malaria, died. His biographer related that in his illness he expressed a wish to burn the *Aeneid*, which he had not finally revised, but that his friends, Lucius Varius and Plotius Tucca, preserved and published it. According to the same authority, he had chosen the Second, Fourth, and Sixth Books—a choice which modern critics would approve—to read to Augustus. When this intention was carried out, is not known, but certainly after the death of Marcellus, which occurred soon after Augustus returned from Spain. The story is well known that Octavia was present when Virgil recited the lines in which Anchises foretold the early promise and the premature death of her son, and that she swooned.[3]

When Augustus on his homeward journey was passing through Campania, a deputation, comprising Quintus Lucretius, whom, though he had been one of the proscribed, he had nominated consul in consequence of the recent riots, praetors, tribunes, and other notables, came to meet him by decree of the Senate—an honour which, as he proudly recorded,[4] had been conferred upon no other Roman. Of other honours which were offered to him he accepted only the foundation of an altar to *Fortuna Redux* (Fortune the Home-bringer), hard by the Gate called Capena, through which on the night of the 12th of October he entered the city, and a senatorial decree that the day of his arrival should be called Augustalia and numbered among the annual holidays.[5] Eight years later games were held on the anniversary, and in the last year of his reign made annual.[6] Though the Senate and the people unani-

Augustus returns to Rome, meeting Virgil on the way. Death of Virgil and publication of the Aeneid.

The Senate confers honours on Augustus.

---

[1] Dio, liv, 10, 1-2. See p. 34.   [2] *Class Rev.*, 1930, pp. 1-3, 57-9.

[3] Donatus, *Vita Verg.*, ed. Brummer, 123-33; Servius *ad Aen.*, vi, 861.

[4] *Mon. Ancyr.*, ii, 34-7. See pp. 147-9.

[5] *Mon. Ancyr.*, ii, 29-33; *C.I.L.*, i², p. 332; Dio, liv, 10, 3-4. Cp. Mommsen, *Res gestae*², &c., p. 46.

[6] Dio, liv, 34, 2; lvi, 29, 1; 46, 4; Tac., *Ann.*, i, 15, 3; 54, 3.

mously desired that he should be appointed controller of
laws and public morals with supreme authority, he declined
the offer, preferring to carry out certain social measures
which he contemplated in virtue of his tribunician power;[1]
but he accepted the consular insignia—the *fasces* and the
consular seat in the Senate—which, since he had abandoned
the consulship,[2] would be useful.

The work which Augustus had done in the last three
years did not conciliate personal enemies or political
opponents. Marcus Egnatius Rufus, an ex-aedile who,
having done good work in saving houses from being destroyed by fire, had been elected a praetor, formed a plot to
murder the First Citizen, whom he had offended by pub-
lishing a vainglorious announcement, and, together with
his fellow-conspirators, was executed.[3]

Plot of Egnatius Rufus.

20 B.C.

The period for which Augustus had received the proconsular power at the commencement of his principate was
drawing to a close, and in the year after he returned from
the East it was renewed—by himself, if Dio was not mis-
informed—for five years, to which five more were soon
afterwards added. At the same time the tribunician power,
which he held for life, was granted to Agrippa, together
with proconsular power, for five years.[4]

18 B.C.

Immediately afterwards a purgation of the Senate was
held, as it had been ten years before. On this occasion also
no senator would resign voluntarily, and Augustus, unwilling to incur odium by expelling undesirable members
on his own responsibility, selected thirty, who, as he afterwards testified on oath, were the best in the whole body,
and attempted through this committee to form a new list
by combining the methods of selection and lot. In the
course of the voting an incident was noticed, which illustrates not only the character of Augustus, but also the

Purgation of the Senate.

[1] *Mon. Ancyr.*, i, 37–9 (the missing Latin is supplied from the *Monumentum
Antiochenum* [*Klio*, Beih. xix, 1927, Tab. 1, following p. 36], 3, 11–21. See
pp. 43–5.
[2] See p. 30.
[3] Vell., ii, 91, 2–3; 92; Dio, liii, 24, 4–6. Was the plot, which Ferrero
(*Grandezza*, &c., iv, 79, n. 3 [Eng. tr., iv, 187, n. ‡]) calls 'an act of reprisal
for the injustice [!] he had suffered', due to fear of punishment?
[4] Dio, liv, 12, 4–5.

nature of his relations with the Senate. It will be remembered that when Octavian removed Lepidus from the Triumvirate he forbore to depose him from the position of Chief Pontiff, notwithstanding the illegality of the method by which he had obtained it.[1] But, while he scrupulously adhered to this forbearance,[2] he systematically insulted Lepidus, all the more perhaps because of the plot for which his son had been executed. For instance, he compelled him to attend the meetings of the Senate with the object of exposing him to the jeers of members, and never asked him for his vote until all the other ex-consuls had given theirs. Undeterred by this example, a famous jurist, Antistius Labeo, inserted the name of Lepidus among those whom he selected. Augustus, in exasperation, threatened to punish him for perjury, doubtless assuming that he had violated the oath by which each member of the committee had pledged himself to select the fittest men. 'What harm have I done', replied Labeo, 'by retaining in the Senate a man whom you even now allow to remain Chief Pontiff?' The feeling of the House was that Labeo had made a very apt retort, and Augustus held his peace. But, as his attempt at selection failed, he himself chose the men whom, after expelling the undesirables, he deemed fittest to make up the number to six hundred—just twice as many as he would have appointed if he had felt free to adopt his own view. Among them, however, were found unsuitable persons, whom he removed in favour of others. He now felt himself in a position to embark upon his scheme of social legislation.[3]

Conspirators executed. But, apparently before he could begin this work, many persons were accused of plotting against him and Agrippa, and although Dio guardedly declines to decide whether the accusations, which he found recorded, were true or false, and does not even hint that they may have been due, wholly or in part, to the recent purgation of the Senate, he states unequivocally that Augustus executed some of the accused.[4] Perhaps it was at this time or when he made

---

[1] *The Architect of the Roman Empire* (44–27 B.C.), p. 117.
[2] *Mon. Ancyr.*, ii, 24–5.
[3] Dio, liv, 13–4; 15, 4–8; Suet., *Aug.*, 37. See p. 39.   [4] liv, 15, 1–4.

his own selection of senators that Augustus wore a breast-
plate under his tunic, while ten of his most robust sup-
porters stood beside his chair, and, if we may trust a statement, perhaps not wholly unfounded, of Cremutius Cordus,
who honoured the memory of the Republican leaders,
other senators were only allowed to approach him singly
and after their clothing had been searched.[1]

One may conclude not only from the testimony of historical writers, but also from that of Augustan poets—
Horace, Propertius, and Ovid—that the laxity in sexual
relations which had been noticeable even in the Ciceronian
age,[2] increased after the cessation of the civil wars. The
sense of security, following a long period of suffering and
anxiety, the prosperity resulting from renewed commercial
activity, encouraged men and women to get all obtainable
enjoyment out of life; even after we have been careful to
avoid inferring overmuch from censorious or erotic verse
we may reasonably suppose that what poets observed or
practised was more than the immorality that exists in every
age; and, as a well-informed critic[3] has remarked, it was
such as 'the old religion, disregarded now by the masses,
as it had long been ignored or abused for political purposes
by their betters, was as powerless as the traditional
morality to check or control'. If Augustus had observed
nothing more reprehensible than the amours of men of
pleasure with the Syrian dancers and the dainty young
freedwomen—the demi-mondaines and cocottes of the day
—whose white arms and slender fingers the more wealthy
adorned with Oriental gems, he might not have thought
it politic to legislate: what impelled him was the growing
repugnance to marriage.[4] While many noble families had
been extinguished in the civil wars others were in danger
of dying out through lack of posterity. In the first year of
the Principate Augustus had framed a law which imposed

Legisla-
tion of
Augustus
relating to
marriage
and
adultery.

[1] Suet., *Aug.*, 35, 1–2.
[2] See *The Roman Republic*, i, 92–4.
[3] Pelham, *Essays*, p. 94.
[4] G. Boissier (*La religion rom.*, i², 1892, p. 84) says that Augustus resolved
to legislate because he was 'sollicité de tant de côtés', amongst others by
Horace (*Carm.*, iii, 24, 25–30). Who can tell whether Horace wrote these
lines spontaneously or under the influence of Augustus?

certain disabilities upon unmarried men;[1] but it provoked
such opposition that, much to the delight of Propertius,[2]
it was repealed. Men preferred mistresses to wives, and
married couples often agreed that it would be pleasanter
to spend their money on luxury and amusement than to
have children who would be an encumbrance and a source
of expense.[3] Ovid, whose experience qualified him to judge,
probably exaggerated little when he wrote[4] that in Rome
the only chaste women were those whom no one had
attempted to seduce. Livy[5] deplored the love of money
and the lust of pleasure that had corrupted the old stern
morality on which the greatness of Rome was founded;
Horace,[6] bidding his countrymen remember that their
dominion rested upon reverence for the gods, and that
they had suffered reverses since they ceased to revere,
lamented the disregard of the marriage tie which was
sapping family life, described the beauty of boys whom the
keenest eye could hardly distinguish from girls, and declared that the generation in which a rich lover dared to
make assignations with a woman in the presence and with
the connivance of her husband was very different from that
in which the hardy sons of austere mothers vanquished
Hannibal.

Augustus seems to have been uneasily conscious that in
attempting to check the prevalent immorality he would
hardly be able to escape the reproach that he had not
always practised what he was about to preach; for his
biographer, while he was careful to refute the scandal-
mongers who charged him with unnatural vice,[7] admitted

[1] Dio, liii, 13, 2.   [2] ii, 7, 1–3.
[3] Cp. the significant words of Ovid (*Amores*, ii, 14, 7), *ut careat rugarum crimine venter.*
[4] *Amores*, i, 8, 43.   [5] Praef., § 12.
[6] *Carm.*, iii, 6, 5–8, 17–44; i, 4, 19–20; ii, 5, 20–4.
[7] Dr. S. G. Owen (Ovid, *Tristia*, ii, p. 40, n. 2), citing Th. Birt, *De amorum in arte antiqua simulacris et de pueris minutis apud antiquos in deliciis habitis,* Marburg, 1892, p. xi, says that the writer gives an interpretation 'no doubt true' of a passage in Suetonius's *Divus Augustus*, 83—*ludebat cum pueris minutis quos facie et garrulitate amabilis undique conquirebat.* Dr. Owen might have added that Suetonius (*ib.*, 71, 1) emphatically denies that Augustus was guilty of unnatural vice; and, whether the charge of paede-rasty is true or false, the evidence with which Birt endeavours to support it is insufficient.

that his best friends were unable to deny his adulteries, and
Dio [1] found in the sources of his *Roman History* that
senators, who urged the First Citizen to enforce marriage by
legislation, did not shrink from alluding in debate to his
gallantries nor even from plying him with questions which
he could not readily answer. But, whether his decision was
spontaneous or formed under such pressure, he concluded,
as not the least illustrious of Italian statesmen has lately
done, that those who were reluctant to marry or to fulfil
the obligations of marriage might be amenable to a com-
bination of penalties and rewards; and in this spirit he proposed to the Comitia, in virtue of his tribunician power, the
law which became known as the *lex Iulia de maritandis ordinibus*. While it was being discussed, he reminded his
fellow-senators how the famous censor, Quintus Metellus,
had exhorted bachelors to marry, not for their own gratification, but because it was a duty, which they owed to the
State, to beget children.[2]

Under this law, as it is described by Dio,[3] men were
required to marry within two years after betrothal;
rewards were to be bestowed upon parents who had at
least three children; and, since freeborn males were more
numerous than females, the children of all men, except
senators, who married freedwomen, were to be legitimized.
Of these provisions the first is recorded by Dio alone;[4] the
others are to be found, amplified, in the writings of the
jurists. The few who study them, however, sometimes find
it impossible to decide whether this or that clause belonged
to the original law about marriage or to others which followed it; for the social legislation of Augustus was spread
over twenty-six years, and, following the law with which
we are at present concerned, and which was subsequently
modified, there were others connected with it.

Besides those which have been already mentioned, the
lex de maritandis ordinibus contained various noteworthy
provisions. All Roman citizens, except senators, their sons,

[1] liv, 16, 3.
[2] Livy, *Epit.*, 59; Suet., *Aug.*, 89, 2. Cp. *The Roman Republic*, i, 92.
[3] liv, 16, 1–2. 7.
[4] Suetonius, however (*Aug.*, 34, 2), says that Augustus shortened the
duration of betrothals.

grandsons, and great-grandsons in the male line, were permitted to marry freedwomen of unblemished reputation;[1] for it was part of Augustus's plan to remove all obstacles to marriage. In certain cases separation between husband and wife was made legally invalid, while a freedwoman, married to her former master, was forbidden, except in certain cases, to separate from him and marry again without his consent.[2] Husbands, on the other hand, were forbidden to dispose, without the consent of their wives, of dowries which they had received.[3] Various privileges were granted to women who had three or more children.[4] Freedmen who had been manumitted on condition of remaining celibate were released from that obligation;[5] those who had two children, or one not less than five years old, were exempt from the duty of rendering certain services to their former owners;[6] freedwomen who married with their patron's consent were, under the *lex Papia Poppaea*, of which more anon, similarly privileged.[7] Bachelors and spinsters were disqualified for inheriting property,[8] and forbidden to be present at public games— a prohibition which was to be relaxed, on a special occasion and on religious grounds, in the following year.[9] If a father or a guardian refused consent to a marriage or withdrew a dowry, the son or daughter or ward had a legal remedy.[10] Two other provisions may have been included in the law: heirs and legatees were released from the obligation of celibacy or widowhood if it was imposed by the testator;[11] any Roman citizen might be a candidate for office at an age as many years below that prescribed by law as he had children.[12]

The marriage law was supplemented—apparently in the same year—by one relating to adultery, in which sumptuary legislation was perhaps included. Of this latter one

---

[1] Ulpian, xiii, 1; *Dig.*, xxiii, 2, 44. Mr. Barrow (*Slavery in the Roman Empire*, p. 182, n. 2) remarks that in *Dig.*, xxiii, 2, 23, this provision is assigned to the *lex Papia*.

[2] *Dig.*, xxxviii, 11, 1, 1.   [3] Gaius, ii, 63.

[4] *Fragm. iuris Rom. Vaticana*, 158, 197, 214.

[5] *Dig.*, xxxvii, xiv, 6, § 4.   [6] *Dig.*, xxxviii, 1, 37 pr. § 1.

[7] *Dig.*, xxxviii, 1, 14.   [8] Ulpian, xxii, 3.

[9] See p. 50.   [10] *Dig.*, xxiii, 2, 19. Cp. Gaius, i, 178, and Ulpian, xi, 20.

[11] *Dig.*, xxxv, 1, 72, 4; 79, 4.   [12] *Ib.*, iv, 4, 2.

provision only, apparently intended to restrict expenditure,[1] is known. It has been suggested,[2] reasonably enough, that both resulted from the law of marriage, for men could hardly be compelled to marry unless they were armed with domestic authority. The same commentator [3] has inferred, perhaps rightly, from a well-known passage in Dio's *History*,[4] that Augustus was opposed to this supplementary legislation and could only be induced to act by a threat to rake up the details of his own adulteries. What Dio says is that Augustus, being pressed in debate by senators, whom he told that they ought to follow his example and control their wives, to explain how he did so, reluctantly made a few remarks about women's dress and modesty. *Patresfamiliae* were allowed by the law in question to kill adulterous daughters and their paramours,[5] husbands, in certain cases, to kill their wives' lovers if they caught them in their own houses.[6] Otherwise adulterers were liable to be banished to an island and to forfeit half their property, adulteresses to the like banishment and the forfeiture of half their dowries and one-third of their fortune.[7] Wives were not allowed to accuse their husbands of adultery; [8] freedmen, freedwomen, and aliens were not punishable for this offence. Men who knowingly married women convicted of adultery or did not divorce wives caught in adultery, were liable to various penalties.[9] Not only adultery, but also unnatural vice was punishable.[10]

Augustus must have been dissatisfied with the results of the marriage law; for twenty-two years later he made it A.D. 4 more severe. A prosecution, to which Dio alludes,[11] for breach of the law relating to adultery can hardly have been unique; and since in the year after the marriage law was passed Augustus revived, formally or virtually, the obsolete enactment which forbade advocates to accept fees,[12] it has been naturally inferred [13] that he anticipated that his

---

[1] Gell., ii, 24, 14–5.   [2] By Ferrero, *Greatness and Decline*, &c., v, 66, n. *).
[3] *Ib.*, 66, nn.*‡, 69–70.   [4] liv, 16, 3–5.   [5] *Dig.*, xlviii, 5, 24 (23).
[6] *Ib.*, 25 (24).   [7] Paul., *Sent.*, ii, 36, 14.   [8] *Cod. Iust.*, viiii, 9, 1.
[9] *Dig.*, iv, 4, 37, 1.   [10] *Inst.*, iv, 18, 4.   [11] liv, 30, 4.
[12] Dio, liv, 18, 2. See *The Roman Republic*, i, 232. Cp. Ferrero, *op. cit.*, v, 168, and W. W. Buckland, *Text-book of Roman Law*, &c., 1921, pp. 23–5.
[13] By Ferrero (*op. cit.*, 100, n. *).

social legislation would stimulate the activity of the courts. The stringent law of A.D. 4, which appears to have been called the *lex Iulia caducaria*, subjected childless married men to the same penalties as bachelors, and provoked such opposition that Augustus was obliged to suspend it for three years, to which two were afterwards added because war was imminent. On the expiration of this period, the final manifestation of his social policy, the *lex Papia Poppaea*, was enacted, alleviating the *lex caducaria* by relieving married men.[1]

17 B.C.
Religious
revival.
It was in the year after the enactment of the law relating to marriage that Augustus accomplished a religious revival which tended to satisfy hopes and aspirations expressed in Virgil's famous fourth Eclogue and Horace's sixteenth Epode.[2] Superstitions, which his biographer noted—for instance, the fancy that if his left shoe was put on before the right, ill luck would follow [3]—were not, indeed, incompatible with religious scepticism: there are strong minds which, while they know that such fancies are absurd, cannot resist the impulse to yield to them. Although there is no direct evidence that Augustus disbelieved in the gods whose temples he had restored, nobody who has studied the history of his reign will challenge the view that he was not animated by religious enthusiasm, and that his motive for reviving old cults was to restore public confidence and to awaken faith in a renewal of divine favour.[4] When George Long wrote those thought-provoking words, 'He who is strictly honest and unbending is not fit for the direction of political affairs',[5] he would have found no lack of fitness in him. If he did not anticipate the judgement of Gibbon,[6] that 'the various modes of worship, which prevailed in the Roman world, were all considered by the people as equally true, by the philosopher as equally false, and by the magistrate as equally useful', one would not be far wrong in attributing to him the view of Swift, as defined by an agnostic, that 'religion, however little regard is paid to it in

---

[1] See pp. 151–2.   [2] See *Class. Rev.*, xxxix, 64.
[3] Suet., *Aug.*, 92, 1.   [4] Pelham, *Essays*, pp, 101–2.
[5] See *The Architect of the Roman Empire* (44–27 B.C.), p. 71.
[6] *Decline and Fall*, &c., i, 1867, p. 36.

practice, is in fact the one great security for a decent degree of social order'.[1] It has been said that he sincerely regarded Apollo as his protector.[2] Who can tell ? Did his allusions to 'the immortal gods' mean more than those of Caesar ? [3] The declaration of Henry of Navarre, 'Je ferai voir à tout le monde que je n'ay esté persuadé par autre théologie que la nécessité de l'estat', may describe the 'theology' of Augustus; but if 'all the world' saw it, he did not go out of his way to aid their vision. Perhaps he found his own convictions expressed by Ovid: [4] 'That gods should exist is expedient; then let us suppose that they do.' No constitutional ruler would refuse to take part in a religious service approved by popular sentiment, even if he were convinced that prayer and thanksgiving are of no avail; or, if intellectual honesty overcame his sense of political expediency, a healthy conscience would bid him abdicate rather than offend. Augustus since his boyhood had been a pontiff; [5] he had become an augur before his Triumvirate; [6] and one may feel sure that in planning the religious revival he gauged the average sentiment of Roman citizens. Although in the poetry of the age the conjugal relations of Jupiter and Juno, the coquetry and the vanity of Venus were made ridiculous,[7] although Cicero [8] put into the mouth of an Epicurean speaker his own contempt for the fancied quarrels of gods and goddesses, although women here and there were attracted by Iris and Jehovah, and men by the speculations of Zeno and Epicurus,[9] although Pliny [10] scornfully denied the immortality of the soul, the belief that Roman deities must be propitiated if they were to favour Romans was not extinct. For Tibullus [11] the gods of the countryside were alive; and Virgil

---

[1] Leslie Stephen, *Swift*, 1882, p. 47.

[2] G. Boissier, *La religion rom.*, ii[4], 89.   [3] *B.G.*, i, 14, 5; v, 52, 6, &c.

[4] *Ars amat.*, i, 635: *Expedit esse deos, et ut expedit, esse putemus.* So also Mucius Scaevola, the Chief Pontiff under whom Cicero had studied Roman law, affirmed that religion, true or false, was essential to the existence of the State. See *The Roman Republic*, i, 78, 228.   [5] Vell., ii, 59, 3.

[6] See the coin figured by H. A. Grueber (*Coins of the Roman Republic*, &c., ii, 404), which corrects a statement of Mommsen in *Res gestae*[2], &c., p. 32.

[7] Boissier, *La religion rom.*, i[2], 204.   [8] *De nat. deor.*, i, 16, 42.

[9] Cp. *The Roman Republic*, i, 79–83.   [10] *Nat. hist.*, vii, 55 (56), 188–90.

[11] i, 10, 45–6.

supported the efforts of Augustus, whom he, like Horace,[1] represented as destined to become after death divine.' The civil wars had produced a reaction towards the old worship in acknowledgement of Rome's victory over the gods of Egypt; and Augustus, who could hardly yet have found time to write the treatise in which he urged his country-men to study philosophy,[2] intended to exploit that move-ment for religious, political, social, and even economic ends. Not only had he revived the adoration of Venus Genetrix and built a temple to his adoptive father, who was both her reputed descendant and the deified hero of the empire,[3] but he also resuscitated obsolete or obsolescent rites[4] and re-established practices of which Varro lamented the loss, nominating a priest of Jupiter for the first time since the dictatorship of Sulla.[5] For the Romans and the Greeks the essence of religion was ritual, and Augustus purposed to satisfy the want. An inscription, in which his purpose and its achievement are minutely recorded, shows that in one respect at least he was perfectly successful: the spirit of bargaining that had characterized the religion of the Republic is evident throughout.[6] The ritual was formulated by regulations as precise as those of which we read in *Leviticus*. Lay worshippers as well as priests must be purged of all uncleanness; the sacrificial victims were selected according to rules which prescribed their sex, their age, their colour; every detail must be performed in exact obedience to prescription, every word spoken as it was set down in the liturgy, lest the deity concerned should take offence and refuse to grant the boon for which his votaries prayed. The time was ripe for the revival which the Emperor planned; for after the victory of Actium a hope manifested itself that the new and better age anticipated by Virgil was beginning or about to begin; and ancient colleges such as that of the Arval Brothers, now re-estab-lished, were honoured by the inclusion among their mem-bers of Augustus.[7]

11 B.C. *(margin note)*

---

[1] *Carm.* 1, 2, 45–6.   [2] Suet., *Aug.*, 85, 1.

[3] *Mon. Ancyr.*, iv, 2; Dio, xlvii, 18, 4. Cp. *The Architect of the Roman Empire* (44–27 B.C.), p. 174.   [4] Suet., *Aug.*, 31, 4.

[5] Dio, liv, 36, 1.   [6] See p. 51, n. 1. Cp. *The Roman Republic*, ii, 71–2.

[7] *Mon. Ancyr.*, i, 45–6. Cp. Paulys, *Real-Ency.*, ii, 1468, 1471–2.

According to tradition, a religious festival had been instituted after a great calamity, which more than one authority of the Augustan Age assigned to 509 B.C., the first year of the Republic. It included expiatory sacrifices offered at night to propitiate the deities of the nether world, Dis Pater (more widely known to modern readers as Pluto) and Proserpine, to whose wrath the calamity was attributed, and was to be celebrated again at intervals of a *saeculum*, or one hundred years, in accordance with which it became known as the *ludi saeculares*. The earliest celebration of which the date is absolutely certain was in 249 B.C.; but there is some reason to believe that the first of the series occurred two centuries earlier. Most probably the festival was repeated in 348, and undoubtedly (after 249) in 149 or 146; but it was omitted in 49, the first year of civil war.[1] If it was to be revived, as Augustus intended, in 17, the year in which the renewal of his proconsular power took effect, what was to become of its character as marking a period of one hundred years? And how would expiatory sacrifices, offered at night, harmonize with an occasion which was to be one of hope and rejoicing, befitting the commencement of a new and happy era? Augustus found a way out of the difficulty. He had been appointed, or had caused himself to be appointed, president of the sacred college of fifteen members—the *XVviri sacris faciundis*; and Agrippa, upon whose support he could rely, and who jointly with him held tribunician power, was one of the fifteen.[2] In the year 18 Augustus had ordered that the Sibylline oracles should be copied anew by members of the college, 'so that', as Dio[3] says, 'nobody else might read them.' The order provided the machinery by which the year 17 might be harmonized with tradition. An oracle was discovered, or said to have been discovered, according to which the last celebration of the festival had occurred, not in 149 or 146, but in 126, and a *saeculum*, by Etruscan reckoning, lasted a hundred and ten years.[4] Thus, while

[1] I ask readers who may wish to control my statements to read pp. 153–5.
[2] *Mon. Ancyr.*, iv, 36–7; *C.I.L.*, ix, 262; Dio, liv, 19, 8.
[3] liv, 17, 2.
[4] Zosimus, ii, 6, 1. Cp. *Paulys Real-Ency.*, i A., 1697–8, 1708.

Augustus gained his point, public opinion was satisfied. In February the Senate decreed that the festival should be held, and entrusted its celebration to Augustus and Agrippa.[1] Augustus purposed to substitute for Pluto and Proserpine Apollo and Diana. A young lawyer, Ateius Capito, who had contrived the interpretation of the oracle, drew up the arrangements,[2] and Horace was requested by Augustus, who indicated the points that were to be emphasized, to compose a poem for the occasion.

Celebra-
tion of the
*ludi
saeculares.*

Since Augustus desired that the festival should attract as many worshippers as could be induced to attend, heralds were dispatched to every town and every village in Italy to announce the celebration, 'which no one had yet seen or would ever see again.'[3] As such a unique occasion might fitly be associated with some act of indulgence, those unmarried persons who had been forbidden by the law relating to marriage to look on at public games were allowed, in this one instance, to do so.[4] On the 26th, the 27th, and the 28th of May torches, sulphur, and bitumen for purification were distributed,[5] and on the following day the celebration began. During the last three days of the month first-fruits of the approaching harvest—wheat, barley, and beans—were given to the members of the college, to be made into sacrificial cakes;[6] for Augustus desired to impress upon all the worshippers the importance of Italian agriculture.[7] On the 31st there was a full moon;[8] and while a subterranean altar in a spot called Tarentum, on the left bank of the Tiber and in the Field of Mars,[9] the scene of the nocturnal services, was illuminated by torches, Augustus sacrificed nine lambs and nine kids to the Fates, or, to use the Greek name given to them in the inscription that recorded the festival, the Moirae, whom, after the

---

[1] *C.I.L.*, vi, 877.

[2] G. Wissowa, *Ges. Abhandl.*, 1904, pp. 204–5; *Paulys Real-Ency.*, 1 A.², 1710. Cp. Zosimus, ii, 4, 2.   [3] Zosimus, ii, 5.

[4] *C.I.L.*, vi, 32323, ll. 52–7. Cp. Dio, liv, 30, 5.

[5] *C.I.L.*, vi, 32323, ll. 30, 48–50; Zosimus, li, 5, 1.

[6] *C.I.L.*, vi, 32323, l. 30. Cp. *Paulys Real-Ency.*, 1 A.², 1716, where Prof. Nilsson adds that, according to a defective passage in the oracle (*C.I.L.*, &c., ll. 30–1), first-fruits were also to be distributed to performers in the games.   [7] Hor., *Carm. saec.*, 29–30.

[8] *Klio*, x, 1910, p. 360.   [9] Val. Max., ii, 4, 5. Cp. pp. 155–6.

sacrifice, he prayed to bless, in return for it, the Roman People, the sacred college, himself, his family, and his household. In the course of the night stage-plays followed; and one hundred and ten chosen matrons—one for each year of the Etruscan *saeculum*—gave a banquet to Juno and Diana, whose images were placed on two seats.[1] On the 1st of June Augustus and Agrippa each sacrificed a bullock on the Capitol to Jupiter, praying him to bless the Roman People; plays were performed in a wooden theatre near the river; the matrons again gave a banquet; and in the night Augustus made a bloodless sacrifice—twenty-seven cakes of three different kinds—to the Ilithyiae, the Greek goddesses of childbirth, to one of whom he prayed for a blessing on pregnant women. On the 2nd Augustus and Agrippa each sacrificed a cow on the Capitol to Juno, praying her also to bless the Roman People. Then in the presence of Agrippa (for Augustus had departed) the matrons knelt to her in prayer; and plays were performed, as on the previous day. In the night Augustus sacrificed a pregnant sow to Mother Earth and prayed for her blessing: once more the matrons gave a banquet, as on the previous day. On the 3rd Augustus and Agrippa offered bloodless sacrifice to Apollo and Diana on the Palatine, and prayed for their blessing. After the sacrifice twenty-seven boys and twenty-seven girls (thrice nine being again deemed a lucky number) assembled on the Palatine, facing the marble temple of Apollo, and, gazing on the figure of the Sun in his four-horsed chariot, sang in the presence of the college of fifteen the hymn which Horace had composed. Passing from the Palatine to the Capitol, they lifted up their voices again;[2] and finally, chariot-races and other festivities, in sequence of the shows that had been held for the amusement of the worshippers on the preceding days and nights, marked the end of the festival.[3]

[1] *C.I.L.*, vi, 32323, l. 100 = Dessau, *Inscr. Lat.*, 5050 (100). Cp. *The Roman Republic*, i, 94, n. 4. The earlier part of the inscription, cited in preceding footnotes, is omitted by Dessau.

[2] See Warde Fowler's *Religious Experience of the Roman People*, 1911, p. 445. His account of the singing differs from Mommsen's, which he notices on pp. 444–5. Cp. Dessau, *Inscr. Lat.*, 5050, n. 42.

[3] Dessau, 5050, (103–6, 115–66). Cp. *Eph. epigr.*, viii, 1899, pp. 269–71,

It remains to consider its effect. How far the social legislation which preceded and followed it, and on which Horace in his official hymn [1] invoked the blessing of the Ilithyiae, was fruitful, it is impossible to tell; but the result would seem to have been small,[2] and in this respect probably that of the religious ceremony was insignificant. But inscriptions prove that during the next two centuries belief in the national deities, despite rationalism, Caesar-worship, and Oriental cults, survived; and perhaps the survival was partly due to the religious policy of Augustus.[3]

Agrippa, having played his part in the festival, returned to the East, accompanied by his wife, whom he or his chief may have thought it imprudent, after the enactment of the law relating to adultery, to leave at home. She had borne him two children, Gaius and Lucius, of whom the younger was still a baby, and the elder not more than three years old. Augustus, who had induced their father to marry her, adopted both, appointing them, if we may trust Dio,[4] his successors in the Principate, in order that he might be less exposed to conspiracy. No man could have been selected, better qualified than Agrippa, to represent the Emperor in the East. He remained throughout on the most friendly terms with Herod, listened at his request to a plea which Nicolaus of Damascus addressed to him on behalf of the Jews resident in Ionia, and forthwith redressed their grievances.[5] Two incidents, attested by inscriptions, show that the deification of Augustus in Asia, which had

Augustus adopts Gaius and Lucius, the sons of Agrippa.

Agrippa's relations with Herod.

and see Hill, *Historical Roman Coins*, pp. 148–50. The games (*ludi*) after June 3 were not, strictly speaking, a part of the festival, but a gratuitous addition. [1] *Carm. saec.*, 13–20.

[2] Tacitus (*Ann.*, iii, 25, 1–2) remarking that the *lex Papia Poppaea* 'had done nothing to make marriage more frequent', adds, 'the number of persons exposed to prosecution was continually increasing. Not a house but was at the mercy of informers'. I quote from G. G. Ramsay's translation. See, however, in regard to adultery, Hor., *Carm.*, iv, 5, 21–2.

[3] Cp. Boissier, *La religion rom.*, i², pp. 301, 321–2.

[4] liv, 18, 1. Ferrero, *Greatness and Decline*, &c., v, 99, n. ‡, conjectures that Augustus's motive was 'to be able to say that, as a law-abiding citizen, he had brought up three children'—Julia and her two boys.

[5] Jos., *Ant.*, xvi, 2. Mommsen (*Res gestae²*, pp. 163–4), commenting on the statement of Josephus (xvi, 3, 3) that Agrippa governed the East for ten years, remarks that he confused Agrippa's first arrival and his final return (see pp. 27–9, 34, *supra*) with the period of his government.

begun even before the foundation of the Principate,[1] was
followed by that of his daughter. In Paphos she received
the title of 'divine';[2] at Eresus in Lesbos she was identified
with Aphrodite.[3] Agrippa, however, was provoked on one
occasion to take strong action on her behalf. In crossing
the river Scamander, then in flood, by night, she narrowly
escaped drowning: Nicolaus, who described this accident,
added that Agrippa imposed a heavy fine upon the inhabitants of the neighbourhood, although they had not been
informed that Julia was coming, and that he himself
induced Herod to intercede for them,[4] which he did successfully. Agrippa in the year before he returned to Rome   14 B.C.
subdued, in conjunction with Polemo, that newly recognized Friend and Ally of the Roman People, the tribes of
the Cimmerian Bosporus, who were struggling to regain
independence.[5]

Two years earlier Augustus had left Rome for Gaul,   16 B.C.
hearing that the Governor, Marcus Lollius, who in another   Augustus
capacity had distinguished himself by chastising the Bessi   returns to
of Thrace, had himself been defeated by Caesar's old   Gaul.
opponents, the Sugambri, Usipetes, and Tencteri, who,
after crucifying Roman citizens,[6] had made an incursion
into his province.[7] Augustus, however, having been
forced to leave it in 27 B.C., when he had only begun the
work of settlement,[8] had enough to occupy him for at least
two years, and, although the news about Lollius may have
hastened his departure, it was not the cause. Nor would it
be safe to accept without confirmation the statements
of Dio[9] that he left because he had incurred unpopularity
by his protracted stay and offended many who violated the

[1] See *The Architect of the Roman Empire* (44–27 B.C.), p. 173.
[2] *J.H.S.*, ix, 243.
[3] W. M. Ramsay, *Cities . . . of Phrygia*, i, 1895, p. 54.
[4] *Fragm. hist. Graec.*, ed. Müller, iii, 350.
[5] Dio, liv, 24, 4–6. See *The Roman Republic*, iii, 215.
[6] Itinerant traders ?
[7] Vell., ii, 97, 1; Strabo, vii, 1, 4; Suet., *Aug.*, 23, 1; Dio, liv, 20, 3–6.
Obsequens (71) assigns the defeat of Lollius to 17 B.C. There is no incon-
sistency between his statement and Dio's; for Dio does not say that it
occurred in the year in which Augustus went to Gaul, and, as C. Winkelsesser
says (*De rebus . . . in Germania gestis*, 1901, p. 7), he sometimes groups
together connected events belonging to more than one year.
[8] See p. 6.   [9] liv, 19, 2.

law of marriage, while by sparing others he incurred the
odium of violating it himself. Unfriendly observers
expressed suspicions that he was going to live abroad with
Terentia, the beautiful wife of Maecenas, undisturbed by
the gossip of the capital.[1] Since Agrippa was busy in the
East, he took with him Tiberius, then praetor, whose
brother, Drusus, he left to perform the praetorian duties,
and deputed his own former lieutenant, Statilius Taurus,
who had done such good service during the Triumvirate,[2]
to govern Italy. When he arrived in Gaul he found it
undisturbed, for the German invaders, fearing his vengeance
and learning that Lollius was prepared to punish them,
gave hostages and recrossed the Rhine.[3]

Why he
did not
invade
Britain.

If Augustus had ever seriously contemplated invading
Britain,[4] he had abandoned his resolve; and the cause of
his inaction is discernible in two passages of Strabo,[5] which
give the official explanation of his policy. The conquest
would be very costly, and it was unlikely that the revenue
would be more than sufficient to defray the expense of the
garrison and the administration: the duties levied at the
Gallic harbours on goods imported from and exported to
Britain were more productive than any tribute; besides,
Britain was too weak to be dangerous, and its conquest
was therefore unnecessary. Nevertheless Augustus must
have foreseen that the conquest of the island, which,
since the conquest of Gaul, could not safely be left independent, would, sooner or later, be inevitable. Late in
his principate two British kings, Dubnovellaunus[6] and
Tincommius, undertook the long journey to Rome to
solicit his aid.[7] Dubnovellaunus, who had been expelled
from the country of his subjects, the Trinovantes, by

British
princes
visit him.

Dio, liv, 19, 3.
The Architect of the Roman Empire (44–27 B.C.), pp. 114, 118.
Dio, liv, 19, 6; 20, 6.   [4] See p. 4.   [5] ii, 5, 8; iv, 5, 3.
[6] So the name is spelt on British coins. In the Monument of Ancyra the
form is Dumnobellau[nus]. Cp. Caesar's Conquest of Gaul², 1911, p. 843, s.v.
Dumnorix.
[7] Mon. Ancyr., v, 54–vi, 1–3. Cp. Anc. Britain, pp. 361–8. The reading
'tin[commius', a correction of 'Tim . . .' printed by Mommsen in Res gestae²,
&c., p. 135 (cp. Ancient Britain, pp. 363–4), is adopted by Sir W. M. Ramsay
and A. von Premerstein (Klio, Beih. xix, 1927, p. 94), who refer to Numism.
Chronicle, xviii, 1918, pp. 97–110, and J.R.S., vi, 126, n. 2.

Cunobeline (the Cymbeline immortalized by Shakespeare),·
was a grandson of Caesar's old antagonist, Cassivellaunus;
Tincommius a son of Commius, who accompanied Caesar in
his second invasion of Britain. How they were received
we are not told; but it is certain that Augustus did not
grant them armed assistance, and we may perhaps infer
from the prominence which is given in the Monument of
Ancyra to their entreaty that it was officially interpreted
as a sign of virtual submission. They were not the only
British princes who paid their respects to the Emperor.
'In our time', says Strabo,[1] 'various chieftains there gained
the friendship of Augustus Caesar by sending embassies
and performing services; placed votive offerings in the
Capitol; and made almost the whole island familiar to the
Romans'. Among them, we can hardly doubt, was
Cunobeline, whose coins, like those of his father, Tascio-
vanus, testify that Roman mythology had already taken
root on British soil, and who, according to Geoffrey of
Monmouth, voluntarily paid tribute to Rome. If there is
any truth in Geoffrey's statement, the tribute must have
been the price paid for moral support; but it was the
jealousy and the fear which Cunobeline's dynasty aroused
in the family of Commius that was to lead, nearly a generation after the death of Augustus, to the Roman invasion.[2]

Eleven years had passed since Augustus first visited
Gaul. During that time the country which Caesar had
conquered, commonly called Gallia Comata—'the land of
the long-haired Gauls'—had been of course governed by
legates of the Emperor; the Province, which, until the
time when he accepted the charge of providing for the
supply of corn, had been under his control, was then transferred by him together with Cyprus to the Senate, because
it no longer needed the presence of an army.[3] In Gallia
Comata, although there was some unrest, owing to dissensions among the tribes and to occasional incursions from
Germany, there was no rebellious movement or none that
chroniclers thought worth mentioning; among the governors
were Agrippa and Tiberius, of whom the former had not

His settlement of Gaul.

22 B.C.

[1] iv, 5, 3.   [2] *Anc. Britain*, pp. 369–71.
[3] Dio, liv, 4, 1. See *The Architect of the Roman Empire* (44–27 B.C.), p. 180.

only ruled the Province in the time of the Triumvirate with conspicuous success, but had also begun, if he had not completed, the preparation of a census.[1] The others, whose names have not been recorded, had doubtless been carefully selected by the Emperor and may be supposed to have been informed, more or less fully, of the measures which he contemplated. These facts seem to have been hardly considered by the writers, who decline to accept the traditional account of what Augustus had already accomplished.[2] While it may be true that he had not had time to complete, one may reasonably suppose that he planned the rearrangement of tribal divisions which has been already described,[3] though, as he doubtless foresaw, it would involve the settlement of various details; and, while we have no knowledge of the work done by successive governors in the eleven years, it is at least probable that they had in some measure prepared for the reorganization which he was about to take in hand.

He had not been long in the country when natives, who, if we may believe Dio, had obtained an audience, complained that his procurator,[4] a Gaul, or perhaps a German,[5] named Licinus, who, originally a prisoner of war, had been freed by Caesar, and was responsible for the collection of the revenue,[6] had abused his office by extortion, to enrich himself and his friends.[7] Reading in Dio's history that one of his methods was to tell those who paid their tribute monthly that December was really (as its name originally signified) the tenth month of the year, and that they must therefore pay for fourteen months instead of twelve, one may be reminded of the complaint of a well-known journalist, that, like many of his colleagues, he had been ordered by a local official to pay income tax twice over on a bonus received in 1927 'on the ground that the financial year 1927–28 had been made the basis of assessment for

---

[1] See *The Architect of the Roman Empire* (44–27 B.C.), p. 111; Dio, liv, 11, 1–2; Suet., *Tib.*, 9, 1. Cp. p. 5, *supra*.

[2] See p. 4. Cp. Ferrero, *Greatness and Decline*, &c., v, 146, n. *.

[3] See pp. 4–5.

[4] See *The Architect of the Roman Empire* (44–27 B.C.), p. 181.   [5] See p. 156.

[6] Strabo, iii, 4, 20; Dio, liii, 15, 3. See Mommsen, *Röm. Staatsr.*, iii, 267–8.

[7] Dio, liv, 21, 2–6.

two years.'[1] We can hardly accept the statement of Dio,[2] though there may have been some slight foundation for it, that Licinus disarmed the anger of Augustus, whose consideration for provincials he must have known, by inviting him to enter his house, showing him gold and silver piled in heaps, assuring him that his motive in collecting the treasure had been to deprive the natives of the power to rebel, and thereupon making him a present of the whole. It would seem, however, that Licinus somehow escaped punishment; and, so far as we can tell, during the reign of Augustus no complaint was made against any other procurator. By legitimate methods, indeed, the revenue must have been considerably increased: for the wealth of Gaul, in which viticulture was developing, had been growing since the end of the civil wars;[3] the fortunes which Caesar and his staff amassed show that even in his time it was great;[4] and the Julian colony of Arelate succeeded to [Arles.] much of the trade which Massilia had lost[5] after its [Marseilles.] treachery in the siege was punished by Caesar. There were landowners so rich that they employed hundreds of slaves.[6] Even before the conquest the maritime tribe of the Veneti carried on trade with Britain in ships of their own construction;[7] the Sequani exported hams to Italy; and wealthy Gauls imported well-bred horses, for which they paid high prices.[8] Since Caesar's time commerce had developed. Gallic pottery was exported to Britain, Spain, Africa, and Italy; for the potters, who had learned to imitate vases imported from the far-famed factories of Arretium in Etruria, eventually succeeded in capturing the [Arezzo.] trade from these rivals, whose productions had begun to deteriorate.[9] Woollen tunics for the hard wear of slaves were manufactured for the Italian market; wine, so

---

[1] *The Times*, Sept. 17, 1929, p. 15, col. 4. See p. 156.

[2] liv, 21, 7–8. Cp. Macrob., ii, 4, 24.

[3] Rostovtzeff, *Social and Econ. Hist.*, &c., pp. 90–1.

[4] *The Roman Republic*, ii, 6.

[5] T. Frank, *Econ. Hist. of Rome*², 1927, pp. 367–8. Cp. O. Hirschfeld, *Kl. Schr.*, 1913, p. 28.   [6] *C.I.L.*, xii, 1025, 4887; xiii, 1747.

[7] *Caesar's Conquest of Gaul*², pp. 86–7.

[8] *Ib.*, p. 19; *The Roman Republic*, ii, 6.

[9] Rostovtzeff, *Social and Econ. Hist.*, &c., p. 512, n. 13; *Bonner Jahrb.*, cxiv–cxv, 1906, p. 179. Cp. *The Roman Republic*, ii, 9.

highly prized that rich Gauls would barter a slave for a jar, was imported from Italy.[1] The revenue derived from the land and from the tribute paid by individuals was augmented by indirect taxation. A duty of two and a half per cent on all imports and exports was levied in the harbours and on the roads leading into Gaul.[2] For this purpose the Province, Gallia Comata, the Alpine provinces, and Germania, after the province so called was created, formed one whole, the financial administration of which was

A.D. 6. centred in Lugudunum.[3] Late in the reign of Augustus a tax of five per cent was levied on legacies and inheritances received by Roman citizens, including those resident in Gaul, except the very poor.[4] In return for these payments the people enjoyed the benefit of improved communication, provided by the roads which Agrippa had constructed, and of defence against German invasion; while humble landowners, who under native rule had been oppressed,[5] were protected by Roman law.[6]

Two most important changes, made in or soon after the stay of Augustus and doubtless by his express command, indicated his resolve to inaugurate a peaceful era of urban development. He was aware, for his adoptive father had probably talked to him about the conquest, the classic narrative of which he had of course read, that the leading tribes of Gallia Comata, which, rivals though they were, had both played a prominent part in the rebellion of Vercingetorix, were the Aedui and the Arverni. The capital of the Aedui, Bibracte, situated on Mont Beuvray, twelve miles west of Autun, was not only a great manufacturing town, whose ramparts, streets, and workshops have been revealed by excavation, but also a formidable hill-fort.[7] Gergovia, the chief stronghold of the Arverni, standing on a mountain, twelve hundred feet above the

---

[1] *The Roman Republic*, ii, 6; Diod. Sic., v, 26, 3–4.

[2] *C.I.L.*, v, 7213; Strabo, iv, 5, 3.

[3] Jullian, iv, 305–6.   [4] Dio, lv, 25, 5. See p. 110.

[5] *Caesar's Conquest of Gaul*², p. 21; *The Roman Republic*, ii, 10.

[6] *Dig.*, i, 18, 6, 2.

[7] *Caesar's Conquest of Gaul*², pp. 19–20, 53, 398; cp. *The Roman Republic*, ii, 8–9, 23, 25. The demonstration of the geographical position of Bibracte (*Caesar's Conquest of Gaul*, 1899, pp. 387–94) has since 1899 been accepted as certain. Nevertheless Prof. G. G. Ramsay (*The Annals of Tacitus*, 1904,

plain, four miles south of the eminence now covered by the streets of Clermont Ferrand, commanded the slopes on which Vercingetorix had routed four of Caesar's legions.[1] Augustus doubtless saw that so long as the two strongholds were occupied in force, they might be rallying points in the event of another rebellion, while their historical associations could not be forgotten and would remind Gallic patriots of their lost independence. He therefore at some uncertain date[2] compelled the inhabitants of Bibracte to settle in the new town, called after him Augustodunum, which was the nucleus of Autun, while Gergovia was abandoned for Augustonemetum, whose site is now dominated by the lava towers of Clermont Cathedral. Augustus wisely tolerated the worship of the goddess Bibracte,[3] which persisted in Augustodunum.

It has often been remarked that in the nomenclature of France there are many traces of the action of Augustus in recognizing the tribal cantons, whose names are familiar to readers of Caesar's *Commentaries*, as administrative units, and the pre-eminence in most of them of central towns. While in the area of the Province the names of the principal cities are derived from those of the Gallo-Roman municipalities out of which they grew—Nice from Nicaea, Narbonne from Narbo, Fréjus from Forum Iulii, Arles from Arelate, Toulouse from Tolosa, and many others— in what was Gallia Comata they are in many cases the outcome of the names of the tribes in whose territories the towns from which they grew were situated, though the tribal did not succeed local names before the end of the third century. Thus the successor of the chief town of the Senones is called Sens, which preserves their name, while its Gallic and Gallo-Roman predecessor was Agedincum;

p. 225, n. 3), who evidently neglected to inform himself, says that Augustodunum (Autun) was 'probably the Bibracte of Caesar'.

[1] *Caesar's Conquest of Gaul*[2], pp. 149–50, 155–8; *The Roman Republic*, ii, 197–9.

[2] Jullian (*op. cit.*, p. 74) suggests 12 B.C., I suppose because in that year there were signs of unrest in Gaul (Dio, liv, 32, 1). G. Bloch (E. Lavisse's *Hist. de France*, i, 1900, p. 366), affirming, on what evidence I cannot discover, that the coinage of Bibracte ceased in 5 or 6 B.C., concludes that the town was abandoned in one of those years. Nothing in A. Blanchet's excellent *Traité des monn. gaul.*, 1905, supports the conclusion.   [3] *C.I.L.*, xii, 2652–3.

Amiens is in the territory that belonged to the Ambiani, whose chief town on the same site was Samarobriva; Paris recalls the name of the Parisii, not of their Gallic and Gallo-Roman capital, Lutecia.

While Augustus accepted the cantonal organization which he found existing in the 'Three Gauls'—Aquitania, Celtica and Belgica—he recognized the constant loyalty which the Remi and the Lingones had manifested in the time of the conquest, perhaps also the repentance of the Aedui and the Carnutes, by granting them the status of allied communities, whose privileges were guaranteed by treaty.[1] The epithet *liberi*, which Pliny bestows upon the Nervii (who had fiercely resisted Caesar), the Suessiones, the Silvanectes, the Leuci, the Meldi, the Segusiavi, the Santoni, the Arverni, and the Bituriges,[2] certainly does not imply that Augustus granted them political independence, and probably means only that they were pardoned by Caesar or his adopted son, freed from dependence upon other tribes, exempted from the jurisdiction of the governor, and indulged with immunity from tribute.

Augustus added Tolosa, Nemausus (Nîmes), Carpento-rate (Carpentras), Avennio (Avignon), Aquae Sextiae (Aix), and Valentia (Valence) to the colonies which his adoptive father had founded in the Province; but, like him, he founded none in Gallia Comata, being doubtless confident that in the course of time the insensible Romanization of the existing cities would attach the tribes more closely to the empire than any attempt to hasten the desired result. In the Province the position of the Vocontii, whose status, like that of the Remi, the Lingones, the Carnutes, and the Aedui, had been guaranteed by treaty, was unique. There the cantonal organization was not replaced, as in the rest of the district, by the municipal. There were, indeed, important towns—Vasio and others—but the canton was not absorbed in their territories.[3] Whether the colonies were all Roman, or in some cases received only Latin rights,[4] is

---

[1] Pliny, *Nat. hist.*, iii, 4 (5), 34; iv, 17 (31), 106; 18 (32), 107.

[2] *Ib.*, §§ 106–7; 19 (33), 108–9.   [3] Rushforth, *Lat. Hist. Inscr.*², p. 14.

[4] Cp. *The Roman Republic*, i, 5–6; iii, 322. Nemausus had Latin rights (Strabo, iv, 1, 12).

doubtful: probably the colonists were not exclusively old
soldiers or Italian immigrants, but included some native
Gauls.[1] But Augustus, whose example was scrupulously
followed by Tiberius, was always, unlike Caesar, chary in
granting Roman citizenship, except as a reward for good
service, and even when Livia asked the favour for a Gaul,
refused.[2] Those Gauls, however, who enlisted as legionaries
of course received the distinction immediately; auxiliaries,
among whom the cavalry were still the best in the imperial
army, on completing their period of service.[3]

Though an imperial mint, for the production of gold and
silver coins, was soon to be established at Lugudunum,
Augustus permitted not only 'free' and 'federated' communities in the Province, such as those of Massilia and the
Volcae Arecomici, but also federated peoples in Gallia
Comata to continue their long-standing issues of coins
(gold, of course, excepted), bearing their tribal names and
the names and titles of their magistrates. Some of these
coins bore portraits of Augustus and Agrippa side by side.[4]
Augustus, however, introduced one reform: the coins of the
several tribes were alike in denomination, weight, and value.[5]

The inhabitants both of the Province and of Gallia
Comata, like the other provincials, had one guarantee for
the justice of the government which Augustus established:
any individual, any community, which felt aggrieved,
could appeal through the provincial council, composed in
the Province of Roman citizens, to the Emperor,[6] whose
representative, moreover, kept him fully informed of noteworthy events. If it is at present impossible to define the
relations between Roman and Celtic law, we know that in
free and federated states civil justice was administered by
their own magistrates and according to their own laws,
while in the others the representative of the Emperor was
responsible.[7] The sovereign authority, however, of course

---

[1] See Cic., *Pro Balbo*, 21, 48, and Jullian, *op. cit.*, iv, 255.
[2] Suet., *Aug.*, 40, 3. Cp. Tac., *Ann.*, iii, 40, and Dio, liv, 25, 1.
[3] Strabo, iv, 4, 2; *C.I.L.*, iii, pp. 907–8.
[4] Jullian, iv, 55.   [5] *Ib.*, p. 86.
[6] We learn from an inscription found at Cos that permission to appeal had
to be granted by the governor of the province to which the appellant belonged (*J.R.S.*, vii, 243).   [7] Jullian, iv, 278.

reserved to itself the adminsitration of criminal and penal law.[1] The golden collar which the guild of boatmen in Lutecia presented to Tiberius[2] was a mark of gratitude for reforms which his stepfather had introduced.

Did the government of Augustus tend to Romanize the Gauls? It has been contended that 'central Gaul [as distinguished from the Province] showed but few signs of Romanization for a century at least'.[3] On the other hand, an historian,[4] whose scrutiny few sources of information escape insists that 'the rural character' of the Gallic communities has been exaggerated,[5] and that the towns 'began to grow rapidly . . . after the reorganization by Augustus'. The foundation of colonies in the Province did not involve the suppression of native institutions, which, indeed, Roman influence tended to bring gradually into conformity with the colonial administration, and which in Gallia Comata were transformed, little by little, into copies of the Roman.[6] Native magistrates assumed Latin names; the chief towns had *basilicae* and *fora* adorned by the statues of famous Romans.[7] The tribal communities, indeed, continued, as in the time of Caesar, to have senates and popular assemblies; vergobrets—the name of these magistrates will be familiar to all readers of Caesar's *Commentaries*— still exercised a reduced administrative power.[8] Nevertheless Romanization was promoted not only by the colonies, but also by the grant of Roman citizenship, however restricted, and of Latin rights, by the adoption of Latin as the official language,[9] by the improved communication that followed the construction of roads, by retired auxiliaries, who, proud of their well-earned citizenship, must have had much to tell their countrymen about the work done by Augustus for countries in which they had served, by the vast amphitheatres of Nemausus and Arelate, built for the

[1] Jullian, iv, p. 287.   [2] Dessau, *Inscr. Lat.*, 4613.
[3] T. Frank, *Econ. Hist. of Rome*, p. 369.
[4] Rostovtzeff, *Social and Econ. Hist.*, &c., p. 501, n. 10.
[5] By O. Hirschfeld (*Kl. Schr.*, p. 112).
[6] Jullian, pp. 319, 327.
[7] *C.I.L.*, xiii, 5380-1; *Panegyrici*, vi [vii], 22. Cp. Jullian, p. 360.
[8] *C.I.L.*, xiii, 1048. Cp. *Caesar's Conquest of Gaul*[2], pp. 21, 505-7.
[9] Jullian, p. 281.

amusement of the proletariat, by the worship of the Emperor, whom the Gauls reverenced equally with their own deities, Esus and Tentates. It is to Augustus that Nîmes, the richest in Roman antiquities of all the cities of Southern France, owes its ramparts, gates,and towers,[1] which he added to the aqueduct already constructed by Agrippa.[2] What wonder that, although, in conformity with the religious toleration which Rome had always practised, he freely permitted the cult of Celtic deities, forbidding only the human sacrifice which was part of Druidical ritual, and which no government that reserved to itself the right of inflicting capital punishment could allow,[3] he was worshipped in Gaul as well as in the East ? Inscriptions mention priests of Augustus at Narbo,[4] at Vienna in the country of the Allobroges,[5] and at Dea and [Vienne.] Vasio[6] in the adjoining territory of the Vocontii.[7] [Die.] [Vaison.]

Before Augustus returned to Rome he entrusted the 13 B.C. government to his younger stepson, Nero Claudius Drusus,[8] who, as we shall presently see, had already made his mark as a military commander. Finding himself in the following year obliged to repel an invasion of the Sugambri, Drusus feared that some of the Gauls, dreading increased taxation, might join them,[9] and, to prevent such a contingency, invited their leaders to attend the dedication of a newly erected altar near Lugudunum, where the cult of Rome and of Augustus was to succeed that of the Celtic deity, Lug.[10] The officiating priest was an Aeduan noble, Vercondaridubnus, who also, like other distinguished Gauls,

Dedication of a altar at Lugudunum for the worship of Rome and Augustus.

---

[1] *C.I.L.*, xii, 3151.

[2] Stuart Jones, *Companion to Rom. Hist.*, 1912, p. 141 and Pl. XXV. Cp. E. Babelon, *Monn. de la rép. rom.*, ii, 555.

[3] Jullian, p. 291. Cp. G. Dottin, *La religion des Celtes*, 1904, p. 34.

[4] *C.I.L.*, xii, 6038. Cp. Rushforth, *Lat. Hist. Inscr.*², p. 47.

[5] *C.I.L.*, xii, 1872, 2605.   [6] *Ib.*, 1585. Cp. Jullian, p. 345, n. 6.

[7] Speaking of a temple of Augustus at Narbo (*C.I.L.*, xii, 392), Jullian (iv, 429) says that 'pour la province Rome et Auguste devaient être . . . ce qu'avaient été Teutatès pour la Gaule ou Minerve pour Athènes . . .'. Granted. But does not the word *divi* in the inscription show that the temple was erected after Augustus's death ? See p. 143.

[8] Dio, liv, 25, 1; 32, 1.

[9] Livy, *Epit.*, 139; Dio, liv., 32, 1. Livy attributes the disturbance in Gaul to the census (see p. 5), to which Dio evidently alludes.

[10] Dio, liv, 32, 1; Livy, *Epit.*, 139. See pp. 157-8.

bore the name of the conqueror, Gaius Julius.[1] Thenceforward every year on the same date, the 1st of August, the chief priest of Gaul and the members of the council of the three provinces, Gallia Lugdunensis, Aquitania, and Belgica, assembled at the altar,[2] which was not in the city, but on the western side of the Saone, on the flank of the hill which adjoined its confluence with the Rhone.[3] Lucterius Leo, a descendant of the chief who, after the surrender of Vercingetorix, had fought against Caesar to the bitter end, was soon to become the priest.[4] Conspicuous in gilt letters on the marble, on which were inscribed the names of sixty tribal communities, were the names Roma and Augustus, to whom jointly the altar was dedicated. There the assembly sacrificed and held high festival. Was its institution designed as a counter-move against that annual assemblage of Druids which Caesar described?[5] What is certain is that it, like the councils presided over by the priests of Augustus at Narbo and elsewhere, was intended to foster loyalty to the Emperor and the sense of membership in the empire.[6]

The mint at Lugudunum.

Hard by in the city was the mint, recently established, which enabled Augustus to retain, without questioning the authority of the Senate, the sole power of coining gold and silver for the empire. He had never interfered with the senatorial mint at Rome, which continued to strike such coins until the year in which the altar was dedicated; but when the mint at Lugudunum was in working order the senatorial issues were no longer needed. Thenceforward the gold coins struck at Lugudunum sufficed for the whole Roman world, the silver for Italy and the Western provinces, a mint at Antioch in Caria helping to supply others. The silver coins of Lugudunum were, however, of course legal tender in the East as well as in the West, and, like the gold, circulated beyond the imperial frontiers. What is

[1] Livy, *Epit.*, 139. Cp. Rushforth, *op. cit.*, p. 18.
[2] Dio, liv, 32, 1. Cp. Rushforth, pp. 16–7.
[3] Since the erection of the altar the course of the Saone has changed, and the confluence was then further northward than now.
[4] Rushforth, pp. 16–8. Cp. *Caesar's Conquest of Gaul*[2], pp. 189–93, or *The Roman Republic*, ii, 226–30.
[5] So Mommsen thought (*Röm. Gesch.*, v, 95–6 [Eng. tr., i, 105]). See *Caesar's Conquest of Gaul*[2], p. 34, or *The Roman Republic*, ii, 15.
[6] Rushforth, *op. cit.*, p. 47.

ramso

brü

u

(E

ıste

ür

called 'token money', that is, coins of bronze, copper, or orichalcum (an alloy of copper and zinc), continued to be issued by the senatorial mint as well as by towns in Gaul, Spain, Africa, and the East. As a rule the portrait of the Emperor appeared on the coins struck in provincial towns, except in those of Athens and other allied communities. The kingdom of Bosporus, being ruled by a vassal ally of Rome, was privileged to strike even gold coins, honouring the Emperor by placing his portrait upon them.[1]

While Augustus was still busy in Gaul, he restored to Cyzicus the autonomy of which he had deprived it as a punishment,[2] and bestowed a sum of money (presumably from the imperial chest) upon the city of Paphos, which had suffered from an earthquake[3] for in whatever sphere of duty he might be, he was constantly thinking of the interests of the empire. Meanwhile his two stepsons, of whose movements he was of course regularly informed, were engaged in military operations in Central Europe. The northern frontiers of the empire were not yet secure. In the year in which he returned to Gaul two Alpine tribes, the Camunni and the Vennii, or Venostes, who, it would seem, had made raids in Northern Italy, were chastised by an ex-consul, Publius Silius.[4] The Pannonians and the Dalmatians, against whom Augustus had himself conducted a successful campaign during the Triumvirate,[5] rose in revolt, but were temporarily repressed; the Norici, who dwelt between the Danube and the Alps, and who had assisted Caesar in the Civil War,[6] were punished with the Pannonians, whom they had joined;[7] the Sarmatians, who ventured to cross the Danube, were driven back.[8] In the following year Drusus and Tiberius, who joined him at Lake Constance, subdued the Raetians, whose territory comprised Eastern Switzerland, the Northern Tyrol, and

Military operations of Drusus and Tiberius in Central Europe 16 B.C.

15 B.C.

[1] H. Mattingly, *Coins of the Roman Empire*, &c., 1, 1923, pp. xvi–xvii, xxii–xxiii, xxix. Cp. Hill, *Historical Roman Coins*, pp. 154–5. Mattingly (p. xvii) remarks that Willers (*Gesch. d. röm. Kupferprägung*, pp. 187 ff.) has given good reasons for thinking that the circulation of the token money issued by the senatorial mint was at first restricted to Rome and Italy.

[2] See p. 35.   [3] Dio, liv, 23, 7. Cp. pp. 136–7, 177–8.   [4] Dio, liv, 20, 1.
[5] *The Architect of the Roman Empire* (44–27 B.C.), pp. 130–5.
[6] See *The Roman Republic*, iii, 19.   [7] Dio, liv, 20, 2.
[8] *Ib.*, § 3.

Southern Bavaria, and who had not only overrun Southern Gaul, but even plundered Northern Italy; deported most of the strongest men of military age; and also overpowered 14 B.C. their southern neighbours, the Vindelici.[1] Next year it was necessary to send an army against the Pannonians, who had not been deterred by their recent punishment, and another against the Alpine Ligurians.[2] In consequence of these successes two new provinces, or rather administrative districts, were created—Raetia, which was strongly garrisoned, and the Maritime Alps;[3] and Drusus, obeying his stepfather, who desired to provide for easy military communication between Raetia and Italy, constructed a road, to be known as the *via Augusta*, along the valley of the Adige.[4] Raetia and the Maritime Alps were governed by military officers, appointed by the Emperor, in virtue of the power which he had taken over from their native rulers.[5]

7–6 B.C. Seven years later a monument, on which were inscribed the names of forty-six Alpine tribes, which had been subdued under the auspices of Augustus (and of which one, the Salassi, had been ruthlessly punished) was erected on the rock now called La Turbie (Tropaea Augusti) above Monaco, commemorating the conquest, which secured the peace of Cisalpine Gaul.[6] Fifteen tribes, whose names were omitted from the list, because they had not revolted,[7] were comprised in the little kingdom, if it may be so called, ruled by Cottius, a client prince, devoted to the Roman interest, who, officially called a prefect, assured the safety of the road that traversed his country, and in whose capital, [Suse.] Segusio, below the Cottian Alps, another monument was erected in honour of his great patron.[8]

---

[1] Dio, liv, 22; Hor., *Carm.*, iv, 4, 17–8; Suet., *Aug.*, 21, 1; *Tib.*, 9, 1; *Mon. Ancyr.*, v, 12–4. Dessau (*Gesch. d. röm. Kaiserzeit*, i, 294) remarks that inscriptions show that the deportation was not thoroughly carried out.

[2] Dio liv, 24, 3.   [3] Rushforth, *Lat. Hist. Inscr.*[2], pp. 39, 41.

[4] Dessau, *Inscr. Lat.*, 208. Cp. Mommsen, *Röm. Gesch.*, v, 18 (Eng. tr., 1, 20) and Rushforth, p. 40.

[5] Mattingly, *The Imperial Civil Service of Rome*, p. 131; Rushforth, pp. 39–41. Sardinia also was placed under military government in consequence of piracy (Dio, lv, 28, 1).

[6] Pliny, *Nat. hist.* iii, 20 (24), 136–7; *C.I.L.*, v, 7817; Rushforth, p. 36.

[7] Pliny, iii, 20 (24), 138.

[8] *C.I.L.*, v, 7231 (Rushforth, p. 39); Suet., *Tib.*, 37, 3; Dio, liii, 26, 5 (who apparently mistook the date); Amm. Marc., xv, 10, 2, 7.

No wonder that when Augustus, leaving Drusus in Germany to guard the frontier, returned to Italy,[1] his reception was triumphal. Since the foundation of the Principate he had visited every province except Sardinia and Africa: while he had virtually completed in Gaul the work of reconstruction, which the outbreak of civil war had forced his adoptive father to leave undone, and his own work in Spain, where he founded new colonies,[2] his stepsons had finished the subjugation of the Alpine tribes, added two new provinces to the empire, and begun the warfare which was to result, after many years, in the subjugation of the Pannonians. The Senate decreed that an altar, to be dedicated to the Peace of Augustus, should be set up in the Field of Mars, and that on it the chief magistrates, the priests, and the Vestal Virgins should celebrate anniversary sacrifices.[3] On this altar, which was not dedicated until the 30th of January, 9 B.C.,[4] is a relief, one of the artistic glories of the Augustan age, in which a 'majestic yet tender'[5] female figure, fondling infant boys, represented the goddess Italia. The consuls, of whom Tiberius was one, exhibited games in honour of the Emperor's return,[6] and Horace, who had already sung the praises of Drusus for his campaign against the Raetians,[7] gave expression to the popular rejoicing,[8] congratulating the Emperor on his settlement of Spain, and even assuring him, perhaps not without subtle irony, that his social legislation had been justified. On the 4th of July Augustus entered the city by night, as he had done on returning from the East; for, said Dio, he was always unwilling to trouble the populace, or, as one may surmise, shrank from the bustle of a popular welcome; but on the following day he held a reception in his house on the Palatine, paid formal respect to official religion by ascending the Capitol and placing the laurel, which entwined his

Triumphal reception of Augustus on his return from Gaul.

13 B.C.

---

[1] Dio, liv, 32, 2.   [2] *Ib.*, 23, 7.

[3] *Mon. Ancyr.*, ii, 37–41; Ovid, *Fasti*, i, 709. Cp. *J.R.S.*, iii, 134–41.

[4] *C.I.L.*, i², p. 320. Cp. Rushforth, *Lat. Hist. Inscr.*², pp. 51–3.

[5] I quote the words of A. W. van Buren (page 137 of the above-mentioned article in the *Journal of Roman Studies*), feeling sure that every one who looks at the illustration of the relief (Pl. IV, facing page 140 of the same article) will see how apt they are.

[6] Dessau, *Inscr. Lat.*, 88.   [7] *Carm.*, iv, 4, 17–8. Cp. 38–40.

[8] *Ib.*, 5, 1–4, 21–8.

fasces, upon the knees of the statue of Jupiter, and immediately afterwards ordered the public baths to be opened free of charge to all comers, for whom barbers were, also gratuitously, provided.[1] Next he made a beginning, which the renewed outbreak of war made it impossible for several years to continue, of providing by a new method for discharged soldiers. In former years and before he returned from Gaul he had planted colonies for their benefit in Gaul and Spain. Disregarding the practice of his adoptive father, who had known how to combine effective discipline with gracious familiarity, he had never since the end of the civil wars addressed, or allowed his stepsons to address the troops as 'comrades';[2] but he was ever mindful of their welfare. Under the scheme which he now unfolded to the Senate, soldiers were to be assured on enlistment that after sixteen years' service—in the case of the Praetorian guards only twelve—they should receive a fixed payment.[3] The amount is uncertain, but was probably less than that ultimately granted[4]—twenty thousand sesterces (about two hundred pounds) for Praetorians, twelve thousand for legionaries. Before the end of the year in which Augustus returned from Gaul, his proconsular powers and those of Agrippa, who had returned from Syria and was now sent to pacify Pannonia, were prolonged for five years.[5]

His scheme for pensioning discharged soldiers.

A.D. 6.

12 B.C.

He becomes Chief Pontiff.

In the following year on the 6th of March,[6] soon after the departure of Agrippa, Augustus accepted the office of Chief Pontiff, for Lepidus had lately died; but when other honours were pressed upon his acceptance by the Senate, he rose from his curule chair and left the House.[7] 'The multitude', he recorded, 'that flocked from the whole of Italy to my election was such as is not reported to have ever been in Rome before'.[8] Perhaps when he saw the throng, whose presence was a compliment inspired by a desire to salute and gaze upon the national hero, he thought

---

[1] Dio, liv, 25, 3–4.   [2] Cp. Suet., *Caes.*, 67, 2, with *Aug.*, 25, 1.

[3] Dio, liv, 25, 5–6. Cp. *Mon. Ancyr.*, iii, 28.   [4] Dio, lv, 23, 1.

[5] *C.I.L.*, xiv, 2230. Cp. Dio, liv, 28, 1 with 12, 4, and see Pelham, *Essays*, p. 62.

[6] *C.I.L.*, i, p. 387; *Mon. Ancyr.*, ii, 28; Ovid, *Fasti*, iii, 420. Dio (see the next note) incorrectly refers the election to 13 B.C.

[7] Dio, liv, 27, 2.   [8] *Mon. Ancyr.*, ii, 25–8.

of the huge majority of voters which, fifty-one years before, had elected his adoptive father, many doubtless influenced by bribes, in the days when popular election was real.[1]

One of the earliest pontifical acts of Augustus was to guard against the circulation of false prophecies which might be dangerous, by ordering all the so-called prophetic writings that could be discovered (except, of course, the Sibylline books, of which he selected those that seemed harmless or likely to be useful) to be collected and burned.[2] But in connexion with his election one naturally thinks first of Caesar-worship, which began in his reign. Before he left Gaul he had become an object of veneration in Italy.[3] Ovid[4] alludes to his statues, to be seen in the chapels of the local spirits, called *Lares compitales*, at cross-roads. The worship of his Genius, or guardian spirit,[5] was officially recognized[6]; and it will be remembered that an altar had been dedicated to the deified abstraction, 'Fortune the Home-bringer', to which his safe return from Asia was attributed. In the preceding volume it has been related that the Senate decreed after the victory at Actium that at all banquets libations should be made in honour of the victor[7]; and in later years, after he was acclaimed *Pater patriae*, the guests used to rise and, as they poured out the wine, salute their absent emperor, 'Father of thy country, Caesar, the best of men'.[8] As Chief Pontiff, he engrafted upon the old religion, which he was striving to revive, worships[9] holding up to reverence the new era, which he had inaugurated by the festival of the *ludi saeculares*, and himself its leading representative.[10] It has been acutely observed that his object in reorganizing the Arval Brotherhood[11] was the glorification of the imperial family[12]; and the decree, passed after the victory at Actium, that priests were to pray for him whenever they prayed for the Senate and

Marginal notes: Caesar-worship and its effect in unifying the Empire.

2 B.C.

---

[1] *The Roman Republic*, i, 242, 252–3.   [2] Suet., *Aug.*, 31, 1.
[3] Hor, *Ep.*, ii, 1, 16; *C.I.L.*, xi, 3303.   [4] *Fasti*, v, 145.
[5] See *The Roman Republic*, i, 70.
[6] *Paulys Real-Ency.*, Suppl. iv, 827.
[7] *The Architect of the Roman Empire* (44–27 B.C.), p. 172.
[8] Ovid, *Fasti*, ii, 637–8.   [9] *Mon. Ancyr.*, ii, 37–41; iv, 21–2.
[10] See Pelham, *Essays*, p. 102.   [11] See p. 49.
[12] *Paulys Real-Ency.*, ii, 1471–2.

the Roman People,[1] is illustrated by the transactions of the
order.[2] The marble temple of Apollo on the Palatine,
which he had planned after defeating Sextus Pompeius,
and dedicated after defeating Antony,[3] and which has been
called [4] 'the most splendid of all the splendid buildings of
Rome', helped to perpetuate the memory of his services.
As Chief Pontiff he was the guardian of the worship of the
national deities; and, since new deities might be added as
readily as new saints to those recognized by the Catholic
Church, his own deification was a consequence which
prayers, thanksgivings, and festivals [5] tended to ensure.
Though with the good sense—may not one include in it the
sense of humour ?—which never failed he emphatically refused to allow a temple to be erected to him in Rome,[6]
though, while he habitually called himself 'Son of the
Deified' (for his adoptive father's deification had been recognized by the Senate and the Roman People[7]), he would
not permit his statue to be placed in the Pantheon,[8] dedicated though it was to his supposed ancestress, Venus
Genetrix, priesthoods for his worship were instituted and
altars erected in his life-time in Bononia, Pisae, Puteoli,
Pompeii, Beneventum, and other Italian towns.[9] If in
Italy such worship was addressed rather to the *numen* of
Augustus—the beneficent power which his career had
manifested—than to himself, the First Citizen; if it was in
this mode that Caesar-worship was established in Roman
houses, where images of Augustus were placed side by side
with the images of the Lares and Penates,[10] still, as it has
been truly said, that worship became the worship of 'the
eternal majesty of the empire'.[11]

[1] *The Architect of the Roman Empire* (44–27 B.C.), p. 172.
[2] *Paulys Real-Ency.*, ii, 1483. Cp. *C.I.L.*, i², p. 305.
[3] *The Architect of the Roman Empire* (44–27 B.C.), pp. 119, 175.
[4] By Pelham (*op. cit.*, p. 104).
[5] *Mon. Ancyr.*, ii, 15–20, 29–33, 37–41; Suet., *Aug.*, 57, 1; Dessau, *Inscr. Lat.*, 95. See Pelham, p. 105.   [6] Suet., *Aug.*, 52.
[7] *The Architect of the Roman Empire* (44–27 B.C.), p. 75.
[8] Dio, liii, 27, 3.
[9] Dessau, *Inscr. Lat.*, 139–40, 6369, 1091, 6361–6362 a.
[10] Hor., *Carm.*, iv, 5, 31–6; *Ep.*, ii, 1, 15–6; Tac., *Ann.*, i, 73, 2. Cp.
Pelham, *Essays*, p. 109, and Warde Fowler, *Roman Ideas*, &c., pp. 132–3.
[11] Pelham, p. 110.

But while in the West the object of the nascent cult was the *numen* or the Genius of the Emperor, in the East and in Africa, where a large proportion of the population was of oriental origin, he was really, it would seem, regarded as divine. Let those who may find it difficult to conceive such a mental attitude reflect that it was in the Hellenistic East that divinity was first attributed to a Syrian of lowly parentage who had attracted disciples as Indian enthusiasts have done in our time,[1] and that, in the nineteenth century, a brotherhood of fakirs in North-western India worshipped a young British officer, John Nicholson—all the more because he repeatedly flogged them for idolatry [2]—and replied to doubters by insisting that there was daily proof of his miraculous power.[3] But what we are concerned with is not so much the beliefs of the worshippers of Augustus as the political effect of the worship. Temples dedicated conjointly to the goddess Roma and to Augustus were erected in the Carian town, Mylasa [4], and in Ancyra, where Augustus was given precedence over Roma [5], to Augustus alone in Caesarea Philippi, [6] in Samaria, which he had given to Herod, who called it after him Sebaste (the Greek equivalent of Augusta),[7] and in Mauretania at Iol, which the founder named in his honour Caesarea.[8] There is no reason to doubt that such foundations signified gratitude rather than adulation: in the Hellenistic East Augustus was described as the Revered Deliverer,[9] Saviour, and Benefactor.[10] If he encouraged the worship of himself by Orientals, it was because he saw that while it was wise to continue the time-honoured toleration of local cults, the political unification

[1] Sir Alfred Lyall, whom I knew intimately, told me that more than one such preacher appeared in the North-western Provinces while he was Lieutenant-Governor, and that their disciples ascribed to them the power of working miracles, which they emphatically disclaimed.

[2] Rice Holmes, *Hist. of the Indian Mutiny*, fifth ed., 1898, and later reprints, p. 321.

[3] Sir Alfred Lyall told me that the alleged proof was, 'He never makes water'! Presumably Nicholson was one of those men who are unable or reluctant to do so in the presence of others.

[4] *C.I.G.*, 2696.   [5] *Paulys Real-Ency.*, Suppl., iv, 824.

[6] Jos., *Ant.*, xv, 10, 3.   [7] Jos., *Bell.*, i, 21, 2.

[8] L. Müller, *Numism. de l'anc. Afrique*, iii, 1862, pp. 105 (No. 55), 106 (No. 56).

[9] *I.G.*, xii, 2, No. 156.   [10] *Ib.*, vii, No. 1836.

of the empire could not be accomplished without the religious unity which Caesar-worship symbolized,[1] and from which, before the rise of Christianity, Jews alone held aloof. It has been truly said that in the provinces the worshippers, who knew how much they owed to the supervision of Augustus, were testifying gratitude for the honour and the privilege of belonging to the Roman empire.[2]

Death of Agrippa.

At Athens, whither he had gone to attend a festival, Augustus learned the news of an event whose consequences were felt throughout the remainder of his life. Agrippa was not destined to begin the campaign which he had planned against the Pannonians, for the mere rumour that so renowned a commander was preparing to attack them,

12 B.C.

stopped their intended revolt. Returning to Italy, he fell sick in Campania. Augustus, on hearing of his illness, instantly returned, and finding that his colleague and lifelong friend was dead, had his corpse conveyed to the capital, where it was laid in state in the Forum; and, after delivering an oration in which he eulogized his public services, directed that the funeral should be conducted with due honours (which, many years later, were repeated with his own), and that he should be interred in the imperial mausoleum.[3] When, after Agrippa's death, Julia bore their third son, Augustus named him, not, like the two elder brothers, Caesar, but, in memory of the father, Agrippa Postumus. When Agrippa's will was opened, it was found that while Augustus was to inherit the greater part of his property, he had bequeathed the baths named after him to the people of Rome, assigning estates for their upkeep to the Emperor, who made them state property, distributing to every citizen four hundred sesterces, which, he declared, were a bequest from Agrippa.[4] Two hundred and forty slaves, whom Agrippa had included in the property which he left to Augustus, and whom he had kept to attend to the aqueducts which he had constructed, were transferred by

[1] See the remarks of G. B. Grundy, *Hist. of the Greek and Roman World*, 1927, p. 484.
[2] G. Boissier, *La religion rom.*, i², p. 170.
[3] Vell., ii, 96, 1; Livy, *Epit.*, 138; Pliny, *Nat. hist.*, vii, 8 (6), 45–6; Dio, liv, 28, 2–5.
[4] *Mon. Ancyr.*, iii, 12–4; Dio, liv, 29, 4–5.

Augustus to the Senate, which became responsible for the
due supply of water.[1] Among the extant letters of Augustus there are none of those which he must have written to
Agrippa; but no one will doubt that Dio, who appreciated
not only the greatness of Agrippa's public services, but also
the nobility of his character, told the truth when he wrote[2]
that Augustus long felt his loss. For, even if in the inscrutable nature of the man who has often, perhaps hastily,
been called cold, there was lacking such heart-felt gratitude
as one would wish to recognize for the self-forgetting friend
and counsellor who had let him have the credit of so many
great deeds, he knew, while he doubtless hoped that
Tiberius might worthily take the place of Agrippa as his
coadjutor, that without the aid of Agrippa at Naulochus
and Actium, he could never have become the First
Citizen and the ruler of the Roman world.

[1] In 11 B.C. Augustus had appointed, in agreement with the Senate, a
consular instead of aediles as manager of the water-supply (*curator aquarum*)
with two senatorial assistants (Frontin., *De aq.*, i, 100–2). Cp. Rushforth,
Lat. Hist. Inscr.[2], pp. 28–9, O. Hirschfeld, *Kaiserl. Verwaltungsbeamten*[2],
pp. 274–5, and *The Architect of the Roman Empire* (44–27 B.C.), p. 136.
[2] liv, 29, 5.

CHAPTER III

Evidence for what is historically important in Augustus's later years is comparatively insufficient.

AUGUSTUS had still five-and-twenty years to live, of which we know less that is historically important than of the period of his prime. Legislation affecting slaves and freedmen, the working of the civil service, provision for the orderly government of Rome and for the security and the amusement of its inhabitants, reform of the Senate—all these are well attested. The general lack of anything that deserves the name of military history need not be regretted by students who can learn from the chronicles of successive campaigns in Central Europe and Galatia how the *Pax Romana* was finally assured. But while it is certain that the provincials continued to owe much to the constant supervision of the Emperor, whose still unflagging industry was supported, after he began to feel the infirmities of age, by the counsel and the co-operation of his elder stepson, we have to deplore even more than in earlier years the lack of information about administrative details (compensated though it is said to have been in one particular by Saint Luke, and lately has been in another by the discovery of the now famous edicts of Cyrene) which was due, partly perhaps to imperial neglect of publicity, partly to lack of intelligent curiosity or to lethargy on the part of so-called historians. On the other hand, one can now learn gradually more of the personality of Augustus. The authentic records,

But his personality becomes more distinct.

including his own letters, of his relations with members of his family—Tiberius, his daughter Julia, his granddaughters Julia and Agrippina, his grandsons Gaius and Lucius—and with intimate friends, besides details of his personal habits, collected by the industry of his biographer, enable us to watch him both in his public and in his private life. Does not this letter, referring to the festival of Minerva in March, help to compensate for the loss of his autobiography? 'We spent the Quinquatria merrily, my dear Tiberius, for we played all day. . . . Your brother [Drusus] complained loudly about his luck . . . but, after losing heavily, he unexpectedly got back a good deal. I lost twenty thousand sesterces. . . . If I had made everybody pay the stakes which I let go, or had kept all that I gave away, I should have won quite fifty thousand.[1]

Tiberius, whom on the death of Agrippa he had accepted as his coadjutor, had already proved himself an able commander, a good administrator, and a competent diplomatist.[2] The author of the *Lives of the Caesars*, who sedulously noted every detail that might illustrate character, relates that in his first campaign the soldiers, noticing that he was inordinately fond of wine, nicknamed him Biberius[3] ('the tippler'). It was generally observed that he had even more than the pride of his Claudian ancestors,[4] and his stepfather tried to excuse to the Senate and the people his ʼstern taciturnity by assuring them that it was a congenital failing, which implied nothing intentionally offensive.[5] While it is certain that he was misrepresented by writers whom he had offended or who clung sullenly to Republican traditions, and whose readers in contempt of popularity he had neglected, unlike Augustus, to conciliate,[6] it is impossible to control fully their particular statements. With the almost incredible abominations laid to his charge by Suetonius[7] we are not here concerned: we have only to do with his character as it revealed itself in the lifetime of Augustus.

During the next three years, while their stepfather was engaged in work which was not sufficiently spectacular to attract the attention of the chroniclers upon whom we have to depend, Tiberius and Drusus were campaigning in Central Europe. Tiberius had only just been chosen as the coadjutor of the Emperor when he was obliged at his bidding to divorce his wife, Agrippina, the only daughter of Agrippa, whom he dearly loved, and who was about to give birth to her second child, and to allow himself to be betrothed to Julia, the daughter of Augustus and the widow

How Tiberius was characterized by ancient historians.

Why Augustus constrained him to marry Julia.

---

[1] Suet., *Aug.*, 71, 3.   [2] Vell., ii, 94, 3–4. See pp. 28, 36, 65.
[3] Suet., *Tib.*, 42, 1.   [4] Tac., *Ann.*, i, 4, 3.
[5] Suet., *Tib.*, 68, 3. Cp. Plin., *Nat. hist.*, xxviii, 2 (5), 23; xxxv, 4, 28.
[6] Tac., *Ann.*, i, 4, 4; 54, 3; iv, 11, 4–5; 53, 3; Suet., *Tib.*, 34. Pelham's estimate of Tiberius (*Outlines of Roman Hist.*[2], 1895, pp. 431–6) is remarkably just. Many passages in the *Annals* (*e.g.* i, 75, 1; iv, 6, 3, 6–7; 20, 4; 31, 1–4) show that Tacitus appreciated his finer qualities.
[7] *Tib.*, 43–4, &c.

of Agrippa.[1] One may divine the motive of Augustus in
forcing him to contract a union which, while it caused grief
hardly to be healed by time and must have permanently
embittered his temper, could only by a stretch of language
be called a marriage of convenience: probably he considered
that, as his stepson had been promoted to a position which
would bring him into close relations with himself and
which might conceivably lead to his becoming his sucessor,
it would be politic to mate him with a member of the
imperial family. It has been suggested that Tiberius reluctantly sacrificed love to ambition;[2] but, if that is true, he
had doubtless another motive. If he had read the *Aeneid*,
he may well have felt that the protestations with which the
poet made Aeneas excuse his desertion of Dido[3] did not
ring like the utterance of a lover; but, as a Roman, he
would have held that to leave her for a patriotic mission,
believed to have been divinely preordained, was a sacred
obligation. But to fulfil his own cost a hard struggle. It
was noticed that when, after his divorce, he happened once
to see Agrippina, he followed, gazing at her dear face with
such tearful longing that she was never again allowed to
appear before his eyes.[4] Immediately after his betrothal,
subordinating personal considerations to the performance
of public service, he undertook the campaign against the
Pannonians which their dread of Agrippa had for the
moment made unnecessary[5]. Encouraged by the news
of Agrippa's death, they again revolted; and, if it is true
that Tiberius sold most of the men of military age as slaves
and deported them, Dio's statement that he disarmed them
is stultified by the narrative of their persistence in rebellion.
Perhaps Augustus accurately gauged the importance of the
campaign; for, although the Senate voted Tiberius a
triumph, he would not allow him to celebrate it, granting
him in compensation only the triumphal insignia.[6] During
the next three years, while Lucius Calpurnius Piso, the

Campaigns against the Pannonians. 12 B.C.

11–9 B.C.

---

[1] Suet., *Tib.*, 7, 2–3; Dio, liv, 31, 2. Agrippina was a grand-daughter of
Atticus, Cicero's ever-faithful friend. As the daughter of Vipsanius Agrippa,
she is called in *Prosopographia imperii Romani* Vipsania.
[2] See Ferrero, *Greatness and Decline*, &c., v, 202.
[3] *Aen.*, vi, 458–64.   [4] Suet., *Tib.*, 7, 2.
[5] See p. 72.   [6] Dio, liv, 31, 2–4.

governor of Pamphylia, repelled raids of the Bessi,[1] Tiberius took the field regularly against the Pannonians and the Dalmatians, who, like the Pannonians, would not acquiesce in the defeats which Augustus had inflicted upon them some twenty years before;[2] but the repeated sub-jugations which Dio chronicled, and which Augustus rewarded, never lasted more than one year. Whether the experienced general's forces were inadequate to the per-manent subjugation of formidable tribes, it is impossible to ascertain from the original authority who could spare no more than a single sentence for his account of each campaign.[3] An important result of the operations was that Dalmatia was made an imperial province because it was evident that, to keep Dalmatians and Pannonians in subjection, armed forces would be required.

Throughout these years the younger brother of Tiberius, already famous as the conqueror of the Vindelici, was busy in his own sphere. Roman society in the capital suspected that Drusus, who showed none of the proverbial Claudian pride, and whose personal beauty was combined with a singularly winning manner,[4] was the son of his reputed stepfather;[5] and if the general belief had no more solid foundation than the gossip of those who remembered that he was born three months after his mother became the wife of Augustus, who had constrained Tiberius Nero to divorce her,[6] it was supported by the love which moved his successor to name Drusus his joint heir with the young Caesars, his two grandsons.[7] After the dedication of the altar at Lugudunum Drusus marched north-eastward into the country of the Ubii, in order to repel the threatened invasion of the Sugambri,[8] who had begun by crucifying twenty Roman centurions;[9] attacked them after they crossed the Rhine or while they were in the act of crossing,

Opera-tions of Drusus in Germany.

---

[1] Vell., ii, 98; Dio, liv, 34, 6. See *The Architect of the Roman Empire* (44–27 B.C.), p. 77.

[2] *Ib.*, pp. 131–5.   [3] Dio, liv, 34, 3–4; 36, 2; Livy, *Epit.*, 141.

[4] Vell., ii, 97, 3.   [5] Suet., *Claud.*, 1, 1.

[6] See *The Architect of the Roman Empire* (44–27 B.C.), pp. 109–10.

[7] Suet., *op. cit.*, 1, 5.   [8] See p. 63.

[9] If Florus (ii, 30, 24) is not confusing this invasion with that of 16 B.C. See p. 53.

somewhere in the neighbourhood of Bonn or Cologne; then crossed the river himself into the country of the Usipetes, north of the Lippe, marched southward into the Sugambrian territory, and devastated it[1] in punishment for the outrages which the tribe had inflicted upon Roman citizens. Thence he embarked his army in the fleet kept permanently for the security of the river, won the friendship of the Frisians, who dwelt between the mouth of the Weser and the Zuyder Zee, which he had just crossed, and invaded the country of the Chauci, east of the Ems. The troops who manned the fleet had already seized the island [Bor-chum.] Burchanis, opposite the Frisian coast, and on the Ems they defeated a flotilla belonging to the Bructeri, who dwelt north of the Lippe; but on the return voyage the ships ran aground on the ebbing of the tide, and Drusus might have perished with his army if they had not been rescued by the Frisians.[2] This tribe and the Batavians, who, like them, had never taken part in the German raids, would seem to have been peacefully incorporated in the empire, to which both rendered valuable services, about this time. Free from taxation, they were always ready to serve under their own chiefs in the imperial armies;[3] and one may reasonably suppose that their friendly attitude was partly due to the winning personality of Drusus, whose universal popularity was soon to be memorably attested. Master of the coast, Drusus, who in the winter returned to Rome and served as urban praetor, crossed the Rhine again in the ensuing 11 B.C. spring and, after defeating the Usipetes, bridged the Lippe with the intention, encouraged by the dissensions of his enemies, of inflicting further punishment upon the Sugambri.[4] The Chatti, who inhabited the country about the head waters of the Weser, had either refused to join them in the previous year or had neglected to send their promised contingent: the Sugambri in exasperation attacked them; and Drusus, after traversing their country

---

[1] Dio, liv, 32, 1–2. It seems doubtful whether it was in this campaign, as Jullian affirms (*Hist. de la Gaule*, iv, 109, n. 4), in 11 B.C., or in 10 that the Gallic chiefs mentioned in the *Epitome* of Livy (141) accompanied Drusus from Gaul.

[2] Strabo, vii, 1, 3; Suet., *Claud.*, 1, 2; Dio, liv, 32, 2–3.

[3] Mommsen, *Röm. Gesch.*, v, 25 (Eng. tr., i, 28). [4] See p. 77.

unresisted, marched against that of the Cherusci, which
extended between the Weser and the Elbe. Shortage of
supplies and the approach of winter prevented him from
crossing the Weser; and, returning towards the Rhine, his
column was attacked in a defile, but saved by the rash confidence of the assailants not less than by the discipline of
the legions.[1] This check did not prevent him from assuring
the results of the campaign by constructing a fort near the
confluence of the Lippe with a tributary[2] and another,
probably on the site of Coblenz, opposite the country of
the Chatti. The young general was rewarded by the
bestowal of the triumphal insignia; but Augustus declined
to sanction the title of *imperator*, which the troops had conferred by acclamation upon their beloved commander.[3]
In the following year Drusus, having again attacked the   10 B.C.
Chatti, who had joined the Sugambri, returned for the
winter to Rome with his brother and the Emperor, who
had once more visited Gaul in order to watch events in
Germany.[4] As consul in the year 9 B.C. he crossed the
Rhine for the last time, subdued the Chatti, advanced
against the Marcomanni of the upper Main, who retreated
before him, turned northward against the Cherusci, whom
he defeated, though not without considerable loss, and
marched eastward to the valley of the Elbe, which, perhaps in obedience to the Emperor,[5] he did not attempt to
cross. A legend arose in this connexion, which Dio, who
was attracted by such stories, and had before observed that
Drusus set out from Rome in disregard of portents, faithfully reported. Drusus, he tells us, set up trophies near

---

[1] Pliny, *Nat. hist.*, xi, 17, 55 (cp. Obsequens, 72); Dio, liv, 33, 1–4.

[2] See pp. 164–5.

[3] Dio, liv, 33, 4–5. Ferrero (*Greatness and Decline*, &c., v, 210, n. ‡),
remarking that the fort which Drusus built to overawe the Chatti must have
been on the site either of Coblenz (Confluentes) or of Mainz, decides for the
former, which he thinks better adapted for defence against the Chatti and
the Tencteri. The reason seems to me sufficient.

[4] Dio, liv, 36, 3–4; Oros., vi, 21, 22.

[5] Dessau (*Gesch d. röm. Kaiserzeit*, i, 420–1) insists that the Emperor's
beloved stepson could have disregarded this prohibition [!], which is attested,
without mention of Drusus, by Strabo (vii, 1, 4), and that it belonged to a
later time [after the Varian disaster ?]. I see no reason to doubt that it was
in force in the time of Drusus, who certainly had some cogent reason for his
retreat.

the river and returned in obedience to a woman of super-human stature, who, speaking in Latin, warned him: 'Whither art thou hastening, insatiable Drusus ? Thou art not fated to see all these things. Depart; for the end both of thy toils and of thy life is already nigh.' 'I cannot', Dio naively added, 'disbelieve; for straightway Drusus did depart, and, returning in haste, died before he reached the Rhine.'[1] He was riding at the head of his troops between the Saale and the Rhine when his horse fell, and his thigh bone was broken.[2] While he was lying in the 'summer camp', not far from the Weser, to which he had been carried, Augustus, [Pavia.] hearing at Ticinum that he was ill, sent Tiberius, who was there also, to visit him.[3] Tiberius, taking advantage of the postal service, drove in one stage of the journey two hundred Roman miles in a day and a night,[4] and found his

[1] Suetonius (*Claud.*, 1, 2) appears at first sight to assign the warning to 11 B.C., but probably told the story in careless disregard of chronological order.

[2] Livy, *Epit.*, 142; Strabo, vii, 1, 3; Flor., ii, 30, 23–4, 26; Dio, lv, 1. Orosius (vi, 21, 15) exaggerates when he says that Drusus almost exterminated the Marcomanni

Jullian (*Hist. de la Gaule*, iv, 112, n. 1), after citing the authorities for Drusus's last campaign, says, 'Après bien d'hésitations, je propose l'itinéraire suivant', which I ignore, thinking that such labour, in default of satisfactory information, is labour lost. I agree, however, with Jullian that 'le nom de Sicambri (*sic*), dont il est question à propos de cette campagne, doit dissimuler celui de quelque peuplade de l'Elbe'. 'Toutes les questions relatives à Drusus', he finally remarks (p. 113, n. 2), 'ont donné et donnent lieu à d'interminables discussions', which, for the most part, he wisely disregards.

[3] Val. Max., v, 5, 3; Tac., *Ann.*, iii, 5, 2. 5; Dio, lv, 2, 1.

[4] As the summer camp was not far from the Weser, the whole drive must have been far more than 200 Roman (about 184 English) miles. Miss A. M. Ramsay (*J.R.S.*, xv, 67) says that Tiberius 'rode . . . *mutato subinde equo* (Val. Max., v, 5, 3), i.e. making use of the posting service', but adds in a foot-note, 'Pliny, *N.H.*, vii, 84, says he drove, but this seems improbable'. Why ? Since Valerius, besides recording the distance, only tells us the self-evident fact that horses were repeatedly changed, is it not safest to accept the statement of Pliny ? That Tiberius rode, unless he was habitually on horseback and had the physical endurance of George Osbaldeston (*Dict. Nat. Biogr.*, xlii, 274) or the war-correspondent, Archibald Forbes, who after the battle of Ulundi rode 110 miles in 20 hours and almost immediately afterwards 170 in 35, finishing in complete exhaustion (*ib.*, Suppl. ii, 1901, pp. 222–3), is, I think, incredible. My view is supported by Suetonius (*Aug.*, 49, 3) and M. Rostovtzeff (*Social and Econ Hist. of the Roman Empire*, Pl. LXIV, p. 366. Cp. *Mitteil. d. K. d. Arch. Inst.*, xxvi, 1911, pp. 268–78, to which Miss Ramsay herself refers in *J.R.S.*, x, 85). Miss Ramsay will, I am sure, pardon this one criticism of her excellent article, even if she cannot accept it.

His death and posthumous honours.

brother still alive. After thirty days of suffering Drusus in his thirtieth year expired: his corpse was conveyed to the 'winter camp' beyond the Rhine, and thence to the Roman Forum, Tiberius walking the whole way beside the bier. After Augustus and Tiberius had delivered the customary eulogies it was cremated in the Field of Mars, and the ashes were deposited in the imperial mausoleum.[1] Augustus in his speech prayed that the gods would make his grandsons follow the example of Drusus and grant to himself an end as honourable as his; wrote verses in his praise, which were inscribed upon the tomb; and published a memoir on his life.[2] It had been intended that Drusus should have a triumph: the Senate gave to him and his sons the name Germanicus, which is recorded on a gold coin;[3] his mother was honoured in consolation for her loss by being enrolled under the law of marriage among the mothers of three children,[4] though her third, the only one whom she had borne to Augustus, was still-born.[5]

But even more significant were the honours spontaneously paid to the dead general by the soldiers whom he had led and the people against whom he had fought. Instinctively making an informal truce, they followed him after he received his mortal injury, while he was being carried to the summer camp, with equal veneration;[6] an

[1] Dio, lv, 2. Mommsen (*Röm. Gesch.*, v, 27, n. 1 [Eng. tr., i, 30, n. 1]), citing Dio, but ignoring the most important part of his narrative, asserts that the cremation took place in the winter camp. It is true that the body of Germanicus was cremated in Syria, where he died, on account of the remoteness of Rome (Tac., *Ann.*, iii, 5, 4. Cp. Suet., *Tib.*, 39, 1); but that does not justify Mommsen in disregarding the testimony of Dio. Livy (*Epit.*, 142) says that the interment took place in the tumulus of Julius Caesar.

[2] Livy, *Epit.*, 142; Suet., *Claud.*, 1, 5; Dio, lv, 2, 2–3. Cp. *Imperatoris Augusti operum fragm.*, ed. H. Malcovati, 1919, p. 29.

Consider this one instance of the difficulties that beset a historian who tries to understand the aims of Drusus and the character of Tiberius. Valerius Maximus (v, 5, 3) sees in the speed with which Tiberius drove from Ticinum to visit his brother a signal proof of fraternal love; Suetonius (*Tib.*, 50, 1. Cp. *Claud.*, 1, 4) affirms that Tiberius, in hatred of Drusus, 'produced a letter in which Drusus discussed with him the question of restoring the Republic'—a statement which no one of sound judgement would accept without conclusive proof. Tacitus (*Ann.*, i, 33, 4) says that Drusus was believed to intend to restore the Republic, but does not impute a motive.

[3] Dio, lv, 2, 3; Hill, *Historical Roman Coins*, p. 161.

[4] Dio, lv, 2, 5. See p. 43.   [5] Suet., *Aug.*, 63, 1.

[6] Seneca, *Consol. ad Marciam*, 3, 1.

altar was erected on the spot where he died;[1] the army set
[Mayence.] up in his honour at Mogontiacum, on the western bank of
the Rhine, a cenotaph, the scene of annual obsequies, in
which Gauls and Roman soldiers jointly took part, and
which was soon to be regarded, next to the altar of Lugudunum, as the most sacred spot in Roman Gaul.[2]

Death of
Octavia.
Octavia, who had served her country and her brother
not less faithfully than Drusus, and whose noble nature,
even if he was as cold as some historians have thought, he
never failed to honour, had died in the year before he lost
the much-loved stepson who was believed to be in truth his
only son. He ordered that her body should lie in state in
the temple of Julius Caesar, in which he delivered the
funeral oration, while Drusus delivered another from the
Rostra, for the mourning was public, and the Senators had
discarded their official dress, the tunic with a purple stripe.[3]

Whatever sorrow Augustus may have felt for the loss of
his sister and his stepson, he did not slacken in the discharge of public duty. Since the time when he decided to
How
Augustus
strove to
reform the
Senate.
17 B.C.
restore a semblance of authority to the Senate his aim had
been to reform it in such wise that it should become an
efficient partner. We have seen how he strove by repeated
purgations to exclude unfit members. In the year before
he paid his second visit to Gaul he increased the fines
exacted from those who without sufficient excuse were
13 B.C.
unpunctual in attendance.[4] During his absence a decree
was passed that certain ex-quaestors, whose age qualified
them for the tribuneship, should be appointed by lot to that
office,[5] which, since he and Agrippa had been invested with

[1] Tac., *Ann.*, ii, 7, 3. Cp. Mommsen, *Röm. Gesch.*, v, 27, n. 1 (Eng. tr.,
i, 30, n. 1).

[2] Suet., *Claud.*, 1, 3; Dio, lv, 2, 3; Eutrop., vii, 13. Cp. Jullian, *Hist. de
la Gaule*, iv, 113. Mommsen (*l.c.*) conjectures that the cenotaph (the *hono-
rarius tumulus* mentioned by Suetonius and the κενοτάφιον mentioned by
Dio) was at Vetera (Xanten). It seems to me more probable that Ihm in his
edition of Suetonius is right in identifying it with the monument at Mogontiacum; for Eutropius surely had in mind the most noteworthy tribute paid
to the memory of the hero. Mommsen says that he was 'doubtless' referring to the tumulus which, according to Florus (ii, 30, 23), Drusus himself
made out of booty taken from the Marcomanni!

[3] Livy, *Epit.*, 140; Seneca, *ad Polyb. de consol.*, 15 (34), 2; Suet., *Aug.*, 61,
2; Dio, liv, 35, 4–5.

[4] Dio, liv, 18, 3   [5] *Ib.*, 26, 7.

tribunician power, had so lost its attraction, that candidates would not come forward. In the year of his return he   13 B.C.
insisted, if we may accept the account which Dio gives in
conjunction with the mis-statement that a purgation of the
Senate was held in that year,[1] that all persons under
thirty-five years of age whose property was not less than a
million sesterces (equivalent to ten thousand pounds)[2] and
who were otherwise qualified should become senators,
actually examining their bodies himself to see whether they
were free from physical disability.[3] Four years later, re-   9 B.C.
membering perhaps that Varro had reminded Pompey
that the business of the Senate must always begin with
sacrifice and prayer,[4] he ordered that whenever a meeting
was held in a temple every senator, before taking his seat,
should offer incense and wine at the altar, and that the
meetings should no longer be held irregularly, but twice
monthly, on the Kalends and the Ides;[5] fixed the number
of members required to constitute a quorum (which
appears to have been reduced in the holiday months,
September and October); and again increased the fines, to
be paid thereafter by one, chosen by lot, in every five, for
inexcusable absence. If, despite these precautions, those
present should be too few to pass a decree, or if a tribune
should exercise his veto, the decision of the majority was
to be recorded as an expression of opinion. Furthermore,
it was enacted that committees, to serve for six months,

---

[1] See pp. 150–1.   [2] See *The Roman Republic*, i, 344–5.
[3] Dio, liv, 26, 3, 8–9. Ferrero (*Greatness and Decline*, &c., v, 163–4),
citing Dio's account of the reform of 13 B.C., says, 'Such were the measures
taken by the man whom every historian has regarded as desirous of founding
a monarchy. He had only to fold his arms and allow the Senate and the
aristocracy to fall into ruin, and he would have found himself and his family
masters of the . . . empire. He preferred, however, to . . . strengthen those
bodies which were the chief obstacles to any attempt at monarchy.' Readers
who may hesitate to acquiesce in Ferrero's implied conclusion that he alone
of all historians has discerned the truth will perhaps consider that Augustus
saw that the monarchy which he had founded, though he was careful to
disguise the fact, would be most effective and most secure if he could induce
the Senate, which he desired to assist him, to undertake its duties seriously.
[4] Gell., xiv, 7, 9. Cp. *The Roman Republic*, i, 79.
[5] In March the second session was to be held on the day before the Ides,
that is, on the 14th; for, since Caesar had been murdered on the Ides, that
day was regarded as ill-omened (Suet., *Div. Iul.*, 88; Dio, xlvii, 19, 1).

should be chosen by lot, to discuss beforehand matters that were to be submitted to the House. All these regulations were inscribed on tablets, conspicuously posted, in order that members, two at a time, might read them and, if they wished, propose amendments or record objections. The First Citizen departed further from traditional practice by calling upon members to state their views on matters of outstanding importance not according to the established order, but as he thought fit, his object being to induce them all to keep their minds on the alert.[1]

But, however much these reforms may have increased the efficiency of the assembly which Augustus desired to co-operate with himself, it tended gradually to become more and more subservient; for, if he tried, as he is said to have done, 'to be democratic',[2] he was attempting an impossibility. One department after another had been withdrawn from the purview of the Senate; it was filled with his nominees; and when he chose to take part in its debates, the reports of which had ceased to be published,[3] though some might venture to oppose or even to contradict him,[4] his opinion inevitably prevailed.[5]

8 B.C. The Julian calendar amended.

In the year after the death of Drusus Augustus was busy both in Rome and Germany. The Julian reform of the calendar had been so imperfectly carried out, either because the pontiffs misunderstood the Dictator's regulations or because they disregarded them under the influence of a religious scruple which held it unlucky for the Kalends of January to coincide with a market-day, that twelve days instead of nine had been intercalated in the years that elapsed since the new reckoning began, and thus what ought to have been the Kalends of January in the year 746 (8 B.C.) fell on the 29th of December, 745. Instead of

[1] Suet., *Aug.*, 35; Dio, lv, 3; 4, 1. Dio (liv, 3, 1), who states incorrectly (see p. 151) that Augustus held both a census and a revision of the Senate in 11 B.C., adds that in the same year, having observed that meetings of the Senate were sparsely attended, he ordered that its decrees should be passed even when less than four hundred were present. The statement, which is comparatively unimportant, may be true, if not of that, of some other year, perhaps 9 B.C.

[2] Dio, lv, 4, 2.   [3] Cp. *The Roman Republic*, i, 319.

[4] See *The Architect of the Roman Empire* (44–27 B.C.), p. 177.

[5] See G. B. Grundy's *Hist. of the Greek and Roman World*, 1927, pp. 460–3.

correcting the error by withdrawing three days from one
ordinary year, Augustus in virtue of his authority as Chief
Pontiff, decided to omit the intercalary day in each of
three successive quadrennial cycles, taking twelve years to
accomplish a reform which, according to modern notions,
might have been accomplished in one. Thus the corrected
calendar was to be inaugurated in 757, and the next inter-
calation was to be made in February of that year.[1]

A.D. 4.

A census, the second which Augustus carried out—this
time without a colleague in virtue of his consular power—
and the first belonging to his principate, showed that the
number of Roman citizens was four millions two hundred
and thirty-three thousand, one hundred and seventy
thousand more than in that which he had held in conjunction with Agrippa twenty years before.[2]

The census of 8 B.C.

It had already been enacted that candidates for office
who brought slaves to intimidate voters should be banished,[3]
and Augustus, although he declined to investigate a charge
of bribery against the newly elected magistrates (for, says
Dio,[4] 'he was unwilling either to punish any or to pardon
them in case of their conviction'),[5] now required all candidates to deposit a sum of money before the elections,
which they were to forfeit if they should be convicted of
corruption. While this rule was unanimously approved,
another, dealing with the evidence given by slaves in
criminal trials, had a mixed reception. Under existing law,
slaves, whose evidence was always given under torture,
were not permitted to testify against their masters. The
new one provided that, in case the evidence of a slave
should be required, he should be sold either to the State or
to Augustus; and those who approved it defended the
evasion of the old law on the ground that it encouraged
unscrupulous masters to conspire against the Emperor and
the magistrates.

Legisla-
tion
against
bribery
and con-
cerning
evidence
given by
slaves.

While Augustus was thus occupied, Tiberius, whom he
appointed to command in Germany, was conducting a

Tiberius
in
Germany.

[1] Pliny, *Nat. hist.*, xviii, 25 (57), 211; Solinus, i, 45–6; Suet., *Aug.*, 31, 2;
Censorinus, xx, 10; Macrob., i, 14, 6. 14. Cp. my *Anc. Britain*, pp. 714–26.
[2] *Mon. Ancyr.*, ii, 5–8. See pp. 150–1, and cp. *The Architect of the Roman
Empire* (44–27 B.C.), pp. 178–9.
[3] Paul., *Sent.*, V, xxx A.   [4] lv, 5, 3.   [5] *Ib.*, § 4.

campaign under his direction, exercised from beyond the
Rhine. It would seem that all the threatened tribes, except
the Sugambri, made overtures for peace, which Augustus, in
default of their submission, refused to grant. The Sugambri
thereupon complied, but soon had reason to repent and to
curse the Emperor, who doubtless considered that the time
had come to avenge the crucifixion of Roman soldiers. Not
only were their envoys arrested—a breach of the law of nations for which Augustus might have pleaded the precedent
furnished by his adoptive father [1]—and confined in Italian
towns, where they committed suicide,[2] but forty thousand
of their fellow-tribesmen were transported by Tiberius into
Gaul and forced to settle near the Rhine.[3] Tiberius was
rewarded with the title of *imperator* and the promise of a
triumph; his soldiers received a donative, because the
emperor's beloved grandson, Gaius Caesar, then a boy of
twelve, was exercising with them for the first time;[4]
Augustus himself accepted the honour, conferred by the
Senate, of having his birthday annually commemorated
by chariot races.[5] While Tiberius was busy in Germany the
subjection of the Pannonians, against whom he had
conducted so many campaigns, was completed (in the sense
that they remained quiet for fourteen years) by Sextus
Appuleius,[6] about whom nothing else that is notable
appears to be known.

The
province
of
Germany.
Before Tiberius returned to Rome to celebrate his
triumph, the province, if it may be so called, of Germany
had been formed, extending from the middle and the lower
Rhine to the Elbe.[7] In it were incorporated the German

---

[1] See *B.G.*, iv, 13, 4–6. Cp. *The Roman Republic*, ii, 92.   [2] Dio, lv, 6, 2–3.
[3] Vell., ii, 97, 4; Strabo, vii, 1, 3; Tac., *Ann.*, ii, 26, 3; Suet., *Aug.*, 21, 1;
Tib., 9, 2; Ps. Victor, *Epit.*, i, 7; Eutrop., vii, 9; Oros., vi, 21, 24. Jullian
(*Hist. de la Gaule*, iv, 103) infers from Tacitus, *Germ.*, 28, that at this time
the left bank of the river was entrusted to the Cisrhenane Germans with the
task of guarding against their compatriots on the right.   [4] Dio, lv, 6, 4–5.
[5] *Ib.*, § 6. Dio (cp. Tac., *Ann.*, xii, 23, 5) adds, that Augustus enlarged the
boundary of the city (a privilege reserved for those who had extended the
boundaries of the empire); but, as Rushforth remarks (*Lat. Hist. Inscr.*², p.
86), the omission of his name in the *lex de imperio Vespasiani* (ll. 15–6) and
the silence of the Ancyran monument are conclusive against this statement.
[6] Mommsen, *Chron. min.*, ii, 135, 590.
[7] *Mon. Ancyr.*, v, 10–12; Jullian, *Hist. de la Gaule*, iv, 135, n. 1. Cp.
p. 87, n. 5.

tribes on the left bank. It would seem that Tiberius, on being appointed commander-in-chief in succession to Drusus, became virtually Governor of Gaul, apart from the 'Province', as his predecessor had certainly been, and also exercised such control as was then possible over the Transrhenane country. The command of the troops remained for some years undivided: there is no evidence that the Cisrhenane district was divided into Upper and Lower Germany before Germanicus, the elder son of Drusus, was sent to co-operate with his uncle.[1] Drusus had provided A.D for the defence of Gaul against German incursions as well as for Roman invasion of Germany. The fort called Vetera (the 'Old Camp'), close to Birten in the neighbourhood of Xanten, and opposite the mouth of the navigable Lippe, was adapted for either purpose. Posts were established along the Meuse, the Weser, and the Elbe; some fifty redoubts were erected along the Rhine;[2] and the foundation of the fort which Drusus built to protect Mogontiacum, and which, like Vetera, not only guarded the passage of the river, but also served as a depot for the storage of supplies, is commemorated by Tacitus[3] and by the modern name, Kastel, derived from *castellum*. Traders and artisans settled round the forts in this as in other provinces.[4]

Naturally it was too early to attempt to organize the government.[5] Assessment of taxation for a half-conquered country, in which renewed outbreaks might be expected, levying of recruits for the imperial army, would have been premature. The Ubii, however, whom Agrippa, mindful of their constant loyalty, had settled on the left bank of the Rhine,[6] but who had not been included in the cantonal union established in Gaul on the dedication of the altar at Lugudunum, erected in their chief town, afterwards called Colonia Agrippina, which, standing upon the site of Cologne, was to become the capital of Lower Germany,

The Ubii erect an altar to Augustus.

---

[1] See p. 112.   [2] Flor., ii, 30, 26.   [3] *Ann.*, i, 56, 1.
[4] J. Colin, *La Rhénanie*, &c., 1927, p. 77.
[5] As Rushforth says (*Lat. Hist. Inscr.*[2], p. 108), 'At first the two Germanies were not provinces proper, but only a military frontier'. I would say 'spheres of military command'. Mommsen, however (*Röm. Gesch.*, v, 31, 107 [Eng. tr., i, 35, 117]) speaks of the 'province' of Germany.
[6] *The Roman Republic*, ii, 92, 138; Strabo, iv, 3, 4.

another altar, of which the priest then or later was a Roman, for the German cantons.[1]

Augustus, ever mindful of the East as well as of the West, had lately been able to undertake the subjugation of the Homonadenses, those brigands who, dwelling on the northern slopes of Mount Taurus, menaced the peace of Galatia—a duty which he had unavoidably postponed

Quirinius subdues the Homona- denses. when that province was formed.[2] The officer whom he selected to conduct the campaign, Publius Sulpicius Quirinius, was a man of low birth, but of invincible resolution and hard, relentless temper, who had risen by dint of sheer merit and, besides chastising the rebellious Gara- mantes,[3] had already subdued the desert tribes of Cyrene. In 12 B.C. he was elected consul, proceeded in the autumn to the East, and there, in consultation with the Governor of Galatia, formed his plans. Probably the consulship had been conferred in order to qualify him for the office of Governor of Syria, the only eastern province in which there was an army sufficient for the task that he was about to undertake. In 12 or 11 B.C., while Drusus was campaigning against the Germans, he was placed in charge of that country, and in this capacity during the next three years

10–7 B.C. conducted the war. The Homonadenses had forty-four fortified villages, which, one after another, were surrounded and reduced by starvation. The successive campaigns were short, for winter began early and lasted long, and on the plateau of Taurus, four thousand to seven thousand feet above the sea, the snow lay deep. Quirinius, who would have approved the line in which Virgil [4] described the Roman way of dealing with a stubborn enemy, had no qualms in adopting such methods as would ensure the permanence of the conquest. Not one man of military age was allowed to remain in the country, four thousand being settled in neighbouring towns. Quirinius was rewarded with the triumphal insignia; and for more than three centuries the descendants of the brigands remained at peace. In the year after the conquest five military colonies,

---

[1] Tac., *Ann.*, i, 39, 1; 57, 2. See Mommsen, *Röm. Gesch.*, v, 28–31 (Eng. tr., i, 31–5).
[2] See p. 14.   [3] See p. 12.   [4] *Aen.*, vi, 835.

Comana, Cremna, Lystra, Olbasa, and Parlais, were founded in the Province and connected by roads, called Augustan, with Antioch, which remained the military centre. In each of them there was stationed a regiment of auxiliary cavalry, for the veterans of which lands were assigned.[1]

It was in the course of the war that, if we may trust Saint Luke,[2] the first enrolment of inhabitants was made in the East of a series which Augustus purposed to conduct throughout the empire. One of its objects was to calculate, by numbering the citizens, future military strength. Augustus discerned that, in order to ensure wise government, it was necessary to ascertain, to classify, and to register minute details. In the judgement of the scholar [3] who by his travels and researches in Asia Minor has done more than any other inquirer to supplement the scanty notices of that country in the works of ancient historians, Luke 'has lit up the obscurity of this dark period, and given us a specimen of imperial administrative method'.

St Luke's account of an enrolment in Syria.

[1] Dessau, *Inscr. Lat.*, 918; Strabo, xii, 6, 5; Pliny, *Nat. hist.*, v, 27 (23), 94; Flor., ii, 31, 41; Tac., *Ann.*, iii, 23, 1; 48, 1–4; *J.R.S.*, vii, 231, 236–8, 240, 257–8, 261–2, 271, 273; xiv, 203. When I wrote the paragraph to which this note belongs I was convinced by the arguments of Sir William Ramsay (*J.R.S.*, vii, 229–31, 237, n. 2) that Quirinius was Governor of Syria between 12 and 6 B.C. as well as in A.D. 6, and that Mommsen (*Res gestae²*, &c., pp. 161–78) was right in regarding the Tiburtine Fragment (Dessau, *Inscr. Lat.*, 918), on which Sir William's arguments were based, as a piece of his *cursus honorum*. Mr. Hugh Last, however, believes that E. Groag (*Jahreshefte d. öster. archäol. Instituts in Wien*, xxi–xxii) 'has shown that connection to be impossible'. 'It looks', Mr. Last adds, 'as if Quirinius had a special command against the Homonadenses, and was not governor of Syria at the time'.

[2] ii, 2. Cp. *Expositor*, Nov., 1912, pp. 385–9, 406–7. 'The decree of Augustus which Luke mentions is commonly interpreted', says W. M. Ramsay (*Was Christ born at Bethlehem?* 1898, pp. 123–4), 'as ordering that a single census should be held of the whole Roman world. This is not a correct interpretation . . . What Augustus did was to lay down the principle of systematic "enrolment" in the Roman world'. In the book from which I quote these words Ramsay held (p. 201) that 'the first enrolment must have taken place in B.C. 6. In *J.R.S.*, vii, 274, he assigned it to 8 B.C. J. Marquardt (*L'organisation financière chez les Romains*, 1888, pp. 366–9 [translated from the German]), remarking that Luke's phrase (ii, 1) ἐν ταῖς ἡμέραις ἐκείναις ('in those days') is vague, argues that the decree of Augustus was made in 27 B.C. See p. 5, *supra*.

[3] Sir William Ramsay (*Expositor*, Nov., 1912, p. 389.) Cp. *J.R.S.*, vii, 273.

This interesting conclusion, has, however, been disputed, if not demolished. It is certain that in the year 6 B.C. no enrolment had yet been held in Cyrenaica.[1] May we, one might ask, provisionally conjecture that it had been ordered, but that the order had not yet taken effect? It must, however, be admitted that Josephus would hardly have neglected to record an event so remarkable.[2]

Deaths of Horace and Maecenas.

Nov. 27.

Towards the end of 8 B.C. Horace, who, like Virgil, one of the best loved of his many friends,[3] had done so much to celebrate the deeds of the First Citizen, to win support for his social and religious reforms, and thereby to make the restored government popular, died, surviving by only a few weeks the patron to whose affectionate friendship he owed his fortune, and who in his last moments commended him to the imperial care of their common friend. Augustus had begged Maecenas to persuade Horace to come to the palace and to live there as his private secretary and, when Horace declined the invitation, had bidden him make use of the house as if he lived there, adding, 'If you are so haughty as to despise my friendship, I am not scornful in return', and insisting that he should write another book of Odes, which was to include one in praise of Drusus, in continuation of the first three.[4] Maecenas, who, if there had not been more in him than the effeminacy which Velleius[5] (who had sufficient discrimination to appreciate his ability), Seneca,[6] and Juvenal,[7] noted as his conspicuous characteristic, would not have been selected by Augustus for high office or accepted as his counsellor,[8] had never hesi-

[1] Prof. von Premerstein (*Die fünf neugefundenen Edikte d. Augustus aus Cyrene* [about which see pp. 92–4, *infra*], 1928, pp. 449–50) remarks that it is evident from the first edict that the number of Greeks whose census was 7,500 *denarii* or more was unknown, which, he says, proves that in 7–6 B.C. there had not yet been held in Cyrenaica the so-called provincial census. The earliest, he adds (pp. 450–1), of which we have sure evidence was that held in Syria A.D. 6–7 [Dessau, *Inscr. Lat.*, 2683; Rushforth, *Lat. Hist. Inscr.*[2], pp. 24–5].

[2] See Prof. J. M. Creed's *The Gospel according to Saint Luke*, 1930 p. 29. He concludes that Luke ante-dated the census of Quirinius, for which see the preceding note, and p. 97, *infra*.   [3] *Carm.*, i, 3, 5–8.

[4] Suetonius, ed. Roth, pp. 296–8, or *Imperatoris Caesaris Augusti fragm.*, ed. H. Malcovati, pp. 13–4.

[5] ii, 88, 2.   [6] *Ep.*, 114, 4–5.   [7] xii, 39.

[8] See *The Architect of the Roman Empire* (44–27 B.C.), pp. 28, 104, 111–2, 114, 116, 144, 158, 177.

tated to remonstrate with him when he gave way to excessive anger. Dio [1] relates that once—perhaps in the previous year, in which alleged conspirators are said to have been punished [2]—seeing that Augustus was about to condemn many accused persons to death, he wrote on a tablet, after trying in vain to approach him through the crowd of onlookers, 'Do rise, executioner: it is high time', and flung it into his lap; whereupon Augustus, who never resented such liberties from him, rose and left the court. Maecenas, forgiving his amour with Terentia,[3] had named him his heir.[4]

How Maecenas remonstrated with Augustus.

Tiberius, after entering upon his second consulship, celebrated his triumph,[5] which he followed up by entertaining the senators at dinner in the Capitol, while his mother entertained their wives.[6] Immediately afterwards he left Rome for Germany, in which fresh disturbances had broken out ;[7] but no military operations were necessary, or none which chroniclers thought worthy of mention. That his work had been done thoroughly became apparent when, two years later, Lucius Domitius Ahenobarbus, the Governor of Illyricum, a grandson of Caesar's implacable enemy, crossed the Elbe, which had barred the advance of Drusus, unopposed, entered into amicable relations with the inhabitants, and set up an altar to Augustus on the further bank.[8] During the absence of Tiberius a festival, held in honour of the return of Augustus from Gaul, was directed by Gaius Caesar, and gladiatorial combats, at which the spectators wore mourning, were exhibited in memory of Agrippa.[9] In consequence of a fire which had damaged buildings round the Forum and had made it necessary to hold the combats in the Field of Mars, commissioners were placed in charge of the slaves previously employed by the aediles as firemen.[10] Augustus added to

7 B.C.

5 B.C. Tiberius and Ahenobarbus in Germany.

[1] lv, 7.   [2] Dio, lv, 4, 4.   [3] See p. 54.
[4] Dio, lv, 7, 5. Cp. *C.I.L.*, vi, 4016, 4032, 4095.
[5] *C.I.L.*, i², p. 181; Vell., ii, 97, 4; Suet., *Tib.*, 9, 2; Dio, lv, 8, 2.
[6] Dio, lv, 8, 2.   [7] *Ib.*, § 3.
[8] Tac., *Ann.*, iv, 44, 3; Dio, lv, 10a, 2–3. Cp. Mommsen, *Röm. Gesch.*, v, 28 (Eng. tr., i, 31) and Winkelsesser, *De rebus . . . Augusti auspiciis in Germania gestis*, 1901, p. 23.   [9] Dio, lv, 8, 3, 5. Cp. liv, 2, 4.
[10] *Ib.*, §§ 6–7.

Augustus
reforms
local
govern-
ment in
Rome.
this temporary measure a reform designed to improve local administration, at the same time ordering that no building over seventy feet high should be erected in a public thoroughfare.[1] Rome was divided into fourteen regions, the government of which was still assigned by lot, as that of the undivided city had been, to the aediles, with whom were associated the tribunes and the praetors, similarly chosen, and subdivided into wards, which were administered by officers elected by their inhabitants.[2] The working of the system must have been at first unsatisfactory; for A.D. 6. thirteen years later seven companies of freedmen, each commanded by a Roman knight and all controlled by a prefect, empowered to punish negligent inhabitants, were organized as watchmen, whose duty was to extinguish fires and to maintain order at night.[3] But, though the growing authority of the Prefect of the City [4] must have gradually weakened the authority which the aediles and their colleagues exercised over the 'regions', the position of the elected officers was still coveted, as that of borough councillors is with us, by ambitious townsmen, and, as a judicious historian [5] has observed, 'the ward-chapels, worships, and festivals formed useful centres of corporate life'. He might have added that by reconstituting the worship of the *Lares compitales*, the tutelary deities of the wards, in whose place appeared *Lares Augusti*, associated with the Genius of the Emperor, Augustus familiarized the freedmen with the fruitful ideas symbolized for provincials throughout the Roman world by the imperial cult.[6]

More important than this municipal organization, though, if it was known to ancient historians, not one had

---

[1] Strabo, v, 3, 7. Cp. Suet., *Aug.*, 89, 2. Seventy Roman feet were equal to about sixty-eight English. Stuart Jones (*Companion to Roman Hist.*, 1913, p. 36) remarks that 'the rule must often have been broken'. I am not so sure. Augustus was in failing health when the rule was drafted; but his stepson and colleague was often in Rome and would hardly have tolerated disobedience.

[2] Suet., *Aug.*, 30, 1; Dio, lv, 8, 7.

[3] *Ib.*, 26, 4–5. Cp. *Dig.*, i, 15, 3, and Rushforth, *Lat. Hist. Inscr.*[2], p. 61.

[4] Cp. *The Roman Republic*, iii, 45, 296.

[5] H. F. Pelham, *Outlines of Roman Hist.*[2], pp. 140–1.

[6] Cp. Rushforth, pp. 59–62.

sufficient discrimination to use his knowledge, was a series
of edicts concerning the province of Cyrene, which Augustus framed in the same year, and which prove what the
present writer [1] had before maintained against adverse
opinion, that he exercised the 'higher command' [2] over
the provinces that had been reserved for the Senate. The
evidence is to be found in that source of information which
has so greatly supplemented the jejune narratives of historians—*papyri*—in this case discovered in the course of
the Italian excavations at Cyrene.[3] It comprises five
edicts, of which the first four are dated 7–6, the last 4 B.C.
The four earlier concerned only Cyrenaica—one of the two
portions of the province of Crete and Cyrene. The first
shows that in this province and, as far as is at present
known, in it alone, criminal judicature was modelled on
that of the permanent courts of Rome.[4] In all the others,
senatorial and imperial alike, the Governor administered
criminal justice without a jury, which was required in civil
cases alone.[5] In Cyrenaica the proconsul had only to give
effect to the decision of his jurors. The edicts that prove,
vindicating the authority of Dio,[6] and illustrate the power
which the First Citizen exercised are the first and the
fourth, which show that he used his right of intervention
in senatorial provinces, at least in response to appeals.[7]
More important, however, was the fifth, which was applicable not only to Cyrenaica, but also to the whole empire.
In it Augustus, communicating to the provincials a translation of a decree relating to extortion, which the Senate
had recently passed, said, 'It will make evident to all the
inhabitants of the provinces what great care I and the
Senate take to prevent any one of our subjects from suffering injustice or extortion.' [8] Before the discovery of the

Augustan edicts in Cyrene.

---

[1] *The Architect of the Roman Empire* (44–27 B.C.), pp. 265–7.
[2] *maius imperium.*
[3] See *J.R.S.*, xvii, 33–48.
[4] *Quaestiones perpetuae.* See *The Roman Republic*, i, 63.
[5] *J.R.S.*, xvii, 41. Cp. Mommsen, *Röm. Strafrecht*, 1899, p. 239.
[6] liii, 32, 5.
[7] *J.R.S.*, xxvii, 43. Cp. von Premerstein, *Die fünf . . . Edikte d. Augustus
aus Cyrene*, pp. 434–5. [See p. 180.]
[8] *J.R.S., l.c.* Cp. von Premerstein, pp. 436–7.

edicts it had been possible for scholars who ignored the significant lines of Ovid [1]

Nec mea decreto damnasti facta senatus,
Nec mea selecto iudice iussa fuga est [2]

A.D. 12. to maintain that once only under Augustus, when he was in extreme old age, had the Senate, exercising criminal jurisdiction in a case which would normally have been tried by a permanent court, condemned a criminal to banishment: [3] the decree which Augustus communicated to the people of Cyrenaica provided for the trial by the Senate of less serious cases of extortion.[4]

Just as the triumphant career of Tiberius seemed to have 6 B.C. reached its zenith, it suffered a check which was destined to last for several years. His stepsons, Gaius and Lucius Caesar, aged respectively fourteen and eleven years, were beginning to manifest qualities which made their grandfather anxious. He had devoted much care to their education, teaching them himself to read, write, and swim, and engaging a learned freedman, Verrius Flaccus, to whom he paid a liberal salary, to give them further instruction.[5] They were being spoiled, however, by flattery, and the elder, despite his extreme youth, was elected consul, an honour which Augustus would not permit him to accept, though he agreed to allow both him and his brother to be designated consuls—the elder then, the younger in his fifteenth year—on condition that they should not enter office until five years later. The Senate decreed further that each, after assuming the dress of manhood, should be permitted to take part in its debates; and each in the year 5 B.C.; of his designation as consul was saluted by the whole body 2 B.C. of Roman knights as *princeps iuventutis*—'leader of the young'[6]—a title which implied that he was regarded as chief

---

[1] *Tristia*, ii, 131–2.
[2] 'You did not condemn what I did by decree of the Senate; my exile was not ordered by chosen jurors.'
[3] Tac., *Ann.*, i, 72, 4; iv, 21, 5. Cp. Dessau, *Gesch. d. Kaiserzeit*, i, 140–1. Prof. McFayden (*Washington Univ. Studies*, x, 1923, p. 243) remarks that in this case there was no court to deal with defamation of character.
[4] *J.R.S.*, xxvii, 47–8. Cp. von Premerstein, pp. 527–8. [See p. 180.]
[5] Suet., *Aug.*, 64, 3; Suet., ed. Roth, p. 264.
[6] Cp. *Mon. Ancyr.*, ii, 46—iii, 6 and (Greek) 7, 11–20, with Ovid, *Ars amat.*,

of those youths who were to become officers of the army.[1]
The numerous coins on which this honour was recorded
made it evident to the Roman world that Augustus had
designated the boys as his successors.[2] Thinking, it is said,
that they needed a lesson, and hoping to bring them to
their senses, he bestowed upon Tiberius the tribunician
power for five years, and offered him as his next sphere of
government Armenia, which, since the death of Tigranes,
had become estranged.[3] One Artavasdes, who had been set
up as king by Augustus, was dethroned by the anti-Roman
faction, and it was this act of hostility that led Augustus to
offer the commission to Tiberius.[4] It might seem that he
desired to impress upon his grandsons that their stepfather,
although he was not, like them, a Caesar, was a more important personage than either of them had yet become.
Tiberius declined the offer and, after resigning his command, prepared to go into retirement. Augustus could only
wait to see what the Armenian faction that rested on
Parthian support would do. The motive of Tiberius was
variously explained. The statement of Tacitus, that one of
his reasons was that his wife, Julia, the daughter of Augustus and the mother of Gaius and Lucius, despised him as
her inferior in birth, will be rejected by all who are not
blind to the patriotism, constantly manifested, of a great
public servant. Not more acceptable are the suggestions
that the proud Claudian would have abandoned the career
in which he had won high distinction because he was dis-
gusted by the amours of the woman whom he had married
in obedience to a Roman sense of duty. Dismissing other
guesses, those who examine the original authorities will find
it safe to accept the explanation which Tiberius himself

Marginal notes: How Gaius and Lucius Caesar were designated successors of Augustus.

Why Tiberius retired to Rhodes.

---

i, 194, Tac., *Ann.*, i, 3, 2, Suet., *Aug.*, 26, 2, Dio, lv, 9, 1–4, 9–10, Mommsen,'
*Res gestae*², &c., pp. 52–8, and Dessau, *Inscr. Lat.*, 106–7, 131–2, 134, 136.

[1] Cp. p. 128.

[2] Hill, *Historical Roman Coins*, No. 108. (p. 169). I cannot undertand why
Dr. Hill says that 'the date of the acclamation . . . as *principes iuventutis* is
not known'. Dio (lv, 9, 10) is wrong in saying that Lucius received the honour
one year later than Gaius. Cp. Hardy (*Mon. Ancyr.*, p. 75) with Mommsen
(*Res gestae*², &c., p. 58).

[3] Vell., ii, 99, 1; Suet., *Tib.*, 9, 3; Dio, lv, 9, 4.

[4] *Mon. Ancyr.*, v, 24–8; Tac., *Ann.*, ii, 3–4. Cp. p. 36, Mommsen, *Res
gestae*², &c., p. 113, and Hardy, *Mon. Ancyr.*, p. 130.

gave when he had no longer any motive for silence—
that he wished to avoid the suspicion of rivalry with the
jealous boys whom his wife had borne to Agrippa, her former husband—an explanation which Velleius Paterculus,
the subordinate officer who so fervently admired him, confirmed in his rhetorical way when he wrote that Tiberius
feared that 'the splendour of his own renown' might mar
their opening career. Tiberius had learned from experience
of public life—perhaps from recollection of the temporary
retirement of Agrippa in favour of the young Marcellus[1]—
that, if he remained in Rome, unpleasantness might de-
velop in his relations with his stepsons and therefore also
with their grandfather. He knew that he was the only
living Roman general of deservedly high reputation, that
he could afford to bide his time, and that, sooner or later,
his country would need the renewal of his services. Therefore, although his mother, after he refused the offer of
Armenia, begged him to remain in Rome, and Augustus even
complained in the Senate that Tiberius was leaving him in
the lurch, he adhered to his resolve, and embarked for
Rhodes, which thirteen years before, on returning from
Armenia, he had found a pleasant resting place.[2]

Tiberius had not long left Rome when Paphlagonia was
annexed on the death of its ruler, Deiotarus Philadelphus,
4 B.C. by his overlord, Augustus;[3] and the following year was
marked by a further development in the eastern part of the
empire. Herod, who ever since the battle of Actium had
been loyal to the victor who had done much to promote the
prosperity of Palestine, and of whose assistance Agrippa
had gladly availed himself,[4] died, leaving a will, to be confirmed by Augustus, which directed that his kingdom
should be divided between his three sons, Judaea being
assigned to the eldest, Archelaus. In the council which
Augustus convened to consider these provisions, the place
of honour was reserved for Gaius Caesar, whose claim to be
acknowledged as the successor designate of his grandfather, already indicated by the title *princeps iuventutis*,

[1] See p. 28–9.   [2] Suet., *Tib.*, 10, 2; 11, 1.
[3] *C.I.G.*, 4154; *Rev. des études grecques*, 1893, p. 251.
[4] See p. 52.

was thus plainly recognized.[1] Archelaus proved himself so
incompetent that, a few years later, Augustus deposed him, A.D. 6.
and Judaea became a Roman province.[2] Disturbances Judaea
followed in consequence of measures which were necessarily becomes
taken for the purpose of taxation;[3] but every care was province.
taken to avoid giving needless offence to the inhabitants.
Since images were abhorrent to the Jews, the portrait of
Augustus was not engraved on the Roman coins; gifts from
Augustus and Livia adorned the temple; and by his order
a bull and two lambs were daily sacrificed there to the
Supreme God.[4]

In the records of the year in which Herod died and of the
next historians, so far as imperfect manuscripts enable us
to see, found little that attracted their attention, except
the discharge of legionaries who had completed their time
of service, and who, as Augustus in the summary inscribed
on the Monument of Ancyra was careful to announce, went
back to their respective municipalities with substantial
pecuniary rewards;[5] but the following year was crowded 2 B.C.
with events which, if they were not of outstanding political
importance, greatly impressed the inhabitants of Rome.
Augustus, who would have abolished the dole that pauper-
ized its recipients if he had not feared that disturbances
would inevitably ensue,[6] followed the example of Caesar,
whose reform had been transient in its effects,[7] by reducing
the number of those eligible to two hundred thousand.[8]
Whatever discontent this measure may have provoked was
doubtless lessened by a series of celebrations which must
have gratified the populace. In August the temple of Mars Spectacu-
Ultor, which he had vowed in the campaign of Philippi to lar cele-
build, if he should succeed in avenging his adoptive father's in Rome.
murder,[9] was solemnly dedicated.[10] In connexion with this
function he provided a spectacle,[11] which was perhaps the

---

[1] Jos., *Bell.*, ii, 2, 4.   [2] Jos., *Ant.*, xvii, 8, 1; xviii, 1, 1.   [3] See p. 123.
[4] Jos., *Bell.*, v, 13, 6; Philo, *Leg. ad Gaium*, §§ 157, 317. Cp. E. Schürer,
Gesch. d. Iüd. Volkes, &c., i, 1901, pp. 483–4.
[5] *Mon. Ancyr.*, iii, 31–3.
[6] See p. 25.   [7] See *The Roman Republic*, iii, 283, n. 6.
[8] Suet., *Aug.*, 42, 3; Dio, lv, 10, 1.   [9] See p. 37.
[10] *C.I.L.*, i², p. 318; *Mon. Ancyr.*; iv, 21–2; Vell., ii, 100, 2; Suet., *Aug.*
29, 1–2; Dio, lv, 10, 2–6.   [11] The first of the annual *ludi Martiales*.

most attractive of any that were given in his reign. Unlike
Tiberius, who in certain respects scrupulously followed his
example, he kept in mind that such exhibitions tended to
keep an urban population which had lost the reality of
political power in good humour; he delighted in watching
them, especially contests in pugilism, from the imperial box
or from the rooms of his friends; and the importance which
he attached to them is evident from the prominence with
which he enumerated all in recounting his deeds.[1] The
nominal management of the spectacle was entrusted to the
brothers Caesar, who were doubtless thus consoled for the
slight which they fancied that they had suffered before the
retirement of Tiberius, and who, with their brother Agrippa
Postumus and boys belonging to noble families, took part
in the equestrian exercise called Troy, which Virgil[2] described. Not only were gladiatorial combats held on the
Field of Mars in a marble enclosure[3] called the Saepta, which
Agrippa had adorned; two hundred and sixty lions were
butchered in the Great Circus; a naval battle between
fleets manned by some three thousand fighting-men, who
represented Persians and Athenians, was exhibited on an
artificial lake; and thirty-six crocodiles were slaughtered in
water with which the Flaminian Circus had been flooded.
The spectators were so numerous that Augustus, in accordance with his usual practice on such occasions, posted
sentries in various parts of the city, to prevent depreda-
tions by burglars and thieves.[4] Ovid[5] noticed the spectacle,
the description of which he left to others, because it gave
opportunities for amorous adventure.

Julia
banished
for
adultery.

It was in the year of these festivities that the incident
occurred, directly resulting from the law relating to adultery
and affecting the reputation of the Emperor's only daughter,
which caused him more distress than any other misfortune
of his life. Tiberius had ceased to live with Julia, and,
although she was approaching middle age, and the mother
of four children, she had lovers, of whom the best known

---

[1] Suet., Aug., 45, 1–2; *Mon. Ancyr.*, iv, 31–48.   [2] *Aen.*, v, 545–603.
[3] See Dio, liii, 23, 1, and cp. p. 91.
[4] *Mon. Ancyr.*, iv, 38–9, 43–8; Vell., ii, 100, 2; Suet., *Aug.*, 43, 1–2; Dio,
lv, 10, 6–8.   [5] *Ars amat.*, i, 175.

was an ex-consul, Iullus Antonius, the son of the Triumvir and of Fulvia. Fond of dress and personal adornment, she was devoted to literature, of which she had read much, and, as we learn from Macrobius, that diligent collector of details which escaped the notice of historians, those who knew the secrets of her private life wondered at the union in one woman of an amiable disposition and sexual depravity. To judge from the specimens which he gives of her conversation, she was witty and apt in repartee. There is no sufficient evidence that her morals were more depraved, lax though they undoubtedly were, than those of countless women, her contemporaries[1]; but they were more provocative of scandal, because she was the daughter of the Emperor and the wife of his illustrious stepson. The story that while she was married to Agrippa she indulged a passion for Tiberius, and that he repelled her advances, may have rested upon nothing more trustworthy than ignorant gossip. In her girlhood Augustus had tried to keep her secluded, sharply rebuking a young man who visited her at Baiae for his presumption; and when he observed her passion for dress and jewels, he may have reflected that the care which he had taken, as an old-fashioned Roman father, to have her taught spinning and weaving had borne no fruit. Once when she dressed simply to please him and he remarked that her attire was now suitable for the daughter of Augustus, she replied archly, 'Yes, to-day I dressed for my father to see, yesterday for my husband'. At last Augustus, who had long suspected her of immorality, was informed that she had been seen engaged in nocturnal revels in the Forum, and, overcome by anger, communicated his discovery in a letter to the Senate. Since he had himself enacted that a father might put to death his daughter if she were detected in adultery, and that if he waived this right, she must be banished to an island,[2] he felt obliged to keep his law, and accordingly banished Julia to Pandateria, opposite the Campanian coast, whither her mother, his divorced wife, voluntarily accompanied her.

---

[1] M. Gelzer, who calls her 'a common whore' (*Paulys Real-Ency.*, x, 485), has perhaps a less sympathetic knowledge of Roman society than of Latin inscriptions.   [2] See p. 45.

Under the same law Antonius and some of her other lovers were executed, the rest, like her, banished. Not content with having enforced the law against his daughter, he would not allow her wine or any luxuries; and when her freedwoman, Phoebe, who was said to have been her accomplice, committed suicide, he remarked that he would rather have begotten her than Julia.[1]

Feb. 5, 2 B.C. Augustus hailed as 'Father of his country'. But in the course of the year there was a memorable session of the Senate, the recollection of which must have consoled the indignant father. The people had sent a deputation to Antium, to offer him the title, which had been informally bestowed upon Cicero after his consulship and by the Senate upon Caesar[2]—'Father of his country'—and afterwards, though he declined it, had so saluted him when he was entering the theatre. But the Senate was not to be denied. On the 5th of February Marcus Valerius Messalla Corvinus, who had been one of the consuls in the year of the victory at Actium,[3] rose in the House, and, addressing the First Citizen, said, 'All good fortune attend thee and thy family, Caesar Augustus; for thus we deem that we are praying for lasting prosperity for the State and happiness for this our city. The Senate in accord with the Roman People hails thee Father of thy country'. Augustus with tears in his eyes replied, 'Having attained my highest hopes, Conscript Fathers, what more have I to ask of the immortal gods than that I may be allowed to retain this your unanimous approval to the very end of my life ?' No wonder that in the closing words of the record of his achievements which, before his last journey, he entrusted to the Vestal Virgins, he proudly commemorated this glorious day: 'While I was holding my thirteenth consulship, the Senate, the Equestrian Order, and the entire Roman People named me Father of my country and decreed that the title should be inscribed in the vestibule of my house and in the

---

[1] Vell., ii, 100, 5; Pliny, *Nat. hist.*, vii, 45 (46), 149; Seneca, *De brev. vitae*, 5, 4; *De benef.*, vi, 12; *De clem.*, i, 10, 3; Suet,. *Aug,.* 64, 2; 65, 1–3; *Tib.*, 7, 2; Tac., *Ann.*, iii, 24, 2–3; iv, 44, 5; Dio, lv, 10, 14–6; Macrob., li, 5.

[2] *The Roman Republic*, i, 282; iii, 331.

[3] *C.I.L.*, i, p. 544. Cp. *The Architect of the Roman Empire* (44–27 B.C.), p. 147.

Augustan Forum under the chariot that had been set up in
my honour by decree of the Senate.'[1]

But little more than a year had passed when he must
have felt how much his country had lost when Tiberius refused to accept that commission in the East. About the
time when he was hailed as Father of his country Phraates,
the King of Parthia, whom Tiberius had induced to restore
the Roman standards, was murdered by his son, Phraataces,
whose mother was his concubine. The anti-Roman party
in Armenia, supported by the murderer, who seized the
royal power, regained the influence which they had lost
when, twenty years before, Tiberius restored Tigranes and
gained his diplomatic victory over Phraates. Augustus
hardly knew how to act. In the absence of Tiberius there
was no one available who could be trusted to deal with so
serious a crisis. Under the stress of necessity Augustus
decided to entrust Gaius Caesar, though he was still only
nineteen, with the mission which Tiberius had declined.

Troubles in Armenia.

Gaius Caesar entrusted with a mission which Tiberius had declined.

The mission had a double aim. After effecting a settlement with the Armenians and the Parthians Gaius was to
proceed to Arabia, and there to complete the measures that
had been taken a quarter of a century before for the promotion of trade with India.[2] The vast peninsula was to be
circumnavigated by fleets starting on one side from Egypt,
on the other from the Persian Gulf. The geographer
Isidorus, who had acquired much information by travel in
the East, and King Juba, who in his study had amassed
a store of Greek documents, placed their services at the
disposal of the prince.[3]

Gaius was now consul. Hoping to increase his prestige,
his grandfather found a wife for him and gave him proconsular authority. Dio relates that when he was on his
outward journey Tiberius visited him in Chios (which he
may have done in order to disabuse his mind of the jealousy

[1] *C.I.L.*, i[2], pp. 233, 309; Dessau, *Inscr. Lat.*, 96, 100–1, 103–5, 107. 5,
110; *Mon. Ancyr.*, vi, 24–7; Ovid, *Fasti*, ii, 127–8; Suet., *Aug.*, 58; Dio, lv,
10, 10; Hill, *Historical Roman Coins*, p. 169. Cp. *The Architect of the Roman
Empire* (44–27 B.C.), pp. 134, n. 2, 147.   [2] See pp. 18–20.

[3] Pliny, *Nat. hist.*, ii, 67, 168; vi, 27, 139–41; xii, 3 (31), 56; xxxii, 1 (4), 10.
Cp. E. H. Warmington, *The Commerce between the Roman Empire and India*,
p. 24.

that he had felt when he himself received the offer of
Armenia), adding the story, which perhaps originated in
the gossip of some attendant who was present at the interview, that he grovelled at the feet of Gaius and of his com-
panions.[1] According to Velleius,[2] the youth treated his
stepfather with the respect due to a superior. Suetonius,[3]
who places the interview in Samos, says that Tiberius there
found that Gaius had become 'estranged through the
slanders of Lollius', whom Augustus had appointed as his
adviser.

Augus-
tus's
letter to
Gaius.

Pursuing his journey, Gaius went on to Syria, where,
towards the end of the year, he must have received a letter
which his grandfather wrote on his own birthday, the 23rd
of September:[4] 'My dearest Gaius, I miss you always, believe me, when you are away from me. Above all, on days
like this my eyes look with longing for my Gaius, and,
wherever you are to-day, I hope you have kept my sixty-
fourth birthday in gladness and good health. For, as you
see, I have passed my sixty-third year, the climacteric
common to all elderly men. But I pray the gods that whatever time remains for me I may be permitted to spend in
a period of the greatest prosperity for our country, while
you are proving yourself a man and learning to succeed to
my position'. Before this letter reached him Gaius met

Between
11 and
8 B.C.

Phraataces on an island in the Euphrates.[5] A few years
earlier Phraates had sent his legitimate sons to Rome with
their wives and children to live under the supervision of
Augustus, who regarded them as hostages.[6] Phraataces, on
first hearing that Gaius was near, had sent an embassy to
Augustus, to demand the restoration of his brothers as a
condition of his keeping the peace; Augustus in reply
ordered him to give up the royal title and to abandon
Armenia; Phraataces, omitting to address him as Augustus

---

[1] lv, 10, 18–9.   [2] ii, 101, 1.

[3] *Tib.*, 12, 2–3. Pliny (*Nat. hist.*, ix, 35 (58), 118) states that Lollius
afterwards accepted bribes for intervening with Gaius on behalf of princes.
Cp. Vell., ii, 102, 1.

[4] Gell., xv, 7, 3.   [5] Vell., ii, 101, 1.

[6] *Mon. Ancyr.*, vi, 3–6; Vell., ii, 94, 4; Strabo, xvi, 1, 28; Jos., *Ant.*,
xviii, 2, 4; Tac., *Ann.*, ii, 1, 2; Suet., *Aug.*, 21, 3. Cp. Mommsen *Res gestae*[2]
&c., p. 142, and Hardy, *Mon. Ancyr.*, p. 148.

and calling himself the King of Kings, made a haughty re-
joinder.[1] Not long afterwards Artavasdes[2] died, and
Tigranes, a son of the Tigranes whom Tiberius had restored,
petitioned Augustus to recognize him as king. Augustus,
fearing hostilities from the Parthians, accepted the gifts
that accompanied the petition and bade him go to meet
Gaius in Syria.[3] Phraataces, who, it would seem, could not
count upon being supported by his subjects in offering resistance, had changed his mind. In his interview with
Gaius he agreed to abandon Armenia and to acquiesce in
the detention of his brothers.[4] Thus the danger of war with
Parthia was for the time averted. Gaius proceeded to
appoint Ariobarzanes, a son of the Median sovereign whose
capital Antony had besieged,[5] King of Armenia. For the
moment it seemed that Gaius had been not less successful
than Tiberius more than twenty years before.[6] But the
anti-Roman party in Armenia resolved to fight. The operations that followed must remain obscure: we only know
that the Armenians did nothing worth recording, except
that one Addon,[7] who was holding a fort named Artageira,
induced the unwary Gaius to come up close to the wall,
pretending that he wished to reveal secrets concerning
Phraataces, and there wounded him. A siege ensued.
When the fort was captured Gaius assumed the title *imperator*, and Ariobarzanes became king, to be succeeded
soon afterwards by his son Artavasdes, who was murdered.[8]
Roman ascendancy was not regained before the reign of
Tiberius; but Augustus knew that he could not have taken
the decisive step of annexing Armenia, which he had deliberately rejected, without the risk of war, which he could
not afford to incur.

Illusory success of Gaius.

Still suffering from his wound, Gaius set out for Arabia,
but only descried the distant northern frontier. His
mission was abandoned. Travelling through Palestine on

His mission abandoned.

[1] Dio, lv, 10, 20.   [2] See p. 95.
[3] Dio, lv, 10, 20–1.   [4] Dio, lv, 10a, 4.
[5] See *The Architect of the Roman Empire* (44–27 B.C.), p. 125.
[6] See p. 36.   [7] or Donnes (Flor., ii, 32, 44).
[8] *C.I.L.*, v, 6416; Dessau, *Inscr. Lat.*, 107. 7; 140, ll. 8–13; *Mon. Ancyr.*,
v, 24–31; Vell., ii, 102, 2; Seneca, *ad Polyb. de consol.*, 15, 4; Rufus Festus,
19; Dio, lv, 10a, 5–7. Dio (§ 7) calls Artavasdes Artabazus.

his return, he passed Jerusalem, but refused to visit the temple, which, as he had doubtless learned from his tutor, Pompey had captured.[1] Weak in constitution and now enfeebled, he asked leave to retire into private life and to remain in Syria; but Augustus urged him to return to Italy. On the 21st of February he died on his homeward journey at Limyra in Lycia.[2] His brother had already died at Massilia on his way to join the army in Spain.[4] Monuments were erected at Athens to the two boys,[5] of whom, as their grandfather wrote,[6] Fortune had robbed him; and in an inscription which became famous, composed by the senate of the Roman colony of Pisa, it was stated that the elder, after his prosperous consulship, had met his death by a cruel fate from wounds received in the service of his country against great and warlike peoples beyond the uttermost limits of the empire.[7]

A.D. 4.
His death.
Aug. 20,
A.D. 2.[3]

Before the two boys died, for whose sake he had gone into retirement, Tiberius returned to Rome. While he was in Rhodes he was still in possession of tribunician power, but only once had occasion to exercise it. He spent much of his time, which he must have often found it hard to while away, in attending philosophical lectures, and, when two professors were in acrimonious controversy, and he spoke in favour of one of them, an onlooker had the audacity to abuse him, but was presently summoned to appear before his tribunal and sent to gaol. His biographer, who sedulously collected all the stories that could tell against him, must have felt that at all events he was a gentleman; for he relates that his attendants, misunderstanding a wish which he had expressed to visit all the sick in the city, gave

Tiberius in Rhodes.

[1] Pliny, *Nat. hist.*, ii, 67, 168; vi, 28 (32), 160; Suet., *Aug.*, 93; Oros., vii, 3, 4–5. Cp. *The Roman Republic*, 1, 215.

[2] Dessau, *Inscr. Lat.*, 140, ll. 26–7, Vell., ii, 102, 3; Tac., *Ann.*, i, 3, 3 (who characteristically remarks that Gaius was carried off either by a natural death or by the craft of Livia); Suet., *Aug.*, 65, 1; Flor., ii, 32, 42; Dio, lv, 10a, 8–9.

[3] *C.I.L.*, i, p. 328. The statement in the *Fasti Gabini* (*C.I.L.*, i, p. 473) that Lucius died on September 19 is incorrect.

[4] Vell., ii, 102, 3; Tac., *Ann.*, i, 3, 3; Suet., *Aug.*, 65, 1; Flor., ii, 32, 42; Dio, lv, 10a, 9.

[5] *C.I.A.* (now called *Inscr. Graec.*), iii, Part I, 444–6.

[6] *Mon. Ancyr.*, ii, 46.　　　　[7] Dessau, *Inscr. Lat.*, 140, ll. 8–14.

orders that they should be laid in a public colonnade, grouped according to their respective ailments, whereupon Tiberius, shocked at the spectacle, spoke, after a moment's hesitation, to every one, 'apologizing even to the humblest and the most obscure'. When he learned that his wife had been banished and divorced, he not only allowed her to keep the presents which he had given her, but did his utmost to induce her father to forgive her; but when, after his tribunician power ended, he asked leave to visit his relations, pleading that he could no longer be suspected of rivalry with his stepsons, whose claim to succeed the Emperor was undisputed, his request was refused. Through the influence of Livia, however, he was allowed to have the title, which veiled his disgrace, of envoy of the Emperor. Despite this concession, he felt that even his life was in peril, for a guest at a dinner-party assured Gaius, who happened to be present, that he was prepared to take ship for Rhodes and bring back his head. Tiberius, supported by his mother, thereupon sued for permission to return to Rome, which Augustus with the consent of Gaius granted, on the condition that he should abstain from taking part in public life; and in the eighth year after his retirement he returned.[1] The time was not far distant when he was to be reconciled to his stepfather, partly, if one might accept the doubtful authority of Zonaras, through the influence of his own divorced wife, partly, doubtless, because he was evidently the one man who could support the old Emperor's declining energies. Augustus had long refused to recall his daughter from banishment, despite the intercession of the Roman people, who felt that she was being harshly treated, and to whose entreaties he is said to have replied in a popular assembly by calling upon the gods 'to curse them with like daughters and like wives'; but at last, under persistent pressure, he so far relented that she was allowed to return from Pandateria to the mainland.[2] In regard to what followed one may be again tempted to trust Zonaras, who relates that she soon made her influence felt. Hostilities, which had been going on in Germany for three years,

A.D. 1.
His reconciliation with Augustus,

---

[1] Vell., ii, 103, 1; Suet., *Tib.*, 11, 2–4; 12, 1; 13; 14, 1; Dio, lv, 10, 1.
[2] Suet., *Aug.*, 65, 3; Dio, lv, 13, 1–1a.

were becoming serious.[1] What was to be done ? Augustus, if he had ever been capable of personally directing operations against such formidable enemies, was becoming enfeebled: Tiberius was Rome's only general. Julia knew that he was indispensable; she was perhaps touched by the efforts which he had made on her behalf; and if any love which she may have felt for him had long since died, we may perhaps believe that she was inspired not only by patriotism, but also by a desire that public life should be reopened to the soldier-statesman who had been her husband and of whose achievements she may well have been proud. Augustus had at last allowed her to return to Rome. Listening to her persuasions and recognizing the necessities of the situation, he adopted Tiberius. One would gladly accept this story if other evidence did not point to the conclusion that Zonaras confused Julia with Livia, that she was never allowed to return to Rome, and that it was Livia alone who influenced the Emperor.[2] What is certain is that he not only adopted Tiberius, but also, perhaps fearing that, if he were left without a rival, he might attempt to seize supreme power, perhaps only intending, in view of the uncertainty of life, to provide for the orderly continuance of the Principate, constrained him to adopt Germanicus, the son of Drusus. Then, having again granted him tribunician power for five years, he sent him to take the field against the Germans.[3]

June 26, A.D. 4.

who adopts him and sends him to suppress German rebellion.

Now that he had settled the question of succession and could attend without distraction to civil affairs, the old man held another revision of the Senate,[4] nominating the ten members whom he most respected and appointing three of them, selected by lot, to examine the qualifications of

Another purgation of the Senate.

[1] Vell., ii, 104, 2; Dio, lv, 13, 1a.

[2] See Melber's note on Dio, lv, 13, 1a (=Zonaras, x, 36). Xiphilinus (=Dio, lv, 13, 1) implies that Julia was only allowed to leave Pandateria.

[3] C.I.L., i², pp. 243, 320; Dessau, Inscr. Lat., 413; Vell., ii, 103, 3; 104, 1; Pliny, Nat. hist., vii, 45 (46), 150; Tac., Ann., i, 3, 3; iv, 57, 5; Suet., Tib., 15, 2; Calig., 1, 1; 4, 1; Dio, lv, 13, 2. 'Suetonius (Calig., 4) says that Augustus had long hesitated whether he should appoint Germanicus his successor in preference to Tiberius. The author (Kroll) of the article on Tiberius in Paulys Real-Ency. (x, 436), remarking that Dio was biased against Tiberius, rejects his statement that Augustus feared that, if he were left without a rival, he would rebel. [4] See p. 39.

the rest. The last revision had evidently been useful, for
few were on this occasion disqualified.[1]

About the same time the *lex Aelia Sentia,* so called after
the consuls of the year, Sextus Aelius and Gaius Sentius,
was passed with the object of restricting the indiscriminate
manumission of slaves. Legislation directed towards this
end had begun in the year of which the outstanding event
was the festival known as the *ludi saeculares.* Slaves regularly, or even irregularly, manumitted had hitherto been
admitted to full citizenship; as the practice of manumission had greatly increased, many worthless characters were
in possession of the franchise; and Dionysius of Halicar-
nassus [2] described the evil results, which he had himself
observed. The first measure designed to remedy this evil,
called after one of the consuls, Junius Silanus, the *lex
Iunia,*[3] enacted that persons who, having been irregularly
manumitted, were still, though in fact free, legally slaves,
should be admitted, not to citizenship but to a new status,
Latinitas Iuniana, which did not include the exercise of
the franchise.[4] In the year in which Augustus was hailed
as Father of his country a further step was taken. By a
consular law known as the *lex Fufia Caninia* it was enacted
that, while an owner of not more than two slaves might
free them both, of numbers between three and five hundred
proportions ranging from half to one-fifth, one hundred,
however large the total might be, was the greatest number
allowed.[5] No restriction, however, was placed on manumissions effected *per censum,* in which master and slave
appeared, when a census was held, before the Emperor,
who, being invested with consular power, could exercise
censorial authority,[6] and the slave's name was recorded

A.D. 4.
Laws for
restricting
manu-
mission of
slaves.

17 B.C.

17 B.C.

2 B.C.

---

[1] Dio, lv, 13, 3.   [2] iv, 23.

[3] There has been much controversy on the question whether the *lex Iunia*
was passed in 17 B.C. or in A.D. 19, under Tiberius. I have adopted the
former view. In 25 B.C., when another Junius was consul, Augustus was
absent from Rome. See pp. 161–4.

[4] Gaius, i, 17; Ulp., i, 12, 16.

[5] Gaius, 1, 42–3; Ulp., i, 12, 16. The *lex Fufia Caninia,* of which Suetonius
was probably thinking when he said (*Aug.,* 40, 3) that Augustus limited
manumission, was enacted in 2 B.C. (Dessau, *Inscr. Lat.,* 9250). Cp. *Paulys
Real-Ency.,* xii, 914, and W. W. Buckland, *Text-book of Roman Law,* 1921,
p. 79.   [6] See *Mon. Ancyr.,* ii, 5–11.

in the list. Under the *lex Aelia Sentia* no slave might receive citizenship on manumission who had not reached the age of thirty, unless the reason for his manumission had been approved either by a committee of five senators and five knights in Rome or by twenty Roman citizens, specially selected, in the provinces; no master under twenty years of age might manumit, except by the process called *vindicta* [1] and with the consent of such a council; and slaves who had suffered certain punishments for crime were to be subject to the same penalties as foreigners who had surrendered in war, being obliged to live at least one hundred Roman miles from the capital, on pain of being permanently enslaved. Such slaves gained nothing by manumission except personal liberty.[2]

Meanwhile Tiberius had begun the operations in Central Europe which, interrupted by journeys made to the capital while his army was in winter quarters,[3] were destined to last for seven years. Soon after he arrived in Germany the Parthian envoys who had been sent to Rome presented themselves before him in obedience to instructions from the Emperor.[4] His enthusiastic admirer, Velleius Paterculus,[5] learned that soldiers who had served under him before his retirement were so overjoyed at seeing him again that they could not restrain their tears, some actually venturing to grasp his hand and saying, 'General, is it really you that we see? Have we then got you safely back?' and reminding him proudly that they had served under him in Raetia, Pannonia, and Germany. After subduing the Canninefates and the Bructeri and receiving the voluntary submission of the Cherusci, he crossed the Weser, and, having cantoned the legions for the winter—for the first time, it would seem, on German soil—near the source of the Lippe, returned in December to visit his adoptive

Marginal note: Joyful reception of Tiberius by the army in Germany.

---

[1] See W. Ramsay, *Roman Antiquities*, 1894, pp. 130–1, or Willems, *Droit public rom.* 1884, p. 144, n. 5.

[2] Dio, lv, 13, 7; Gaius, i, 13, 18–20, 38, 44; Ulp., *Fragm.*, i, 11–3. 100 Roman were equivalent to about 92 English miles.

[3] Dio, always on the look-out for motives which are not obvious, says (lv, 27, 5) that these visits were due partly to fear that Augustus might take advantage of the absence of Tiberius to appoint some one else.

[4] Suet., *Tib.*, 16, 1. See p. 102.

[5] ii, 104, 4.

father. In the following spring he went back to the seat of war, defeated a host of the Langobardi beyond the Weser, and advanced as far as the Elbe, where he joined the fleet, which had moved thither from the Rhine, circumnavigating, for the first time in Roman history, the peninsula of Jutland. Then, repelling an attack, he led back the legions into winter quarters and returned again to Rome. The exploit of the fleet was followed by the dispatch of an embassy, in which the Cimbri and neighbouring tribes, who had watched its appearance with amazement, petitioned for the friendship of the Emperor and the Roman people.[1]

In order to secure the conquests of Drusus and his own, Tiberius saw that it was necessary to subdue a kingdom which had been established by Maroboduus, a chief of the Marcomanni, who had studied Roman methods, in the country which is now Bohemia. Five legions, stationed in Illyricum—probably not less than five-and-twenty thousand men [2]—with the German army on the Rhine, were available; but Tiberius, deeming them insufficient for so great an enterprise, sent orders to two consulars, Aulus Caecina, the Governor of Moesia,[3] and Silvanus Plautius, to join him with five more legions, then serving in Macedonia and Syria. These reinforcements had not arrived when he took the field. His plan was that he himself should march northward from Carnuntum (now Petronell, near Vienna) in the north of Pannonia, and in the territory of Marododuus join Sentius Saturninus, a legate of the Emperor, who was to advance from the Rhine with the German army up the valley of the Main.[4] The plan, however, was frustrated by a revolt of the Pannonians and by a Dacian invasion of Moesia, which occurred before the

His plan
for secur-
ing
Roman
conquest
frus-
trated.

[1] Vell., ii, 105, 1. 3; 106, 2–3; 107, 3; Pliny, *Nat. hist.*, ii, 67, 167; *Mon. Ancyr.*, v, 14–8.

[2] See *Caesar's Conquest of Gaul*[2], pp. 559–63.

[3] I can see no reason to doubt that Dio (lv, 29, 3) whose statement Mommsen (*Röm. Gesch.*, v, 36 [Eng. tr., i, 40]) accepts, but H. M. D. Parker (*The Roman Legions*, p. 83) is inclined to regard as an anachronism, was right in saying that in A.D. 6 Moesia was already a Roman province. Cp. Mommsen, v, 20 (i, 22) and *Class. Rev.*, xxxviii, 192.

[4] Vell., ii, 108–9; Parker, *op. cit.*, pp. 83–4, compared with Vell., ii, 109, 5, and 112, 4.

junction could be accomplished; and, in spite of difficulties of transit, an order to return to the Rhine was conveyed to Saturninus, who was forcing his way with axe and fire through the dense Hercynian forest.[1] The work of Tiberius in Germany was stopped.

War in Asia Minor and Gaetulia.

Meanwhile there was war in distant provinces. In Asia Minor the Isaurians made marauding raids, for which they were severely punished; the Gaetulians, who rebelled against Juba and ravaged neighbouring country, were subdued by a consular, Cornelius Lentulus Cossus.[2] In Rome the Emperor had financial difficulties to contend with.

Discontent in the army.

A.D. 5.

A.D. 6.

Augustus provides for military pensions.

Learning that there was serious discontent in the army, not in Germany alone, he had proposed in the Senate that money should be raised annually to establish a fund for the provision of adequate pensions.[3] As the proposal proved unwelcome, he deposited in a newly-formed military treasury, in his own name and that of Tiberius, a sum to be administered by a board composed of three ex-praetors, who were to be chosen by lot. Contributing to the fund from his privy purse,[4] he promised to make further contributions yearly, and accepted others from client kings, but none from private citizens. The amount raised being insufficient, he requested every senator to propose in writing new sources of revenue and to send the proposals to him for consideration. Approving none, he established a tax of five per cent on inheritances and legacies, except those received by near relatives or poor persons, announcing that he had found mention of the tax in Caesar's memoranda.[5] In this year the supply of imported grain was so inadequate that it was necessary not only to restrict the quantity that might be purchased, but also to send gladiators and slaves who were ready for sale away from the city, while Augustus and others dismissed many of their attendants, leave of absence was granted to senators,

---

[1] Dio, lv, 28, 7; 29, 2; 30, 4; Vell., ii, 109, 5; 110, 2.

[2] Vell., ii, 116, 2; Flor., ii, 31, 40; Dio, lv, 28, 3-4. [3] Cp. p. 68.

[4] *Mon. Ancyr.*, iii, 35-9, shows that in A.D. 6 Augustus's contribution was 170 millions of sesterces (£1,700,000). See p. 137.

[5] Rostovtzeff (*Paulys Real-Ency.*, vi, 2387) observes that this was an encroachment on the rights of the Senate, the necessity of satisfying the army being more urgent than the constitutional scruples of Augustus.

and Augustus ordered that no public banquets should be held on his birthday.[1] It was in this year that, in consequence of destructive fires in the city, the permanent corps of nocturnal watchmen, to which allusion has already been made,[2] was organized. The discontent of the masses was such that revolutionary projects were openly discussed and incendiary placards were posted up. Before the year ended, however, the supply of grain became sufficient to allow the Emperor to recall the gladiators, and an exhibition was given in honour of Drusus, whose memory was still cherished by the populace.[3]

Discontent due to scarcity of grain.

It is time to describe the events that had led to the Pannonian revolt and the military operations that followed. When Tiberius was preparing for his campaign against Maroboduus, Valerius Messalinus, the Governor of Illyricum, was sent to accompany him with an army to which the Dalmatians were required to furnish a contingent. While the men who composed it were assembling, some of them mutinied and defeated legionaries who were sent to punish them. The rest, stimulated by a Dalmatian chief, named Bato, joined the mutineers, and soon afterwards a Pannonian tribe, led by another Bato, attacked Sirmium, the chief town of the province. Dalmatians and Pannonians alike were exasperated by taxation, which had been relentlessly enforced; and those who had served as auxiliaries in the Roman army were formidable enemies.[4] Roman citizens and traders settled in the Province were massacred. The attempted onslaught on Sirmium was stopped by Caecina, who defeated Bato near the Drave; but meanwhile the Dalmatians ravaged the country between Salonae and Apollonia, and defeated a Roman army. Recruits were hastily raised in Italy, for Augustus, addressing the Senate, declared that, unless due precautions were adopted, the enemy might within ten days be seen in Rome. Tiberius, fearing that they intended to invade

Dalmatian and Pannonian revolt. [Mitrovitza.]

[1] Dio, lv, 23, 1; 24, 9; 25; 26, 1–3; Suet., *Aug.*, 49, 2; Dessau, *Inscr. Lat.*, 5402, 5584, 5598.

[2] See p. 92.

[3] Dio, lv, 26, 4–5; 27, 1–4.

[4] Vell., ii, 110, 5. Cp. Mommsen, *Röm. Gesch.*, v, 35 and n. 1 (Eng. tr., i, 39 and n. 1).

Italy, sent Messalinus to oppose them, following with the bulk of the army. The Dalmatian Bato, after gaining a victory over Messalinus, was himself overpowered by an ambuscade, joined his namesake, and with him took post on a mountain, where they were both vanquished by the Thracian, Rhoemetalces, who had been sent against them by Caecina, but, when Caecina appeared in person, resisted his attack. Caecina was obliged to return to Moesia, which was being ravaged by Dacians and Sarmatians; and, while Tiberius and Messalinus were detained in Siscia,[1] the Dalmatians induced many Pannonians to join the insurrection. Tiberius instantly moved against them; but, knowing the country well and being lightly equipped, they were

A.D. 6–7. able to avoid battle. In the ensuing winter some invaded Macedonia, where they were again defeated by Rhoemetalces, while those who remained in Dalmatia took

A.D. 7. refuge in the spring, when it was invaded by the Roman army, in mountain strongholds, from which they made occasional raids. Augustus thereupon sent the youthful Germanicus to join his adoptive father [2] with a force which included freedmen, some of whom he had himself freed for the purpose, paying their former owners the amount of their value and the cost of their maintenance for six months. The expense of the war was daily increasing; the nocturnal watchmen had to be paid; and Augustus, being obliged to devise extraordinary expedients for raising revenue, introduced a tax upon the sale of slaves,[3] at the same time forbidding the money generally given to the

---

[1] See *The Architect of the Roman Empire* (44–27 B.C.), pp. 132–3.

[2] See p. 106. According to Dio (lv, 31, 1), Augustus suspected that Tiberius was protracting the war in order to prolong his own command. Ferrero (*Greatness and Decline*, &c., v, 316, n. §) thinks it more probable that he allowed the public to believe that he sent Germanicus as likely to succeed where Tiberius had failed. I believe that, Germanicus being popular, Augustus thought it well to send him in order to allay the anxiety of the populace and to give him an opportunity of learning the art of war. Cp. Vell., ii, 129, 2, and *Paulys Real-Ency.*, x, 436.

E. von Nischer (*Hist. Zeitschr.*, cxl, 1929, pp. 104–5), reviewing Parker's *Roman Legions*, rejects the view that the volunteers in Germanicus's army were liberated slaves. Following von Domaszewski, he holds that they were Roman citizens in the provinces. Parker (p. 82) accepts Dio's statement, which (cp. Macrobius, i, 11, 32) seems to me quite credible.

[3] Dio, lv, 31, 4.

praetor for gladiatorial shows to be so expended. As
dearth of corn was again causing anxiety, he appointed
two consulars to regulate the supply, and, seeing that the
populace were also troubled by the prolongation of the
war, pretended, in order to humour them, to believe a
report about a female impostor, who was said to have
practised divination.[1] Perhaps it was at this time that he
was so despondent that, if we may believe Pliny,[2] he contemplated suicide; but not long afterwards he provided
against any recurrence of scarcity by creating an office, the
holder of which, called *praefectus annonae*, was always a
member of the equestrian order, for regulating the supply
of grain.[3]

Germanicus began his command by repelling an attack
on the part of the two Batos. In the following year
Augustus, although age and increasing feebleness compelled him to entrust to consulars the duty of receiving,
and, except in extremely important matters, of replying
to embassies, and to cease attending the meetings of the
popular assembly, braced himself to undertake a journey
to Ariminum, in order that he might be at hand to consult
with Tiberius or Germanicus on the conduct of the war.
Meanwhile the Pannonian Bato surrendered with his whole
force, and soon afterwards fell into the hands of his namesake, who, infuriated by such desertion of the national
cause, forthwith put him to death; but in consequence of
the surrender Pannonian resistance virtually ceased.[4]
Early in the following year Tiberius returned to Rome, and
was welcomed in the suburbs by Augustus.[5] He had indeed
deserved such a reception, for he had overcome the difficulty of feeding his troops, and, as Velleius[6] enthusiastically
related, he had devoted himself throughout the war to the
care of sick and wounded men, as if he had nothing else to
do, providing them with medical attendance and suitable
nourishment, maintaining discipline by example and

Marginal notes:
Establish-
ment of
an office
for regula-
ting the
supply of
grain.

A.D. 7.
A.D. 8.

A.D. 9.
Enthusi-
astic
reception
of
Tiberius
in Rome.

---

[1] Dio, lv, 29–31; Vell., ii, 111, 1; 112, 2. 4–5.
[2] *Nat. hist.*, vii, 45, 149. Pliny leaves the date uncertain. Was he reporting
a threat which was not seriously meant?
[3] Tac., *Ann.*, i, 7, 3; Rushforth, *Lat. Hist. Inscr.*, p. 31.
[4] Dio, lv, 32, 3–4; 33, 5; 34, 2–7.
[5] Dio, lvi, 1, 1.   [6] ii, 114, 1–3.

Augustus congratulates him on his generalship.

admonition, never without necessity by punishment. It was perhaps about this time that Augustus wrote to him, 'Farewell, Tiberius, most agreeable of men, be all success yours in the war that you are waging for me . . . Farewell, most valiant of men and most conscientious of commanders': 'I have only praise, my dear Tiberius, for your conduct of campaigns, and I am sure that amid so many difficulties and with such apathy in your army no man could have acted with more judgement than you. All who accompanied you agree that to you was applicable the familiar line,

One man by his vigilance saved our country.

'When I hear and read that you are worn by incessant toil, may the gods confound me if my own body does not wince in sympathy; I implore you to spare yourself, lest news of your being ill should be the death of your mother and me and endanger the Roman people in the person of their future ruler. If you are not well, it matters nothing whether I am well or ill. I pray the gods to preserve you for us and to grant you health now and always if they do not hate the Roman people'.[1]

A.D. 9.

In the course of the year Germanicus captured several Dalmatian forts; but, as resistance continued, Augustus again sent Tiberius into the field. Seeing that the weary troops longed to stop the war, and fearing mutiny, Tiberius formed three divisions, two of which he assigned respectively to consulars, Plautius Silvanus and Marcus Lepidus, while he himself with Germanicus marched against Bato. Silvanus and Lepidus defeated their opponents; Tiberius, after vainly pursuing the elusive Bato, besieged him in a fort called Andetrium,[2] standing on a rocky height a few miles from Salonae, in which he had taken refuge. Bato had abundant provisions, and his fol-

[1] Suet., *Tib.*, 21, 4–7. Cp. H. Malcovati, *Imp. Caesaris Augusti operum fragm.*, 1919, pp. 8–10 (xi, xii, xiv). The line, 'One man . . . country', was quoted from Ennius, *Ann.*, 370 v², Augustus naturally substituting *vigilando* for *cunctando*.

[2] Dio, lvi, 12, 3–4. Cp. Strabo, vii, 5, 5; Plin., *Nat hist.*, iii, 22 (26), 142; Ptol., *Geogr.*, ii, 16, 7; and Dessau, *Inscr.*, *Lat.*, 2478. Andetrium was on the site of Much.

lowers outside prevented supplies from being conveyed to the Roman camp. Nevertheless Tiberius held his ground. At last Bato, seeing that further resistance was hopeless, though he could not induce his ignorant followers to surrender, sent a herald to ask for terms. Many Dalmatians, who had made a sally and failed to make their way back into the stronghold, were hunted down in the adjacent forests and slain by the exasperated soldiers; those who remained, capitulated in despair. While Tiberius was arranging terms, Germanicus captured another fort, and submission became general. Bato had sent his son to Tiberius, promising for himself and his remaining followers to surrender on receiving a pledge of pardon. The pledge was presently given. Bato came by night to the Roman camp, and next day was conducted to the tribunal on which Tiberius was sitting. It is said that he asked nothing for himself, even thrusting his head forward to await a stroke of the lictor's axe,[1] but made a speech on behalf of his followers. Tiberius asked him why the Dalmatians had so long persisted in rebellion. 'You Romans', Bato replied, 'are yourselves to blame; for you send to protect your flocks not dogs nor shepherds, but wolves.'[2]

The Dalmatians finally subdued.

All Italy rejoiced when this war, which had cost so much blood and treasure, and which seemed to later generations the most exhausting that had been waged against a foreign foe since the war with Hannibal,[3] was successfully ended. One fact is enough to show the magnitude of the operations: the legions that fought under Tiberius were supported by seventy cohorts of auxiliary light infantry and fourteen regiments of cavalry [4]—in all, about fifty thousand men.[5] Those who belonged to Dalmatia and Pannonia were transferred to provinces in which their loyalty would not be exposed to temptation, and their places were filled by others from Spain.[6] The title *imperator* was awarded

Rejoicings in Italy.

---

[1] This, if Dio's statement (lvi, 16, 2) that the required pledge had been given is true, seems incredible.   [2] Dio, lvi, 13–6; Vell., ii, 114, 4; 115, 1–4.
[3] Suet., *Tib.*, 16, 1, with which cp. *Hermes*, xxv, 1890, p. 351. It is called in an inscription (Dessau, 2673) the Batonian war.   [4] Vell., ii, 113, 1.
[5] G. L. Cheesman, *The Auxilia of the Roman Imperial Army*, 1914, p. 53.
[6] *Ib.*, p. 72. Cp. G. B. Grundy, *Hist. of the Greek and Roman World*, 1927, p. 483.

to Tiberius, who, the Senate decreed, should in due course celebrate a triumph; two triumphal arches were to be erected in Pannonia; Germanicus and the other divisional commanders received the triumphal insignia; Germanicus was authorized to hold the consulship before the customary time; Drusus, the son of Tiberius and of his first wife, Agrippina, was privileged to attend the Senate before he should become a senator. Hardly had these decrees been passed when news was announced of a disaster, the most appalling that had befallen Rome since the army of Crassus perished on the plain of Carrhae.[1]

The Varian disaster.

Publius Quintilius Varus, formerly Governor of Syria,[2] had recently succeeded to the command in Germany, a position which he probably owed to his marriage with Claudia Pulchra, a grand-niece of the Emperor.[3] He had had little experience of war, and one can hardly account otherwise for his appointment, except on the supposition that no competent man was available. Neglecting to consult officers who had served under his predecessors and knew the inhabitants, refusing to listen to natives whose good faith would have been apparent to any one of sound judgement, he acted as if the province had been long accustomed to Roman rule. Before he arrived many Germans had been associating in a friendly spirit with Roman soldiers who spent the winter among them; but certain tribes, particularly the Cherusci, resented the treatment which they had undergone. Varus, as Velleius [4] remarked, fancied that he could administer justice like a praetor in Rome. When he proceeded to levy taxes, as he had done in Syria, his exactions provoked exasperation; [5]

[1] Vell., ii, 117, 1; Dio, lvi, 17; 18, 1. See pp. 174–6.
[2] Jos., *Ant.*, xvii, 5, 2; 10, 9; *Bell.*, ii, 5, 1.
[3] *Prosopograph. imp. Rom.*, iii, 118–20.
[4] ii, 118, 1.
[5] Sir E. Creasy (*The Fifteen Decisive Battles of the World*[31], 1883, p. 118) says that Varus, 'accustomed to govern the depraved . . . natives of Syria . . . thought that he might gratify his licentious . . . passions with equal impunity among the . . . pure-spirited daughters of Germany. . . . The Romans now habitually indulged in those violations of the domestic shrine', &c. This rhodomontade was presumably based upon the statement of Florus (ii, 30, 31), *Vari Quintilii libidinem ac superbiam haud secus quam saevitiam odisse coeperunt.*

but in the presence of three legions,[1] which he personally
commanded, the tribal leaders dissembled. It happened
that two young men, Arminius [2] and his brother Flavus,
sons of Sigimerus, the ruler of the Cherusci, had served in
the Roman army and had been rewarded by the gift of
citizenship.[3] Arminius, observing the fatuity of the Governor, resolved to liberate his fellow tribesmen, and communicated his design to others. His father, who had also
served in the army and received citizenship from Augustus,[4] warned Varus in vain. Never doubting that he might
safely advance into the country of the Cherusci, Varus encamped for the summer near the western bank of the
Weser, probably in or near the site of Blomberg.[5] Arminius,
who, speaking Latin fluently,[6] had much intercourse with
him, informed him in conjunction with a chief named
Segimerus that certain distant tribes (doubtless the Chauci
and the Bructeri [7]) were in revolt. Deaf to warnings given
by Sigimerus and another loyal native, Segestes, a brother
of Segimerus, he did not suspect that the revolt had been
planned in order to lure him away from the camp. On the
evening before the day which the conspirators had fixed
for the outbreak of the other tribesmen whom they had
roused, Segestes, Arminius, and leaders in his confidence
supped with Varus as his guests. Segestes besought Varus
to have himself, Arminius, and the other chiefs present
arrested, assuring him that the disaffected Germans would
not stir if their leaders were in custody, and that the sequel
would discriminate between the innocent and the guilty.
Even this warning, self-evidently honest, was disregarded,

---

[1] Mommsen (*Röm. Gesch.*, v, 42 [Eng. tr., i, 46]) says that the Varian
disaster was 'due to the inexperience of the young soldiers' as well as to 'the
want of head and courage in the general'. To call the three legions young
soldiers is misleading. See H. M. D. Parker, *The Roman Legions*, p. 85.
Von Domaszewski (*Westd. Zeitschr.*, xxi, 1902, p. 187, n. 3), remarking that
the auxiliaries belonging to the army of the Lower Rhine were three or four
times as many as those in the army of Varus (Tac., *Ann.*, i, 49, compared
with Vell., ii, 117, 1), concludes that the paucity of cavalry and auxiliary
infantry must have contributed to the disaster.

[2] P. von Rohden (*Paulys Real-Ency.*, ii, 1190–1) remarks that it is doubtful whether the name Arminius is of German or Roman origin, adding that
with the German name, Hermann, it has nothing to do.

[3] Vell., ii, 118, 2.   [4] Tac., *Ann.*, i, 58, 2–3.   [5] See pp. 166, 172.
[6] Tac., *Ann.*, ii, 10, 3.   [7] See p. 173.

and Arminius with his fellow conspirators was suffered to go free.[1] They, or the communities which they influenced, had induced the credulous Governor to entrust them with detachments from the legions, explaining that they needed them for guarding various places and escorting provision trains for the supply of his army.[2]

Varus had originally intended to march by the military road to Vetera, the winter camp on the Rhine, near the site of Xanten,[3] but now moved north-westward across a pathless country to deal first with the local revolt. While the distant communities were slaughtering the detachments that had been entrusted to them, the conspirators escorted the column on its departure, then asked permission to go and assemble their tribesmen, pretending that they desired to aid the Governor in subduing the insurgents. Suddenly, joined by forces which had been awaiting their arrival, they fell upon the legionaries while they were felling trees which hindered their progress, making paths and constructing causeways where the ground was impassable, constantly encumbered by their wagons and baggage cattle, and followed by women, children, and soldiers' servants. First assailing the column with missiles, the Germans soon gathered confidence to press forward against an enemy whose weapons, like those of Caesar's troops when they were surprised by the onslaught of the Nervii,[4] were not ready for instant use, and who, bewildered by the unexpected attack, unable to preserve orderly array, impeded by wind, rain, and fallen branches, and slipping on damp soil, could offer no effective resistance. Their auxiliaries—cavalry, archers, and slingers—were too few.[5] What was to be done? Evidently the only course was to make for the fort of Aliso. Encamping at nightfall on high ground, the legionaries, having burned or abandoned wagons and superfluous baggage, advanced next morning in somewhat better order, for the ground was now open; but, as many

[1] Tac., *Ann.*, i, 55, 3.

[2] Dio, lvi, 18, 2–5, 19, 1–4; Vell., ii, 117, 2–4; 118. The narrative of Florus (ii, 30, 34) contains a grotesque absurdity, which Mommsen (*Röm. Gesch.*, v, 41, n. 1 [Eng. tr., i, 45, n. 1]) thought it necessary to correct.   [3] See p. 87.

[4] See *Caesar's Conquest of Gaul*[2], p. 77, or *The Roman Republic*, ii, 45.

[5] See p. 117, n. 1.

were struck down, they were forced to plunge again into woods. The column struggled on painfully in a confined space, cavalry and infantry attacking the enemy promiscuously, sometimes wounding each other by mistake and injured by falling boughs. They encamped again as best they could; but the rampart was barely half complete. At dawn rain fell again; the wind blew hard; the enemy was reinforced; and a cavalry officer, Vala Numonius, deserting his comrades, rode away with his regiment in the hope of reaching the Rhine. The legions were in the region now called the Lippischer Wald,[1] not far west of Detmold, when Varus and some of his staff, already wounded and dreading the savage vengeance which, if they were made prisoners, the Germans would surely wreak, committed suicide. Hearing of what they had done, the men abandoned hope: some followed the example of their general; the rest, except a few who escaped while the enemy were plundering and darkness came on, were all captured or slain. Of the prisoners some were crucified, others buried alive, others decapitated by priests, who nailed the heads to trees in a sacred grove; the corpse of Varus, which some of his men had begun reverently to cremate, was mutilated, his head taken to Maroboduus and by him sent to Augustus, who gave it decent burial.[2]

Immediately after the disaster the exultant Germans attempted to capture Aliso; but the commandant, Lucius Caedicius, and his archers prevented them from storming the fort, cut their way out on a dark night when their stores were exhausted, and, hampered though they were by the presence of women and children, made their way safely to the winter camp. Fortunately two of the five legions that had held the province when Varus began his march were under the command of his nephew, Lucius Asprenas, an experienced soldier, who conducted them to the same refuge.[3]

Augustus, old and worn by the anxieties of the Pannonian

Distress of Augustus.

---

[1] See pp. 173–4.

[2] Dio, lvi, 19, 4–5; 20–1; 22, 1–2; Vell., ii, 119, 3–5; 120, 4; Tac., *Ann.*, i, 61; *Germ.*, 37; Suet., *Aug.*, 23, 1; Flor., ii, 30, 32–4; Oros., vi, 21–6. Cp. pp. 109, 111. Dio (lvi, 22, 4) says that some prisoners were afterwards ransomed and set at liberty on condition of their remaining outside of Italy.

[3] Vell., ii, 120, 1–2; Frontin., *Strat.*, iv, 7, 8; Dio, lvi, 22, 2a.

war, was so deeply distressed that, as his adoptive father
had done after the disaster at Atuatuca,[1] he refused for
some time to let his hair be cut or his beard shaved, was
heard to cry repeatedly, 'Quintilius Varus, give me back
my legions', and during the rest of his life observed the
anniversary of the great calamity as a day of mourning.[2]

His efforts to repair the disaster. Nevertheless he did his utmost to repair it, ordering
watch to be kept nightly in the city to prevent disorder,
sending away Gauls and Germans who served in his bodyguard, lest they should create any disturbance, and pro-
longing the terms of provincial governors, to keep the
subject peoples loyal under experienced men. With his
customary respect for religion as an instrument for sus-
taining public confidence he vowed to give a series of
games in honour of Jupiter, the Best and the Greatest, if
prosperity should be restored, but would not allow the
festivals commonly held in the autumn to be celebrated.
A temple in the Field of Mars had been struck by a
thunderbolt; locusts had appeared in the city; a rumour
that a statue of Victory in Germany, facing eastward,
had turned towards Italy, was believed not only by the
populace, but, if we may trust Dio, who regularly
chronicled such stories, also by the Emperor. Dreading
an invasion of Italy, though he learned with relief that
Cisrhenane Germany was secure and that, thanks to the
prompt action of Asprenas, the insurgents had not ventured to approach the Rhine, Augustus endeavoured to
raise troops and, as comparatively few citizens of military
age were available and, moreover, reluctant to enlist, dis-
graced a certain number, who were selected by lot—
one fifth of the younger, one tenth of the older men—condemned a few, who even then shrank from service, to
capital punishment, and, having raised an additional force
of retired veterans and freedmen, dispatched them under
Tiberius, who had promptly returned from Dalmatia, to
join the two legions that were now alone available for the
protection of the province.[3]

---

[1] See *Caesar's Conquest of Gaul*[2], p. 116.
[2] Suet., *Aug.*, 23, 2; Oros., vi, 21, 27.
[3] Suet., *Aug.*, 49, 1; Dio, lvi, 23; 24, 1–5. See pp. 180–1.

The province, indeed, except that portion which extended west of the Rhine, was virtually lost, for no legions were raised to replace the three that had been annihilated;[1] and, although Germanicus struggled in the two years that followed the death of Augustus to reconquer Germany, the seventh after the Varian disaster was the last in which an attempt was made to extend the empire to the Elbe.[2] Arminius could boast that 'the Roman standards were still in the German groves, hung up to the gods of his fatherland.'[3] 'We Romans', wrote Tacitus, who had affirmed that he was 'in real truth the Liberator of Germany', 'honour him not as he deserves.'[4] Needless to speculate on the question whether Tiberius was wise in declining an enterprise which Augustus, whose policy was his standing model,[5] would assuredly have refused to sanction. Roman armies might have penetrated into Germany from the Rhine, the Danube, and the North Sea; and if they had held their ground, the barbarian invasions might perhaps have been repelled. But Rome could not afford the expenditure which such operations would have entailed.[6]

Trans-rhenane Germany lost.

A.D. 15–16.

A.D. 16.

While the triumph of Tiberius for the successful conclusion of the Pannonian war was of course postponed, he was welcomed as a conqueror, entered Rome wreathed with laurel and wearing a toga embroidered with purple, then, in the presence of the senators, took his seat between the consuls beside the Emperor on a tribunal in the Field of Mars, whence, after formally greeting the assembled citizens, he was escorted to various temples.[7] It was probably in the following year that an arrangement was made, destined to be permanent, by which, notwithstanding the loss of Varus's legions, the force that guarded the Rhine was strengthened by five, withdrawn from Spain, Illyricum, and Vindelicia.[8] Though Tiberius resumed command, no

Tiberius welcomed in Rome.

A.D. 10.

The Rhine secured.

---

[1] H. M. D. Parker, *The Roman Legions*, pp. 78–90.

[2] Tac., *Ann.*, i, 56–70; ii, 5–26. Cp. Mommsen, *Röm. Gesch.*, v, 48–50 (Eng. tr., i, 53–5).

[3] Tac., *Ann.*, i, 59, 5.   [4] *Ib.*, ii, 88, 3.   [5] *Ib.*, i, 77, 4; iv, 37, 4.

[6] Cp. Jullian, *Hist. de la Gaule*, iv, 150–2. I am glad to find that my view was also that of Mommsen (*Röm. Gesch.*, v, 52 [Eng. tr., i, 58]).

[7] Suet., *Tib.*, 17, 2.   [8] Parker, *op. cit.*, p. 92.

military movement was recorded, and the next year was little more eventful. Tiberius spent the summer on the east of the Rhine and ravaged various districts, but did not venture far into the interior, evidently deeming it enough to show that Romans could still invade Germany. His biographer learned that, mindful of the rashness of Varus, he consulted his staff, though he had hitherto relied solely on his own judgement, before taking any important step, was careful to see that no baggage, except what was absolutely indispensable, should encumber the army, took his meals sitting on the grass, and often slept in the open

Tiberius celebrates his triumph. air.[1] Early in the autumn he returned to Rome, to celebrate his postponed triumph, which took place on the 23rd of October.[2] His lieutenants, for whom he had obtained the triumphal insignia, accompanied him, and, before entering the Capitol, he alighted from his chariot to kneel at the feet of the Emperor.[3] Remembering perhaps the humane example of Pompey,[4] he treated Bato with rare generosity, not only sparing him the fate that had befallen so many hostile leaders on days of triumph, but also giving him presents and allowing him to live thenceforth at Ravenna as a political prisoner.[5] In the following

A.D. 12. Tiberius and Germanicus in Germany. year he returned to Germany, alone, for Germanicus, then consul, was of course detained in Rome, where he was the idol of the populace; but he remained prudently inactive.

A.D. 13. Next year Germanicus held sole command, but, eager though he must have been to win glory by avenging the Varian disaster, was restrained by the cautious Emperor or by Tiberius, whose authority over every province had been made equal to his.[6]

[1] Dio, lvi, 24, 6; 25, 2; Suet., *Tib.*, 18.
[2] The date, Jan. 16, A.D. 12 (*C.I.L.*, i², pp. 231, 308), has been corrected on the evidence of a lately discovered fragment of the Praenestine calendar (Wissowa [*Hermes*, lviii, 1923, pp. 373–4]). The date, Jan. 16, found in the uncorrected Praenestine calendar—*Ti. Caesar ex Pan.* [nonia laureatus urbem intr]*avit*—is now referred to the preliminary celebration mentioned by Suetonius. See p. 121. The words in square brackets have been conjecturally restored by Wissowa.
[3] This act of homage was commemorated, as Hill says (*Historical Roman Coins*, p. 172), 'on the magnificent cameo at Vienna, known as the Gemma Augustea'. [See p. 181.]   [4] See *The Roman Republic*, i, 301.
[5] Suet., *Tib.*, 20, where Bato is incorrectly called 'the Pannonian'.
[6] Vell., ii, 121, 1; Suet., *Tib.*, 21, 1. 'Tiberius', says Mattingly (*Coins of*

The wars in Dalmatia, Pannonia, and Germany had so engrossed public attention that an important administrative act, which occurred in the year before Germanicus conducted his first campaign, was unnoticed by every historian except Josephus[1] and St. Luke.[2] Quirinius,[3] who is best known in connexion with the census that is said to have been held at the time of the birth of Jesus,[4] was sent by Augustus after the annexation of Judaea to conduct the survey and valuation of the country. The registration of property for the purpose of taxation and the inquiry that was made into domestic life were alike obnoxious to Orientals, and serious disturbances ensued. More interesting doubtless to the Roman public were the announcements in the following year that Julia, the grand-daughter of the Emperor, and the poet, Ovid, had been banished[5]—the former by the authority conferred in the law relating to adultery, the latter by exercise of the Emperor's consular power.[6] The place of Julia's banishment was an island, Trimera, in the Adriatic; and there, while the most notorious of her paramours, Decimus Silanus, warned by the Emperor's abandonment of friendly intercourse, went into voluntary exile, she spent the remainder of her life.[7] Her grandfather must have been deeply incensed by the slur which she had cast upon his social laws; for he caused a luxurious mansion which she had built to be destroyed, refused to allow a child whom she afterwards bore to be reared—an act which, perhaps because such infanticide, sanctioned by early Republican usage, was not in Roman law a crime, has been inadequately

A.D. 6. Quirinius conducts the valuation of Judaea.

A.D. 7. Banishment of the younger Julia and Ovid.

the Roman Empire in the Brit. Mus., i, lxx), 'as full colleague, held a unique position in the closing years of Augustus, and this fact is reflected in his bearing the tribunician power and the "imperator" title . . . on coins'.

[1] *Ant.*, xvii, 13, 5; xviii, 1, 1. Cp. *Expositor*, Nov., 1912, p. 390.
[2] *Acts*, v, 37.   [3] See pp. 88–9.   [4] See pp. 89–90.
[5] Suet., *Aug.*, 65, 1; Tac., *Ann.*, iii, 24, 2–3; Ovid, *Tristia*, i, 10, 41–2; iv, 4, 43–6. Cp. S. G. Owen's edition of ii, 1924, pp. 9–10. Tacitus says that Augustus 'gave the harsh names of sacrilege and treason to offences between the sexes . . . overstepping the provisions of his own law'; but I am not sure whether he is referring to the banishment of the Julias, or to the punishment of their paramours, or to both.
[6] Cp. H. F. Pelham, *Essays*, p. 88, and p. 45, *supra*.
[7] Tac., *Ann.*, iii, 24, 5–6; iv, 71, 6–7.

noticed—and directed in his will that neither she nor her mother should be interred in his mausoleum.[1]

Ovid, who during more than a quarter of a century had been writing poems which made him a welcome guest in the fashionable world,[2] was staying with a friend in Elba when he was startled by news of an imperial edict, banishing him to an island, Tomi, in the dreary region through which the Danube discharged its waters into the Black Sea.[3] Writing there in the hope of assuaging the resentment of the Emperor, he attributed the punishment to his poem, the *Art of Love*, published eight or nine years before, and to the concealment of a grave offence, which he had unintentionally witnessed and ought to have disclosed.[4] Since he took great pains to defend the poem, we may be sure that to it his banishment was partly due;[5] and readers who are not familiar with it or *Amores*, which had preceded it, will presently be able to judge whether the conjecture that connects the exile of the poet with that of Julia, and assumes that both, while they tended to bring the law of marriage into contempt, were believed to have corrupted her, is right. Before the publication of *Ars amatoria* Ovid had written a poem,[6] which he recommended to his feminine readers,[7] telling them how to beautify the complexion, but to bear in mind that character and wit were more enthralling than mere beauty. In *Ars amatoria* he began by declaring that he might be trusted as a past master of the art, and that the love of which he was about to write might be indulged without disrepute. Then, addressing men, he told them where pretty girls were to be met—in the theatre, in the Circus, and at gladiatorial combats. Let them rest assured that all women were open to seduction, not forget to whisper endearing words about

Ovid's *Art of Love.*

[1] Suet., *Aug.*, 72, 3, 65, 4; 101, 3. Cp. W. Ramsay and R. Lanciani, *Manual of Roman Antiquities*[15], 1894, p. 475.

[2] *Ex Ponto*, i, 7, 27–33. Cp. Owen, *op. cit.*, p. 4.

[3] *Ex Ponto*, ii, 3, 83; *Tristia*, i, 10, 41; ii, 4, 45.

[4] *Tristia*, ii, 209; iii, 6, 11–4. Cp. Owen, *op. cit.*, pp. 4, 10. The date of *Ars amatoria* is attested by the line, *Nunc iuvenum princeps, deinde future senum* (i, 194) addressed to Gaius Caesar. See p. 94.

[5] Cp. Ps. Victor, *Epit. de Caesaribus*, 1, 24.

[6] *De medicamine faciei.*   [7] *Ars amat.*, ii, 199–208.

their beauty, their slender fingers, and their tiny feet, and remember that gold might induce the reluctant to yield to persuasion. The story (which Ovid told anew) of Mars and Venus, caught by Vulcan, would serve to show how a lover should treat a rival. After explaining why he himself preferred connexion with women to paederasty, he recommended that they should be caressed where caresses would give them the greatest pleasure. Women should take care not only of their complexions, but also of their coiffure and of their dress, but on no account allow their lovers to see them while they were engaged in their toilette. Let them shun the society of men whose effeminate appearance might suggest that they themselves had lovers.[1] The poem, which was not devoid of humour, speedily became so popular that quotations were scribbled on the walls of Pompeii;[2] and those who consider how it encouraged infringement of the social laws will hardly wonder that the weaker lines, *Remedia Amoris,* which Ovid wrote to appease moralists who insisted that it would corrupt others besides the readers for whom it was intended, produced little effect, and that neither the piteous lamentations nor the flatteries which he wrote in exile mollified the Emperor.

Often in his last days Augustus must have thought of what he and those who worked under him had done for the welfare of his country. He may well have felt that the prayer which he uttered when he thanked the Senate for the honour which he valued most, the title of 'Father of his country', had been fulfilled. Uppermost in his mind perhaps was the recollection that, so far as it had been possible for human ingenuity, he had kept the promise, made on that opening day of his Principate, to restore the Republic; for the power which he had since exercised was a free gift from the Senate and the Roman People, who saw that his supremacy was indispensable and that without it Rome and the peoples for whose government Rome was responsible could not prosper. Plots, indeed, had been formed

Achievements on which Augustus could reflect in old age.

[1] *Ars amat.,* i, 29, 33–4, 89, 135–6, 165–6, 269–70, 619–22; ii, 561–90, 683–4, 719–20; iii, 105, 197–208, 135–68, 169–96, 209–50, 437–8, 811–2.
[2] H. Bornèque, *Ovide: l'art d'aimer,* 1924, p. vii.

against his life by individuals who detested the new régime, and perhaps there was some foundation for the story [1] that he heeded the remonstrance of Livia, who implored him to be more merciful in dealing with such conspirators, though the instance which Dio gives of his clemency rests upon an invention of Seneca.[2] Step by step, he had trained the Senate to co-operate with its president, the First Citizen; and if he foresaw that the ultimate result would be its complete subservience, he may have believed that the evil, if he so regarded it, was inevitable and not without compensation. The senatorial privilege of wearing a tunic adorned with a purple stripe was awarded to the sons of senators when they became of age.[3] The popular assembly, to which Augustus had nominally restored the rights, suspended under the Triumvirate, that it had formerly exercised, was, indeed, deprived of electoral freedom by the powers of nomination and commendation which, like his adoptive father, he reserved for himself and occasionally used;[4] but he knew that such loss could not be avoided without a recrudescence of the anarchy that had prevailed in the Ciceronian age; and, if citizens with long memories missed the excitement of contested elections, he could congratulate himself on the knowledge of human nature that had led him to establish the long series of public spectacles which provided excitement of another kind. But what of the legislative power that had belonged to the Comitia ? It has been truly said that he restored it because he desired to use what reverence remained for ancient institutions in order to give effect to his own wishes;[5] and one of his reasons for accepting permanent tribunician power was that it enabled him to submit proposals to the assembly. He might honestly maintain that the restored legislative power was not wholly unreal; for

---

[1] Dio, lv, 14–21.

[2] *De clem.*, i, 9. Dio, trusting to Seneca, misdated the conspiracy of Cn. Cornelius Cinna. Cp. *Paulys Real-Ency.*, x, 370–1.

[3] Suet., *Aug.*, 38, 2. Cp. H. Mattingly, *The Imperial Civil Service of Rome*, 1910, p. 59.

[4] *The Roman Republic*, iii, 330; *The Architect of the Roman Empire* (44–27 B.C.), p. 184. Cp. H. F. Pelham, *Essays*, p. 135, and Rushforth, *Lat. Hist. Inscr.*[2], pp. 85–6.　　　　[5] W. W. Buckland, *Text-book of Roman Law*, p. 7.

he had been unable to give effect to the laws relating to
marriage until they had been substantially amended.[1]
While, however, as the First Citizen, who claimed to have
restored the Republic, he was generally careful to avoid
interference with judicial procedure,[2] he did not hesitate
in certain cases to use influence to procure condemnation;
the mere fact of his withdrawing friendship was sufficient
to bias the court against an accused man or to induce him
to go into exile;[3] and more than once he personally exercised judicial powers in Rome.[4]

Two great benefits were alone enough to render his
principate memorable: the happiness of the provinces,
which Caesar had done his best to promote, was generally
assured;[5] the campaigns of Drusus, Tiberius, Germanicus,
and the ruthless conqueror of the Homonadenses had
established for generations the *Pax Romana*, in consequence of which local industries had revived, and economic
progress had been stimulated, not only in Asia Minor and
Syria, but also in Gaul, Spain, and Africa.[6] In the East
protected princes had introduced Roman methods of administration.[7] Doubtless Augustus saw no reason to regret
that, notwithstanding the gradual Romanization of the
provinces, he had been chary in granting the franchise,
which the citizens of Italy, jealous of their dominant position, were unwilling to share.[8]

Much had been done for the efficiency and the content-

---

[1] See p. 46.

[2] Suet., *Aug.*, 56, 1. 3; Dio, liv, 3, 2–3.

[3] McFayden, *Washington Univ. Studies*, x, 1923, pp. 239–40; p. 123, *supra*.

[4] McFayden, who remarks (*op. cit.*, p. 240) that Mommsen's assertion that
Augustus frequently exercised formal judicial powers is supported only by
Dio, lvi, 2–3, and Suetonius, *Aug.*, 33, apparently forgets the passage in
which Dio records the interference of Maecenas. See p. 91, *supra*.

[5] In Sicily and Asia, however, less fortunate than Cyrenaica (see p. 93),
the governors were still completely independent in criminal jurisdiction.
Towards the end of the reign the proconsul of Asia, L. Valerius Messalla
Volesus, executed 300 persons in one day (Seneca, *De ira*, ii, 5, 5).

[6] Rostovtzeff, *Social and Econ, Hist.*, &c., pp. 73, 90–1; *Anatolian Studies*,
1923, pp. 380–1. Rostovtzeff (p. 73) remarks that 'evidence about the life
of the larger cities ... in the Augustan age is very scanty. None of the larger
commercial and industrial cities has been excavated; many could not be'.

[7] See Stuart Jones's remarks (p. 125 of his masterly essay in *The Legacy
of Rome*).

[8] Suet., *Aug.*, 40, 3. Cp. Rostovtzeff, *op. cit.*, p. 82.

ment of the force by which the peace had been won. Augustus had insisted that young nobles should undergo that preliminary training[1] which had fallen into disuse, and the period was lengthened from one to two years;[2] youths belonging to senatorial families were trained in the equestrian exercise called Troy;[3] and Gaius Caesar, as *princeps iuventutis*, directed the games that were annually held on the 1st of August by the temple of Mars Ultor.[4] Exercises were performed by free-born youths of humbler families in towns of Italy and the Western provinces;[5] and shirkers received a warning when Augustus sold into slavery a Roman knight who had mutilated his sons to prevent their serving in the army.[6] To prevent military force, however, from being obtrusive, no troops, except the Praetorian guards, whom on the foundation of the Principate Augustus had separated from the legions,[7] his bodyguard, and the urban cohorts, commanded by the Prefect of the City, who was responsible to him alone,[8] were stationed in Italy.[9] The legionary officers were still chosen, as they had been since the time of Marius, after which the cavalry was furnished by provincials and subjects of dependent princes,[10] from the Roman knights, who in pre-Marian times had been brigaded with the legions.[11] In the West the legions were composed of Italians and Roman citizens from the old Gallic province[12] and from Baetica; in the East principally of Galatians and Cappadocians, to whom citizenship was given, as it had been by Pompey and Antony, if not

[1] Cic., *Pro Cael.*, 5, 11.
[2] *J.R.S.*, xiv, 158; *Klio*, Beih. iii, 1905, p. 62.
[3] *J.R.S.*, xiv, 159.   [4] *J.R.S.*, xiv, 161.
[5] *Ib.*, p. 165.   [6] Suet., *Aug.*, 24, 1.
[7] Dio, liii, 11, 5. Cp. *The Architect of the Roman Empire* (44–27 B.C.), p. 29, and p. 120, *supra*.
[8] Rushforth, *Lat. Hist. Inscr.*², pp. 61, 94. Cp. *The Roman Republic*, iii, 45, 296, and p. 92, *supra*.
[9] Rostovtzeff, *op. cit.*, pp. 41–2. Cp. H. M. D. Parker, *The Roman Legions*, pp. 91–2.
[10] *Caesar's Conquest of Gaul*², 1911, pp. 579–81; *The Roman Republic*, iii, 470.
[11] Mr. Parker (*op. cit.*, p. 211), citing Josephus (*Bell.*, iii, 6, 2, which refers to the time of Vespasian) and Dessau (*Inscr. Lat.*, 2326), says that legionary cavalry—120 in each legion—'seems to have been resuscitated by Augustus'.
[12] Gallia Narbonensis.

on enlistment, on their discharge.[1] The auxiliaries, recruited mainly from Gaul, Spain, and Galatia, were now regularly attached to the legions, and the citizenship which they received on completing their term of service belonged also to their descendants.

A navy, properly so called, the Romans had never had. The fleet that forced Hamilcar Barca to evacuate Sicily was raised for the occasion by voluntary contributions;[2] and the squadrons of Augustus, manned largely by his own freedmen, and stationed at Misenum, Brundisium, and Ravenna, were privately organized in virtue of his consular power, which was also the authority that empowered him to maintain soldiers in Italy for the suppression of brigandage.[3] It was doubtless by these squadrons that piracy was suppressed in Sicilian, Sardinian, and other waters.[4]

While the military training of youth was well provided for, there was still no national system of education; and if Augustus had time to ponder the consequences he could hardly have been pleased.[5] The elder Seneca[6] deplored the demoralization of the rising generation which was evident at the close of the Augustan age. Promising boys were no longer commended, as they had been in the days of Cicero, to the care of distinguished men, from whom they might learn much.[7] Suetonius,[8] indeed, mentions a freedman of Atticus, who commented to his class of private pupils on Virgil and other Augustan poets; but Roman history was still neglected. Rhetoric, which had no relation to life or to Roman law, produced the declamators who were conspicuous in the period.

The capital, which the Emperor and Agrippa had adorned with many noble buildings,[9] had been secured against the re-

---

[1] Parker, op. cit., pp. 170–1 (cp. Mommsen, Röm. Gesch., v, 315 (Eng. tr., i, 342)); O. Cuntz (Jahreshefte d. österreich. arch. Institutes, xxv, 1929, pp. 70–81).   [2] The Roman Republic, i, 7.

[3] Suet., Aug., 49, 1; Stuart Jones, Companion to Roman Hist., p. 260; Dessau, Inscr. Lat., 2819, 2826; Rostovtzeff, op. cit., p. 41. Cp. Mommsen, Röm. Staatsr., ii², 855, 864, and Pelham, Essays, p. 88.   [4] Dio, lv, 28, 1.

[5] See The Roman Republic, i, 84, Rostovtzeff, op. cit., p. 48, and A. Gwynn, Roman Education from Cicero to Quintilian, 1926, pp. 128–9, 133, 149, 154–5, 158.   [6] Controv., 1, pr. 8–9.

[7] See The Roman Republic, i, 86.   [8] Gramm., 16.

[9] Mon. Ancyr., iv, 1–8, 12–6; Suet., Aug., 29, 1–2. See p. 34.

currence of conflagrations by the fire-brigade; its supply of food was now assured; the Prefect of the City kept criminals in awe; and, though brigandage had not yet been completely suppressed, much had been done for the safety of the country roads.[1] Caesar's municipal law was in working order.[2]

The conditions of Italian agriculture had been changed. In the last days of the Republic, when Domitius Aheno- barbus promised an allotment out of his vast demesnes to every centurion and every legionary in Corfinium if they would hold the fortress against Caesar, smallholders were being transformed into tenant farmers; [3] and, since slaves were rarely employed on the land, the process of trans- formation had increased.[4] Horace,[5] many of whose poems illustrate the change, writes of an old peasant, working as the tenant of a veteran soldier on a plot of confiscated land which had formerly been his own. Perhaps the change was partly due to the dread of another servile insurrection,[6] which had existed since the rebellion of Spartacus, partly to recognition of the fact that servile labour was expensive and inefficient.[7]

Country towns in Italy, such as Ocriculum[8] (now Otricoli) in Umbria, bore witness in their public buildings to the prosperity that had followed the establishment of the *Pax Romana* and to the public spirit, allied with inter- urban rivalry, that led local magistrates and councillors, of whom many were freedmen who had made money in busi- ness, to expend part of their gains in embellishing them. Readers of Horace [9] will remember how he ridiculed the pompous official, naively displaying his badges, whom he met at Fundi on his journey to Brundisium; and those to whom the work of the most popular of Roman poets is a closed book may recognize the type if they have had experience of local politics in an English borough.

---

[1] Pelham, *Essays*, p. 307. Cp. p. 131, *infra*.
[2] Cp. *The Roman Republic*, iii, 323 with *The Architect of the Roman Empire* (44–27 B.C.), pp. 16, 196.   [3] *The Roman Republic*, i, 106.
[4] Rostovtzeff, *op. cit.*, p. 65.   [5] *Sat.*, ii, 2, 122–36.
[6] T. Frank, *Econ. Hist. of Rome*[2], 1927, p. 356.
[7] R. H. Barrow, *Slavery in the Roman Empire*, 1928, p. 97.
[8] Strabo, v, 2, 9.
[9] *Sat.*, i, 5, 34–6. Cp. T. Ashby, *The Roman Campagna*, &c., pp. 44–5.

The clerical work in these municipalities was commonly done by slaves, whose lot was comparatively fortunate. To readers who have not studied the subject slavery in the Roman world may seem less tolerable than it really was; and under Augustus it had become ameliorated. Though offending slaves were still occasionally flogged and branded. the observation of Martial,[1] that masters who inflicted such punishments 'left an indelible record of their own infamy', is significant; and the rich freedman, Vedius Pollio, who fed the lampreys in his fish-pond on slaves who provoked his anger, received a rebuke, which he could never have forgotten, from his guest, the Emperor. The story, told by Dio,[2] illustrates the characters of both. While they were dining together the cup-bearer broke a crystal goblet, whereupon Pollio ordered that he should be thrown into the pond. Falling on his knees, the slave implored the protection of Augustus, who tried to persuade his host to refrain from such barbarity. Seeing that he was unmoved, Augustus spoke as the Emperor: 'Bring all the drinking vessels like this or any others of value that you possess, that I may use them.' When they were brought Augustus ordered them to be broken: Pollio, indignant but cowed, remained silent. In a case in which a master whose obscenity was notorious was murdered by his slaves Augustus declined to punish them;[3] and the gradual limitation of the irresponsible power of masters was doubtless partly due to the influence of the Stoic philosophy, partly to the growing recognition of the fact that slaves worked better when they were treated humanely.[4] The law was beginning to grant them some protection. Though their evidence in criminal trials was still given under torture, the practice was greatly restricted.[5] Augustus commissioned Tiberius, then a very young man, to purge the workhouses on the pastures in Southern Italy, in which men who shrank from military service had taken refuge and kidnapped travellers were confined by bandits, of

---

[1] iii, 21.   [2] liv, 23, 1–4.

[3] Seneca, *Nat. quaest.*, i, 16, 1, quoted by Barrow, *Slavery in the Roman Empire*, p. 55.   [4] *Ib.*, pp. 46, 97.

[5] *Ib.*, pp. 31, 35. Cp. *The Roman Republic*, i, 91, and Strachan-Davidson, *Problems of the Roman Criminal Law*, ii, 126–7.

whom many were fugitive slaves; but such large estates were tending to become less numerous.[1] Slaves who had some capacity for business found opportunities for making money. Many kept shops.[2] Inscriptions [3] refer to slaves of slaves, who, as in the time of Horace,[4] called their masters *dominus* or, *magister* and were employed by them in lucrative undertakings.[5] Physicians, surgeons, and oculists were still, as in the Ciceronian age,[6] generally freedmen or slaves; an inscription [7] records that a slave who practised in all three professions, earned enough to pay fifty thousand [£500.] sesterces for manumission and died worth four hundred thousand. Even for the average domestic slave who lacked such ability life had some compensations. On the day of the festival called *Matronalia* (the 1st of March) mistresses still waited on their slaves.[8] Besides the recreations provided by the clubs to which many slaves belonged,[9] they might attend the theatre and the public games, and, like the frequenters of our (so-called) lavatories, scribbled the names of their favourite racehorses on walls and made bets on their chances of victory.[10] Slaves, indeed, sometimes rose to office in their clubs, taking precedence over fellow-members who were free.[11] There are, moreover, inscriptions illustrating the family life of slaves, which, after two thousand years, one can hardly read without emotion: for instance, 'To Eucopion, who lived six months and three days, the sweetest and most delightful babe, who, though he could not yet speak, was our greatest joy . . . his parents wrought this monument.'[12] Slaves, says the author of an excellent book on slavery under the Empire,[13] often spent part of their savings in commemorating the lives of fellow slaves whom they remembered with affection. The clubs to which they belonged were not interfered with; but

---

[1] Suet., *Aug.*, 32, 1; *Tib.*, 8; Barrow, pp. 74–5.   [2] *Ib.*, p. 105.
[3] Dessau, *Inscr. Lat.*, 1771, 7440 a and b, 7888.   [4] *Sat.*, ii, 7, 79.
[5] Barrow, p. 102.   [6] *The Roman Republic*, i, 104.
[7] Dessau, 7812.   [8] Warde Fowler, *The Roman Festivals*, p. 38.
[9] Suet., *Aug.*, 32, 1. Cp. Cic., *In Pis.*, 4, 9; Mommsen, *De collegiis*, &c., 1843, pp. 77–8, 96 n. 18, 102, 121; *Paulys Real-Ency.*, iv, 408; *The Roman Republic*, i, 330; ii, 145–6; iii, 285; and Barrow, p. 169.
[10] Petronius, 70, quoted by Barrow, *l.c.*   [11] Barrow, *l.c.*
[12] Dessau, 8487.   [13] Barrow, p. 159.

Augustus, following the example of Caesar,[1] dissolved all clubs, guilds, and religious associations, except those of ancient origin and others that seemed likely to be useful to the State. He had, indeed, reason to believe that treasonable plots might be formed under the pretext of religion.[2]

Freedmen and their descendants formed a large proportion of the population, and racial mixture was already conspicuous.[3]   Another result of manumission, which Augustus may have observed when he was trying to check the abuse of the practice, was the spread of Oriental religions by freedmen who had introduced them when they were enslaved.[4] In one respect the condition of freedmen was better than that of liberated slaves in the modern world: no difference of colour prevented them from making good their new position.[5] Petronius doubtless exaggerated the vulgarity, ostentation, and ignorance of the typical wealthy freedman; but his amusing sketch did not exceed the legitimate bounds of satire. One can easily believe that a man like Trimalchio might have spoken of Diomede and Ganymede as brothers and of Helen as their sister; that when he confessed, euphemistically, that for fourteen years in early life he had been his master's 'darling', he should have added that there was no disgrace in obeying a master's orders; that he was dead drunk in his own house; that he asked his guests to excuse him for making rumblings in his stomach; and that he gave instructions that on his sepulchral monument should be inscribed that he 'started with very little and left thirty millions of sesterces'.[6] But Petronius was a genial satirist, not an impartial historian. The institution of the office of *sevir Augustalis*,[7] for the superintendence of Caesar-worship in municipalities, if the object was to give freedmen an outlet for ambition, was successful: rich freedmen who filled the office spent their

---

[1] See *The Roman Republic*, iii, 285.

[2] *C.I.L.*, vi, 2193; Suet., *Aug.*, 32, 1. Cp. *Class. Rev.*, xxxviii, 106, and *Paulys Real-Ency.*, iv, 408.

[3] *J.R.S.*, xiv, 1924, pp. 110–1; Barrow, p. 211.

[4] A. M. Duff, *Freedmen in the Early Roman Empire*, 1928, pp. 204–6.

[5] Lord Cromer, *Ancient and Modern Imperialism*, 1910, p. 95; Barrow, p. 235.

[6] Petronius, *Sat.*, 59, 75, 78, 47, 71.

[7] *Paulys Real-Ency.*, ii, 2351. Cp. Rushforth, *Lat. Hist. Inscr.*², pp. 63–6.

money, of which their freeborn fellow-townsmen often had little, with local patriotism.[1] While Augustus stopped indiscriminate manumission, his law relating to marriage released freedmen who were fathers of two free children from the services which they had sworn to render to their former masters.[2] But freedmen were subject to certain disabilities: though they might serve in the auxiliary corps and in the fleet, they were excluded from the Praetorian guards, the urban cohorts, and, generally, the legions;[3] if we may accept the arguments of Mommsen,[4] they were deprived by Augustus of the franchise; and, it need hardly be added, they could not become senators.[5] In the year A.D. 5. after Tiberius was restored to favour a law was passed, under which their daughters might be appointed Vestal virgins, since noble families had become reluctant to allow theirs to accept what had once been regarded as an honour; but though the concession was appreciated, it would seem that no freedman's daughter was chosen.[6] Augustus, like the Republican magistrates and Caesar, was obliged to entrust the clerical work of his own part in government to the slaves and freedmen of his household; for no free Roman would have accepted employment which had always been regarded as servile.[7] But the slaves who did such work, for which they were apparently paid, felt honoured rather than degraded: there were many Syrians and Greeks who, proud of having served the Empire as clerks in the newly created Civil Service, recorded the devotion which they had come to feel to Augustus and to Rome.[8] After the foundation of the Principate it was obviously necessary that in the imperial provinces the chief financial authority

---

[1] Barrow, p. 199. Cp. p. 130, *supra*.

[2] *Dig.*, xxxviii, 1, 37 pr., cited by Duff, *op. cit.*, pp. 15–6.

[3] Duff, p. 66; Barrow, p. 195.

[4] *Röm. Staatsr.*, iii, 440–1. Mommsen, remarking that from the beginning of the Principate freedmen did not use the tribe to which they belonged as part of their designation, adds that such use may be regarded as a mark of the right to vote.   [5] Barrow, p. 195.

[6] Dio, lv, 22, 4–5. May one suppose that Augustus, as Chief Pontiff, declined to appoint any of those who, as Dio says, were chosen by lot in the Senate?

[7] See G. B. Grundy, *Hist. of the Greek and Roman World*, p. 471.

[8] Barrow, *op. cit.*, pp. 131–2, 150.

should be a deputy of the Emperor, not, as under the Republic, a magistrate.[1] Augustus saw that for such offices knights were the best fitted, not senators, who had other work to do, nor, though there were exceptions, imperial freedmen; for, as this narrative has shown, he found it necessary to keep freedmen in check.[2] His freedman, Licinus, indeed, was procurator of Gaul;[3] but, as a rule, he entrusted only subordinate posts to them. The qualifications for knighthood were still free birth, good character, and the possession of four hundred thousand sesterces;[4] and though the time-honoured use of the word *equites*,[5] de- [£4000.] noting not only those who each possessed a troop-horse provided by the State, but also men of business and others whose property amounted to the required sum, was still recognized,[6] membership of the equestrian order, properly so called, which could only be entered by a grant from the Emperor, was necessary for those who desired to become military officers and for the civil posts which those who had served as such could alone obtain.[7]

The *publicani*, or syndicates of moneyed men, who had farmed the taxes under the Republic, and whose extortion

---

[1] Mattingly, *The Imperial Civil Service of Rome*, p. 27. Cp. Suet., *Div. Iul.*, 76, 3.

[2] Mattingly, *op. cit.*, pp. 44, 64. Cp. Dio, lii, 25, 1–5, and pp. 107–8, *supra*.

[3] See p. 56, and cp. *The Architect of the Roman Empire* (44–27 B.C.), p. 186.

[4] Suet., *Aug.*, 39, 40, 1. In 38, 3 Suetonius writes, *reddendi equi* [Augustus] *gratiam fecit eis qui maiores annorum quinque et triginta retinere eum nollent* (permitted those who were over thirty-five years of age and were unwilling to retain their horses to surrender them). Mommsen (*Röm. Staatsr.*, iii, 492), insisting that *gratiam fecit* must mean 'excused', not 'permitted', proposed to read *mallent* (see M. Ihm's edition, 1907, p. 74) and to translate, 'excused those from returning the horse who were over thirty-five years of age and desired to retain it'. Madvig (so I learn from Mattingly, *op. cit.*, p. 51), proving in his third edition (p. 253) of Cicero's *De finibus* (cp. Livy, iii, 41,4) that *gratiam facere* may mean 'to permit', retained the reading *nollent* and translated the passage substantially as I have done. Professor J. C. Rolfe in the Loeb edition of Suetonius (vol. i, 1920), accepting Mommsen's interpretation of *gratiam fecit*, but retaining *nollent*, translates *reddendi* by 'formally surrendering'.

Mattingly (p. 52) remarks that the action of Augustus in allowing knights to retire at the age of thirty-five was 'undoubtedly meant as a concession' to those who did not desire equestrian rank.

[5] See *The Roman Republic*, i, 18.   [6] See p. 179.

[7] Dio, liii, 17, 7; Suet., *Aug.*, 38, 3; *Tib.*, 41. Cp. Mattingly, *op. cit.*, pp. 52, 58–9.

had caused so much misery to provincials in the Ciceronian age, were still employed under Augustus and, as we learn from familiar passages in the New Testament as well as from inscriptions, under his successors in the first century; but Augustus, to whose vigilance the provinces owed so much, took care that they should be kept under strict control. It was their duty to collect payments in kind, customs duties, and the fixed sums paid by the senatorial provinces;[1] but it would seem that the tax on inheritances and legacies as well as the tribute of the imperial provinces was levied directly.[2] The law of Caesar, which had restricted the right of serving on juries to men of senatorial and equestrian rank, was amended by Augustus, who, observing perhaps that the service had come to be regarded as a burden, restricted it to the knights, and, in civil suits involving small sums, to an additional class, composed of men whose pecuniary qualification was two hundred thousand sesterces—one half of that of the former.[3]

Since the revenue from the imperial provinces was supplemented by what the emperor derived from his own estate, including mines and quarries, which was continually increased by legacies and confiscations, and from Egypt, which he treated as his own property, and since the clerical business of both, in so far as it was supervised by him, was transacted by the same men—his freedmen and domestic slaves—his private purse and what may be called the Crown property tended to become confused with his magisterial revenue.[4] Like his adoptive father, he claimed, or at least exercised, the right to dispose of the State's resources[5] —for the benefit of the State. Under the settlement that had been made on the foundation of the Principate he was

---

[1] Cp. Mattingly, pp. 77, 106, with *The Roman Republic*, i, 13, 25–6, 123–8, 130–1, and *The Architect of the Roman Empire* (44–27 B.C.), pp. 184–6.

[2] Cp. Rostovtzeff (*Philol.* Suppl. ix, 3, 1902, pp. 385, 407–8) with Mattingly pp. 79–80.

[3] *The Roman Republic*, iii, 284; Suet., *Aug.*, 32, 3; Mattingly, pp. 63–4. The minimum age fixed for the additional class of jurors was 25: in the passage cited from Suetonius *xxv* should be read instead of *tricensimo* (*J.R.S.*, xix, 222–3).

[4] See Rostovtzeff, *Social and Econ. Hist.*, &c., p. 55.

[5] Suet., *Div. Iul.*, 76, 3; App., iii, 20–1, §§ 74, 79; Dio, xliii, 45, 2; Rostovtzeff, p. 57.

to have supreme control of the finances,[1] and so long as the imperial power, which had been then conferred upon him for ten years and was periodically renewed,[2] lasted, he could not be required to account for the manner in which he exercised such control. Nevertheless he made it clear by the emphasis with which he recorded in the *Monument of Ancyra*[3] benefactions the cost of which he had defrayed out of the 'Crown property' or what he called 'my own money', that he drew a sharp distinction between such expenditure and that of the public funds[4] which he was entitled to disburse.

Perhaps he may have felt, even after Tiberius was recognized as his adopted son, that the desire which he had expressed in an edict[5]—that in his dying moments he might be allowed to hope that the foundations which he had laid for the State would remain unshaken—was hardly certain of fulfilment. For he must surely have reflected that in the constitution which he had devised when he attempted to engraft monarchy upon a restored republic there was one weakness—the question, sure to recur, in the absence of hereditary right, towards the end of every reign, of providing for the succession of another emperor. He himself had raised Tiberius, whose fitness was indeed indisputable, to so high a place that no other candidate would have a chance of supplanting him; and his example was not forgotten.[6] Did he believe that Caesar-worship, which had established itself not only in Africa and Asia, but in some degree also in the Western provinces and Italy,[7] might serve as a further guarantee ?

If Augustus permitted himself to reflect upon his past achievements, he remained to the end a devoted public servant. After the consulship of Germanicus he accepted a renewal of his government for a fifth decennial period, of which he doubtless felt that he would not live to see the end, at the same time renewing the tribunician power of

To the last he remained a public servant. A.D. 13.

---

[1] *The Architect of the Roman Empire* (44–27 B.C.), p. 180.
[2] See p. 39.   [3] *Mon. Ancyr.*, iii, 9–12, 34–5, 37–43.
[4] *Ib.*, i, 32–5. Cp. O. Hirschfeld, *Kaiserl. Verwaltungsbeamten*[2], p. 7, and see p. 177, *infra*.   [5] Suet., *Aug.*, 28, 2.
[6] Cp. G. B. Grundy, *Hist. of the Greek and Roman World*, p. 455.
[7] See pp. 69–72.

Tiberius. Since increasing weakness constrained him to avoid unnecessary fatigue and generally to transact business in his own house, the Senate, deferentially sanctioning a privilege which he already exercised, decreed that whatever he might enact in conjunction with Tiberius, senatorial counsellors for whose assistance he had asked, the consuls, the consuls designate, and other advisers whom he might select, should have the same force as if it had been approved by itself in its entirety. Finding that the tax on bequests, which he had introduced seven years before,[1] was likely to provoke disturbances, he sent a paper to the Senate, charging the members severally to devise other expedients for raising money and hoping that if, as he expected, they could not, they would confirm the tax and relieve him from odium. Germanicus and Drusus were forbidden to vote, lest their fellows should suspect that they were influenced by him. Learning from a report of the debate and of the proposed expedients that the senators would rather submit to any other tax, he substituted one to be levied on lands and houses, and commissioned agents, in conformity with a census which was in progress, to prepare a schedule of the properties of individuals and of towns. The senators, as he had foreseen, expected that the proposed levy would be even more burdensome than the existing tax, which was therefore, however reluctantly, confirmed.[2] The census, completed in the ensuing year, showed that the number of Roman citizens was four millions nine hundred and thirty-seven thousand—seven hundred and four thousand more than in that which had been held twenty-one years before.[3] During the purification that immediately followed, a flash of lightning obliterated the first letter of CAESAR in the inscription on the pedestal of a statue of Augustus which stood upon the Capitol. Since the letter signified 'one hundred' and in the Etruscan language *aesar* meant 'a god', seers concluded that on the hundredth day thereafter,

May 11,
A.D. 14.

---

[1] See p. 110.

[2] Dio, lvi, 28. Cp. liii, 21, 4–5, and Suet., *Aug.*, 35, 3. See Dessau, *Gesch. d. röm. Kaiserzeit*, i, 134–5.

[3] *Mon. Ancyr.*, ii, 8–11; Suet., *Aug.*, 97, 1.

the 19th of August, the Emperor would become divine. The populace were in a mood to heed such prophecies; for a total eclipse of the sun had recently occurred, and, although it had of course been duly predicted, it remained for the ignorant a portentous phenomenon.[1] Tacitus[2] doubtless had authority for the pithy sentences in which he described the diversities of public opinion when it was believed that the end of the reign was near: a few enthusiasts talked of the blessings of liberty; the majority had learned by experience that only monarchy could avert the horrors of civil war; the discontented looked forward to the chances of a revolution from which they might have something to gain.

Diversities of opinion in expectation of his death.

Tiberius, immediately after his censorial work in co-operation with his adoptive father was finished, set out for Brundisium, intending to resume the administration of Illyricum. Augustus, who proposed to accompany him on the first stage of the journey, was looking forward to a recreative tour.[3] Just before he started he had completed the record of his reign which is called the *Monumentum Ancyranum*, and which had not before been carried beyond the events of the year 2 B.C.[4] There is some ground for believing that he directed that his grandson, Agrippa Postumus, whom he had adopted ten years before, but afterwards banished for various depravities to an island near Corsica,[5] should after his own demise be put to death; but Tacitus argued that for this deed,

[1] Suet., *Aug.*, 97, 1–2; Dio, lvi, 29, 3–5.   [2] *Ann.*, i, 4, 2.

[3] Vell., ii, 123, 1; Suet., *Aug.*, 97, 1–3; *Tib.*, 21, 1. Dio (lvi, 30, 1–2) affirming that Augustus shortly before his death went secretly to the island Planasia, to which he had banished Agrippa Postumus (lv, 32, 2) on account of vices, which Velleius (ii, 112, 7) also attests, and was supposed to be about to be reconciled with him, remarks that some people believed that Livia, fearing that he intended to make Agrippa his successor instead of Tiberius, attempted to poison him! Von Domaszewski (*Gesch. d. röm. Kaiser.*, i, 1909, p. 248) believes that Augustus did go to Planasia, longing to see his grandson once more. Every one of sound judgement will agree with Dessau (*Gesch. d. röm. Kaiserzeit*, i, 477) that it would be a waste of words to dwell on the improbability of this story, the absurdity of which Mr. M. P. Charlesworth (*Amer. Journ. Philol.*, xliv, 1923, pp. 149–50, with which cp. *Class. Rev.*, xli, 55) conscientiously demonstrated.

[4] Suet., *Aug.*, 101, 4; Dio, lvi, 33, 1. Cp. Mommsen, *Res gestae²*, &c., pp. 1–2, and Hardy, *Mon. Ancyr.*, pp. 162–3.

[5] Suet., *Aug.*, 65, 1. 4; Dio, li, 1. Cp. n. 3.

His recreative tour.

[Capri.]

[Posilipo.]

[Pozzu-oli.]

which soon followed, he was not responsible.[1] From Astura in Latium he sailed along the Campanian coast, suffering on the voyage from diarrhoea, despite which he enjoyed four days of repose and social diversion at his villa in Capreae. Those who have felt the charm of that restful island, which, seen from Naples, its lofty rugged outline rising higher and still higher northward, appears to dominate the bay, may imagine how he delighted in the prospect of the open sea extending westward towards far Sardinia and, on the opposite side, of the Surrentine peninsula, Pompeii, Vesuvius, and Pausilypum. As the ship was passing Puteoli, the crew and the passengers of a merchantman which had just arrived from Alexandria, dressed in white, decked with garlands, and burning incense, saluted him, exclaiming that it was to him that they owed life, liberty, and prosperity. He was so delighted at this spontaneous welcome that he gave every one of his attendants forty pieces of gold, only requiring them to swear that they would spend the money on the purchase of Alexandrian wares. From Capreae he crossed to Naples, where he attended a gymnastic contest which had been established in his honour, and then, although his bowels were still weak, accompanied Tiberius as far as Beneventum. After he had bidden him farewell he returned to Campania, and, having become seriously ill on the journey, halted at Nola, where he took to his bed, sending a messenger to recall Tiberius, who hastened instantly to see him and received his final admonitions.[2] On the 19th of

[1] *Ann.*, i, 6, 2–4. Tacitus remarked that it was incredible that Augustus would have slain his grandson to secure his stepson's [Tiberius's] safety, and that it was more probable that the 'murder of a youth detested equally by Tiberius and by Livia was the work of both'. Ramsay, commenting on the passage, says, 'the real object of Tacitus in exonerating Augustus is to whitewash him at the expense of Tiberius and Livia'.

[2] Dio, who relates (lvi, 31, 1) that the death of Augustus 'was not immediately made public', because 'Livia, fearing that as Tiberius was still in Dalmatia, there might be some revolutionary movement, concealed the fact until he arrived', remarks that 'this is the statement made by most writers, including the more trustworthy', but adds that 'there are some who have affirmed that Tiberius was present during his illness and received certain injunctions from him'. Velleius (ii, 123, 2–3), than whom on such a point there is no better authority, states this distinctly, and so also does Suetonius (*Aug.*, 98, 5; *Tib.*, 21, 1).

August, the anniversary of the day on which he entered His death,
upon his first consulship, feeling that he was about to die, will,
he summoned his friends, asked them whether he seemed funeral,
to them to have fitly played the comedy of life, and deifica-
quoted two lines from a Greek play:[1] tion.

> 'Since well I've played my part, all clap your hands
> And from the stage dismiss me with applause.'

Perhaps Dio was not far wrong when he remarked that
he thus expressed his own view of the vanity of human life.
Then, dismissing his friends, he kissed his wife, murmuring,
'Live mindful, Livia, of our marriage: farewell,' and
dying as he spoke.[2]

A saying of Livia has been preserved, which reveals her
character and partly his. Asked how she had contrived
to obtain such commanding influence over her husband, she
answered, 'by being scrupulously chaste, cheerfully doing
whatever pleased him, never meddling with his affairs, and
pretending neither to hear of nor to notice the favourites
with whom he had amours.'[3]

Magnates of various communities in rotation carried the
corpse on a bier night after night to Bovillae, a few miles
from Rome, where a party of knights met them and conveyed it into the city. Next day the senators assembled,
the magistrates among them, in token of mourning, without
their purple-bordered togas. An imperial freedman then
read the will, dated April 13 of the previous year, a form-
ality which senators were forbidden to perform. Besides
Tiberius and Livia, many legatees were named. Forty
millions of sesterces were bequeathed to the populace, one [£400,000.]
thousand to every one of the Praetorian guards, five
hundred to every member of the urban force, three hundred
to every legionary; to boys whose patrimony the deceased
had inherited while they were still of tender age the whole

---

[1] Ἐπεὶ δὲ πάνυ καλῶς πέπαισται, δότε κρότον | καὶ πάντες ἡμᾶς μετὰ χαρᾶς
προπέμψατε (Com. Att., frg. 111, p. 544, n. 771). O. Crusius (Philol., lxxiii,
1914, p. 320) reads the first line differently—Ἐπεὶ δ' ἐπαίχθη μοι καλῶς τὸ
παίγνιον—but the meaning remains the same.

[2] C.I.L., i², p. 326; Vell., ii, 123; Suet., Aug., 98, 1–2. 5; 99; 100–1; Dio,
lvi, 30, 1. 5; 31, 1; Tac., Ann., 1, 5, 5–6; Jos., Ant., xviii, 2, 2; Bell., ii, 9, 1.

[3] Dio, lviii, 2, 5.

amount was to be repaid with accumulated interest. Two
provisions must have been noticed by all who heard them:
Julia, although she was to receive bequests, was not
recalled from exile, and not to be interred in the imperial
mausoleum.[1] Did her father give a thought to the babe,
her grandchild, whom he had not allowed to live ?

Four documents which the Emperor had drafted were
brought into the Senate House and read aloud by Drusus,
the son of Tiberius. One contained minute directions for
the funeral; another the manuscript, finished just before
his recent tour, in which he had recorded those acts of his
life that seemed to him memorable, copies of which he
ordered to be inscribed upon bronze columns around his
shrine, and of which two other copies, the Monument of
Ancyra and the Monument of Antioch,[2] are still extant; the
third embodied statements relating to the troops, the
revenues, the public expenditure, the moneys in the
treasuries, and everything else concerning the imperial
administration; the fourth, injunctions for the guidance of
Tiberius and the public. They were advised to restrict
manumissions, for fear of filling the city with a rabble, to
grant citizenship sparingly, in order to preserve the distinction between Romans and subjects, to entrust public
business to men of practical ability, but never to any one
person, and not to attempt to enlarge the imperial
dominions.[3]

In preparation for the funeral the corpse of the Emperor,
enclosed in a coffin, was laid beneath a couch of ivory and
gold, adorned with purple and golden coverlets. An image
of the deceased, clad in triumphal garb, was borne from the
palace by the magistrates designate and placed upon the
couch; another, of gold, was carried from the Senate House;
a third lay upon a triumphal chariot. Behind them were
to be seen images of the Emperor's ancestors and of his
deceased relatives, except that of Caesar, who was regarded as a demi-god,[4] of other famous citizens, including

---

[1] Suet., *Aug.*, 100, 2; 101, 1–3; *Claud.*, 6, 1; Dio, lvi, 32, 1–4. Cp. Tac.,
Ann., i, 8, 1–3.

[2] See *The Architect of the Roman Empire* (44–27 B.C.), p. 182, n. 1.

[3] Suet., *Aug.*, 101, 1. 4; Tac., *Ann.*, i, 11, 6–7; Dio, lvi, 33.

[4] Cp. *The Roman Republic*, iii, 276.

Pompey, and of representatives of nations added in the Principate to the empire. The couch was laid upon the Rostra, and then Tiberius, standing upon the Julian Rostra, hard by the temple of the deified Caesar, delivered an oration in eulogy of the Emperor. Finally the couch was carried through the Triumphal gateway to the Field of Mars, senators and knights with their wives, Praetorian guards, and citizens following in procession. The corpse was laid upon a pyre in the Field of Mars: priests moved round it, followed by the knights and the urban guards, all who had received decorations casting them upon it. The centurions present applied torches to the pyre; and five days later, Livia collecting the charred remains, placed them in the tomb.[1]

On the 17th of September Augustus by decree of the Senate was declared divine; priests were assigned for his worship, and Livia, whom in his will he had named Augusta, was made his priestess. By a vote of the Senate a shrine was erected to him in Rome; others elsewhere by various communities.[2] But it was sufficient glory to have been the architect of the Roman Empire.

[1] Suet., *Aug.*, 100, 3–4; Dio, lvi, 34; 42.
[2] *C.I.L.*, i², pp. 244, 329; Rushforth, *Lat. Hist. Inscr.*², p. 68; Vell., ii, 124, 3; Tac., *Ann.*, i, 8, 2; Suet., *Aug.*, 101, 2; Dio, lvi, 46, 1–3.

PART II

THE GALLIC TRIBAL COMMUNITIES UNDER AUGUSTUS

AS all students of Gallo-Roman history will remember, Strabo [1] says that under Augustus there were sixty tribal communities in Gaul, whereas Tacitus,[2] speaking of the time of Tiberius, reckons sixty-four. Various attempts have been made to explain or to reconcile the discrepancy.[3] Many readers will perhaps feel that the question is not sufficiently important to call for research; but, remembering that the number recorded on the famous altar at Lugudunum agrees with that given by Strabo, who doubtless copied it, they may be inclined to accept the suggestion of Camille Jullian that Tacitus combined the list given on the altar with that of the Iberian tribes of Aquitania, taking account only of those which ranked as *civitates* (organized communities),[4] or (as W. T. Arnold held) [5] with that of the four German tribes—Nemetes, Vangiones, Triboci, and Rauraci [6]—which, after the time of Caesar, were incorporated in Gaul.

DID AGRIPPA PROVIDE FOR THE DEFENCE OF THE GALLIC EASTERN FRONTIER?

Jullian,[7] remarking on the persistence with which the Romans, long before 12 B.C., when Drusus became Governor of Gaul, protected the left bank of the Rhine, holds that Agrippa posted legions and their auxiliaries in permanent camps along the river. E. Ritterling,[8] citing Pliny[9] and Tacitus,[10] insists that this was not done until the time of Drusus, in consequence of the defeat of Lollius,[11] and that the bulk of the legions were before quartered in the country of the Lingones and the Remi. Jullian[12] replies that the incorporation of the Lingones in Belgica, mentioned by Pliny,

---

[1] iv, 3, 2.   [2] *Ann.*, iii, 44, 1.

[3] See C. Jullian, *Hist. de la Gaule*, iv, 90, n. 8, and G. Bloch (E. Lavisse's *Hist. de France*, i, 180, n. 3.

[4] Jullian (*l.c.*) remarks that Tacitus would then have counted 12 between the Garonne and the Loire, 25 in Celtica, 18 in Belgic Gaul, and the nine Aquitanian tribes afterwards known as *Novem Populi*—altogether 64.

[5] *Studies of Roman Imperialism*, 1906, p. 86.

[6] Ubii, according to Jullian.   [7] *Op. cit.*, p. 103 and n. 6.

[8] *Bonner Jahrb.*, cxiv–cxv, 1906, pp. 159–60.

[9] *Nat. hist.*, iv, 17, 106.   [10] *Hist.* i, 54.

[11] See p. 53.   [12] p. 135, n. 7.

may have belonged to the last days of Augustus, that the usage (*vetere instituto*) alluded to by Tacitus may date from the time of Caesar, and that Ritterling's view conflicts with the facts that the Remi and the Lingones were not only far from the frontier, where there was the chief danger, but were also allied peoples, who had always been faithful to Rome. I agree with Jullian. As Gaul was not rebellious under Agrippa, troops must have been available, and it would have been folly not to keep them ready on the frontier. But as the Sugambri crossed the Rhine in 16 and perhaps also in 12 B.C.,[1] the defensive arrangements were evidently imperfect until Drusus improved them.

THE VEXED QUESTION OF AN ALEXANDRIAN SENATE

Much has been written on the question whether the Alexandrian senate, if it ever existed, was abolished by Augustus. The answer depends upon the meaning of three Greek words in the report of the reply (printed in H. I. Bell's *Jews and Christians in Egypt*, 1924, pp. 24–5, ll. 66–72) which the Emperor Claudius made to an Alexandrian deputation—Περὶ δὲ τῆς βουλῆς ὅ τι μέν ποτε συνῆθες | ὑμῖν ἐπὶ τῶν ἀρχαίων βασιλέων οὐκ ἔχω λέγειν, ὅ τι δὲ ἐπὶ τῶν | πρὸ ἐμοῦ Σεβαστῶν οὐκ εὔχεται σαφῶς οἴδατε. Καινοῦ δὴ | πράγματος νῦν πρῶτον καταβαλλομένου ὅπερ ἄδηλον εἰ συνοί|σει τῇ πόλει καὶ τοῖς ἐμοῖς πράγμασει ἔγραψα Αἰμιλλίωι Ῥήκτωι | διασκέψασθαι καὶ δηλῶσέ μοι εἴ ται καὶ συνείστασθαι τὴν ἀρχὴν δεῖ | τόν τε τρόπον, εἴπερ ἄρα συνάγειν δεῖ, καθ᾽ ὃν γενήσεται. I translate thus: 'Concerning the senate, what was your custom under your kings of old I cannot say, but you are well aware that you had none under the Augusti who preceded me. Since then this is a new proposal now first mooted, and since it is uncertain whether it will be advantageous to the city and to my interests, I have written to Aemilius Rectus to hold an inquiry and to inform me whether the authority should be constituted and, if this should be decided on, in what way it is to be done.' I agree with Mr. Bell about the meaning of οὐκ ἔχω λέγειν; but Mr. J. G. Milne, who still holds that Augustus 'took away from the chief city its power of self-government',[2] evidently agrees with Professor Rostovtzeff,[3] who remains unconvinced by Mr. Bell's arguments, that the words merely evade the question, meaning 'I have nothing to say'. Let him speak for himself. 'I can quite easily', he writes, 'envisage the

[1] See pp. 53, 63, 158–9.
[2] *J.R.S.*, xvii, cp. Milne's *Hist. of Egypt*³, 1924, pp. 282–5.
[3] *Social and Econ. Hist. of the Roman Empire*, 1926, p. 571.

Permanent Secretary at Rome minuting: "Say that we can't discuss the arrangements which were definitely abolished by Augustus, but offer them an inquiry to keep them quiet."' He insists that if Claudius, who must have already known or have been informed by his advisers of the facts, had been aware that Alexandria had never had a senate, he would have said so to the deputation. But the question is, not whether Alexandria had ever had a senate, but whether, if such a senate ever existed, it had been abolished by Augustus. Mr. Bell [1] thinks it 'improbable that, had Augustus abolished a senate, Claudius, who more than once refers to his policy as a precedent, should not have mentioned the fact', and [2] 'should even speak of the request for its introduction as a new proposal "now for the first time mooted"'. Sir Frederic Kenyon,[3] who, in agreement with A. Stein,[4] takes οὐκ ἔχω λέγειν as I have done, infers from the sentence in which the words occur that the petitioners who waited upon Claudius pleaded that they had once had a senate, but could not produce cogent evidence, and concludes, I think decisively if he is right in his interpretation of the Greek, that they had certainly not had one within recent memory; for, if they had, and it had been abolished by Augustus, Claudius's profession of ignorance would have been childish. [Readers will observe the mis-spelling of the papyrus.]

THE DEPUTATIONS THAT WAITED UPON AUGUSTUS IN 19 B.C.

Dio [5] relates that in 19 B.C., after Gaius Sentius was elected consul, Augustus refused to accept the position, which had been kept open for him, of his colleague, whereupon factious quarrelling and murders induced the senators to vote a guard for Sentius, who was reluctant to use it. The senators accordingly sent envoys to Augustus, who appointed one of them, Quintus Lucretius, to the vacant consulship, and hastened to return to Rome. As the magistrates had prepared to meet him on his homeward way, he entered the city by night. Augustus, as I have said in my narrative,[6] recorded in the Monument of Ancyra [7] that by decree of the Senate some of the praetors and tribunes, with the consul Lucretius and prominent citizens, were sent to Campania to meet him, 'an

---

[1] *Op. cit.*, p. viii. Mr. Bell (p. 9) rightly holds that Dio (li, 17, 3—a passage which no reader of sound judgement would deem relevant) 'may merely mean that Augustus refused a senate'.

[2] *Journ. Egypt. Archaeol.*, xii, 1926, p. 317.

[3] *Edin. Rev.*, July, 1925, pp. 37–8.   [4] *Preuss. Jahrb.*, 1925, p. 65.

[5] liv, 10, 1–2. 4.   [6] P. 38.   [7] ii, 34–7.

honour which', he added, 'up to this time has been decreed to no one but myself'.

Mommsen [1] asserts that no one versed in Roman affairs will hesitate to prefer Dio's statement to that of Augustus, who, he says, in stating that Lucretius met him in his capacity as consul, whereas he really did so as a private individual, though he returned as consul, having received the appointment from Augustus, shrewdly disguised the truth, in order to avoid mentioning that, after the restoration of the Republic, there had been any civil commotions. If, he adds, Lucretius had come to him as consul, he would undoubtedly have given precedence in the Monument to Lucretius, and have written, not *pars praetorum et tribunorum plebi cum consule Q. Lucretio et principibus viris*, but *consul Q. Lucretius cum parte praetorum et tribunorum plebi et principibus viris.*

Dr. Hardy,[2] remarking, less dogmatically, that 'it is surprising that' [in the Monument, Lucretius] 'should be mentioned after the praetors and tribunes', observes that, if Dio's narrative is correct, 'two companies of magistrates were to have met Augustus, one actually sent as envoys on the subject of the interrupted consular elections, the other a purely complimentary mission, which was forestalled by the rapid nocturnal entry of Augustus. Lucretius', he continues, 'accompanied the first mission, but not as consul, though he returned as consul on the designation of Augustus. . . . It may be assumed that Augustus confused and combined the two missions, ignoring the facts that there had been disorders in Rome, and that he had made Lucretius consul in an irregular manner.'

I undertake to prove that Mommsen and Hardy are both wrong. To begin with, I can see no reason for questioning the statement of Suetonius,[3] which neither Mommsen nor Hardy notices, but which was of course accepted by Teuffel,[4] that Lucretius was consul on the 21st of September, 19 B.C., when Virgil, with whom Augustus had crossed the Adriatic on returning from the East, died at Brundisium. If it is true, it follows that the envoys whom the Senate sent to Augustus had met him while he was still in the East, and that Dio was right in saying that Augustus then nominated him consul. Why should Augustus have alluded to civil commotions, which must have been notorious, in recording the honour conferred upon him by the complimentary Senatorial deputation? The argument that, if Lucretius had been already consul when he met Augustus in Campania, Augustus must have mentioned him before the praetors and the tribunes, is simply trivial. Lucretius

---

[1] *Res gestae*[2], &c., p. 48.   [2] *Mon. Ancyr.*, pp. 68–9.   [3] ed. Roth, p. 296.
[4] *Gesch. d. röm. Lit.*[5], 1890, § 224, 1. 3 (Eng. tr., i, 1891).

undoubtedly, as Hardy says, accompanied the first mission, and returned as consul on the designation of Augustus; but why Hardy should go on to say that Augustus 'confused and combined the two missions' I cannot see, unless he was prejudiced by the comments of Mommsen. There was no reason why he should say anything about the first mission, the disorders in Rome, or his own appointment of Lucretius as consul: all that he was concerned with in describing the honour conferred upon himself was the fact, certified not only by the testimony of Dio, but also by that of Suetonius, that Lucretius was then consul. That the complimentary mission, which Dio, if he was aware of it, omitted to describe, was not forestalled by the nocturnal entry of Augustus, is absolutely certain. That Augustus, though he was doubtless capable of disguising truth when he could do so safely, would, to glorify himself, have minutely described a complimentary mission, stating where he received it, and have made a gross mis-statement, sure to be obvious to many of his readers, about a well-known consul, is incredible. Mommsen, though he was a great scholar, perhaps, as Freeman called him, the greatest of all time, was not infallible, and his arguments must be scrutinized as closely as those of lesser men.

SOME ERRORS OF CASSIUS DIO

As Pelham remarks,[1] in agreement with Mommsen,[2] Dio,[3] who says that Augustus in 19 B.C. accepted the consular power for life, must have misunderstood his authorities. No other ancient writer makes the statement; if it had been true, Augustus would certainly have recorded his acceptance in the Monument of Ancyra, and doubtless Suetonius [4] would have done the same when he spoke of Augustus's consulships. Dio's words (τὴν δὲ τῶν ὑπάτων [ἐξουσίαν] διὰ βίου ἔλαβεν, ὥστε καὶ ταῖς δώδεκα ῥάβδοις ἀεὶ καὶ πανταχοῦ χρῆσθαι, καὶ ἐν μέσῳ τῶν ἀεὶ ὑπατευόντων ἐπὶ τοῦ ἀρχικοῦ δίφρου καθίζεσθαι) in which he affirms that Augustus, in consequence of his [alleged] acceptance, was 'entitled to use the twelve rods (*fasces*) always and everywhere and to sit on the curule chair between the two consuls', point, says Pelham, to the conclusion that Augustus merely received the consular insignia, as he had done in 43 B.C.

Dio,[5] contradicting, perhaps inadvertently, Augustus's express statement,[6] affirms that in 19 B.C. he accepted the superintendence

---

[1] *Essays*, p. 66.   [2] *Röm. Staatsr.*, ii³, 872, n. 2.
[3] liv, 10, 5.   [4] *Aug.*, 26, 2–3.
[5] liv, 10, 5. Cp. 30, 1, and Suet., *Aug.*, 27, 5.
[6] *Mon. Ancyr.*, 3, 11–20 (Greek).

of public morals and the censorial power for five years. As Dr. Hardy observed,[1] 'Suetonius and Dio . . . contradict one another', and 'both make statements demonstrably incorrect. If Suetonius had known of the *censoria potestas* spoken of by Dio, he would not have' said that Augustus was 'without the title of censor'. Moreover, in the two later years—8 B.C. and A.D. 13—in which Augustus held a census he acted in virtue of the consular power which he had specially assumed.[2] Fr. Blumenthal[3] infers from Augustus's statement that he held the census by his consular *imperium*, that he purged the Senate by the same authority, and considers that the grain of truth in Dio's assertion that Augustus received censorial power in 19 B.C. for five years is that he received from the Senate special authority for holding a census.[4] Mommsen, he adds, is wrong in thinking that a purgation of the Senate could be held only in connexion with a general census, and Augustus distinguishes between the three *lustra* and the three *lectiones senatus*. The *lectio* assigned by Dio[5] to A.D. 4 was not counted by Augustus because it was carried out not by him, but by commissioners (*tresviri legendi senatus*).

According to Dio,[6] the Senate in 19 B.C. gave Augustus the power of making such laws as he might think fit. Pelham,[7] remarking that Dio connects with this power the legislation which Augustus, after recording his refusal of the office of superintendent of laws and public morals, described in the Monument of Ancyra—'The domestic measures which the Senate then desired to be carried out by me I effected as holder of the tribunician power' (ἃ δὲ τότε δι' ἐμοῦ ἡ σύγκλητος οἰκονομεῖσθαι ἐβούλετο, τῆς δημαρχικῆς ἐξουσίας ὢν ἐτέλεσα)—suggests that Dio's statement may have been 'a confusion with the *ius edicendi*', which was given to Augustus (Dessau, *Inscr. Lat.* 244) at some unspecified date.

THE PURGATION OF THE SENATE IN 18 B.C.

Augustus recorded that he had purged the Senate thrice. The first purgation was in 29 B.C., two years before the foundation of the Principate.[8] Before the dictatorship of Sulla such a revision had regularly preceded a census, and it did so in 29.[9] Augustus

---

[1] *Mon. Ancyr.*, pp. 47–8.
[2] Mommsen, *Res gestae*[2], &c., pp. 28–9. See p. 85, *supra* and Pelham, *Essays*, pp. 64, 70.
[3] *Klio*, ix, 1909, pp. 498–9.   [4] Cp. Hardy, *Mon. Ancyr.*, p. 57.
[5] lv, 13, 3.   [6] liv, 10, 6.   [7] *Essays*, p. 93, n. 1.
[8] *The Architect of the Roman Empire* (44–27 B.C.), pp. 177–8.
[9] *Ib.*, p. 178.

held a census three times [1]—in 28 B.C., 8 B.C., and A.D. 13. He does not give the dates of the second or the third revision; Dio [2] alone gives that of the second (18 B.C.); and if, as Hardy thought,[3] he implies [4] that it was immediately followed by a census, his mistake as Hardy recognized,[5] does not require us to reject his statement about the revision. Other mistakes of Dio, who in his narrative of the events of 11 B.C.[6] reports a census following a revision of the Senate, are noticed by Hardy;[7] but Dio is doubtless right in saying [8] that there was a revision—evidently the third of those recorded by Augustus—in A.D. 4; for, as Hardy observed,[9] 'the very peculiarity of the method ['he nominated ten senators whom he highly esteemed and appointed three of them, selected by lot, to examine the qualifications of members'[10]] adds probability to the story, since Suetonius[11] in an enumeration of new officials created by Augustus speaks of *triumviratum legendi senatus*'.

THE AUGUSTAN LEGISLATION ON MARRIAGE

Suetonius[12] relates that Augustus, having made stringent alterations in the *lex de maritandis ordinibus*, could not enforce it without abolishing or mitigating a part of the penalties and allowing three years' exemption from the obligation to marry after the death of a husband or a wife, besides increasing the rewards; and that the knights even then persistently demanded its repeal at a public show after the children of Germanicus had been born. Dio[13] says that in A.D. 9, on the occasion of spectacles held in celebration of the return of Tiberius, which occurred in the spring, the knights demanded abrogation of the law that affected unmarried and childless persons alike. According to a speech which Dio[14] attributes to Augustus, he had granted [before A.D. 9] 3 years' respite to persons who would be liable to punishment if they violated a recent law relating to marriage, and afterwards 2 years' more. After the speech, says Dio,[15] he increased the rewards of parents and distinguished between bachelors and childless married men, granting both an additional year in which to obey the law. Then (in A.D. 9) the *lex Papia Poppaea* was enacted by the consuls, M. Papius Mutilus and Q. Poppaeus Secundus.

Since Augustus granted 3 + 2 years' respite, it is clear, if we

---

[1] *Mon. Ancyr.*, ii, 1.   [2] liv, 13, 1.   [3] *Mon. Ancyr.*, p. 56.
[4] ? In liv, 10, 5.   [5] *Op. cit.*, p. 57.   [6] liv, 35, 1.
[7] Pp. 57–8.   [8] lv, 13, 3,   [9] P. 59.
[10] δέκα βουλευτὰς οὓς μάλιστα ἐτίμα προβαλόμενος, τρεῖς ἀπ' αὐτῶν ἐξεταστὰς ἀπέδειξεν, οὓς ὁ κλῆρος εἵλετο.   [11] *Aug.*, 37.   [12] *Aug.*, 34, 1.
[13] lvi, 1, 2.   [14] lvi, 7, 3.   [15] lvi, 10.

reckon back from A.D. 9, that the grant began in 4, which, as
P. Jörs [1] remarks, must have seen the enactment of a law intermediate between the *lex de maritandis ordinibus* and the *lex Papia
Poppaea*. This law made the *lex de maritandis ordinibus*, which
penalized unmarried persons only, more severe, for, as we may
infer from Dio, though he does not record the fact expressly—
because, as Jörs says, the intermediate law did not last—it also
penalized childless married couples. Dio's statement about the
demand for repeal is inconsistent with that of Suetonius, for the
children of Germanicus were so young in A.D. 9 that, according to
the latter, the law could not have been that of 4, and must therefore have been that passed in 9—the *lex Papia Poppaea*—whereas
Dio plainly had in mind the intermediate law of 4. Jörs suggests
that Suetonius was alluding to a second demand of the knights;
indeed, if Dio's statements are correct, he must have been, for,
after the knights demanded the abolition of the law that penalized
both unmarried and childless men, they also demanded that of the
lex Papia Poppaea.

It should be added that the reason why the law of A.D. 4 was
suspended in 7 was that war was then imminent. Ferrero [2] observes
that comparison of Suetonius with Dio will show that, whereas
Dio has forgotten the law of A.D. 4 [or rather, does not expressly
mention it, because it was twice suspended, and did not last] and
speaks only of the *lex Papia Poppaea*, Suetonius confuses these
two and represents them as one legislative act. All, he adds, 'is
explicable if we admit that the words of Suetonius, *nisi adempta
demum lenitave parte poenarum* ("without abolishing or mitigating
a part of the penalties") refer to the *lex Papia Poppaea*, which was
an alleviation' of the intermediate law of 4.

Bouché Leclercq [3] suggests doubtfully that Augustus's legislation on marriage remained from 28 B.C. to A.D. 9 in a tentative
state as edict and senatorial decree, and was not confirmed by a
vote of the citizens until the later date—in the enactment of the
lex Papia Poppaea. Ferrero,[4] however, with whom I agree, thinks
it 'impossible to deny that the *lex de maritandis ordinibus* was
approved in 18 B.C., for in the *Acta ludorum saecularium* [*C.I.L.*,
vi, 32323] people are alluded to *qui tenentur* [who are bound] *lege
de maritandis ordinibus* and in 9 B.C. the Senate gave Livia the *ius
.trium liberorum* [reward bestowed on the parents of three children]
(Dio, lv, 2, 5).

[1] *Die Ehegesetze d. Augustus*, Marburg, 1893, pp. 49–60.
[2] *Greatness and Decline of Rome*, v, 295, n. *.
[3] *Rev. hist.*, lvii, 1895, p. 264.
[4] *Op. cit.*, p. 65, n. *.

LUDI SAECULARES BEFORE 17 B.C.

Only one of the various dates to which the earlier celebrations of the *ludi saeculares* were assigned by our original
authorities is absolutely certain—249 B.C. According to Valerius
Maximus,[1] the first was in the consulship of L. Valerius
Publicola [otherwise called Poplicola] (509 B.C.), according to
Eusebius[2] in 449 (?). Varro, whose words are quoted by Censorinus,[3] says that a celebration was ordained by the *Xviri*,[4] after
consulting the Sibylline books, in consequence of many portents;
and, he adds, they ordered that it should be repeated every hundredth year. The mention of the *Xviri* implies that the celebration to which Varro referred was later than 367 B.C., for the *Xviri
sacris faciundis* were first appointed in that year. Mommsen[5]
held that Varro was referring to the celebration of 249, and seems to
have believed that it was the first; but how he would have reconciled that opinion, if it was really his, with the fact that Varro and
Antias assigned the fourth celebration to 149, and Cassius Hemina
to 146,[6] he could not have satisfactorily explained; and the passage
which he quoted[7] from a scholiast's report of a statement of
Verrius Flaccus—*carmen saeculare et sacrificium institutum . . .
Diti et Proserpinae primo bello Punico Xvirorum responso*—proves
only that a celebration was ordained in 249, not that it was the
first. Perhaps it is just possible that the *Xviri* mentioned by Varro
were those commonly called the Decemvirs (*Xviri legibus scribun-
dis*) appointed in 449, and that, their power being absolute,[8] they
inspected the Sibylline books; but it is practically certain that
Varro was, as Mommsen says, referring to the celebration of 249.
Nevertheless, I am inclined to believe that, like Eusebius (?), he
assigned the first to 449; for, since both Antias and Varro affirmed

[1] ii, 4, 5.

[2] According to Dr. J. K. Fotheringham's edition (p. 194), Eusebius seems
to place the first celebration in 452, but, according to Nilsson (see p. 155,
infra), he places it in 449, with which Nilsson equates the year of Abraham,
1565.   [3] xvii, 8.

[4] According to the Vatican MS., Censorinus wrote *XIIviri*, which is
historically meaningless. Fr. Hultsch remarks in his *apparatus criticus* that
the common reading is *XVviri*: this is obviously out of the question, for the
sacred college did not contain fifteen members until the dictatorship of
Sulla, 81 B.C. (Livy, *Epit.*, 81; Ps. Victor, *De vir. ill.*, 75, 11). Mommsen's
correction (*Röm. Chron.*², 1859, p. 181, n. 351) is obviously right.

[5] *Op. cit.*, p. 180.   [6] Censorin., xvii, 11.

[7] *Op. cit.*, p. 181, n. 351. Mommsen's quotation is substantially, but not
exactly, identical with that given in *Pseudacronis scholia* ed. O. Keller, i,
1902, p. 471.   [8] Livy, iii, 32, 6.

that the celebrations were to be held every 100th year, and
Varro referred the fourth to 149, it is not unreasonable to suppose
that he dated the first 300 years earlier. Censorinus,[1] after reporting
the celebration ordered by the *Xviri*, goes on to say that, according
to the 'commentaries' of the *XVviri* and edicts of Augustus, the
repetition was to be in every 110th year, and adds that Horace in
the *Carmen saeculare* [21–2] designated that time—*Certus undenos
decies per annos Orbis ut cantus referatque ludos*. Then, after remarking on the discrepancy between the authorities, he says [2] that
the first celebration has been assigned to the 245th year of the city
[509 B.C.]—[that is, to the date given in the received chronology
for the foundation of the Republic]—adding that, according to the
XVviri, the date was the 298th year [456 B.C.]. The next, he continues, was in the 408th year [346 B.C.] or, according to the *XVviri*,
the 410th [344 B.C.]; but, I may remark, Lachmann, commenting
on the text of Censorinus, substituted 406th (*sexto et quadringentesimo*) [348 B.C.] for 408th (*octavo et quadringentesimo*) and
408th for 410th, at the same time filling up a lacuna in the text
after the mention of the consuls of the 298th year by the words
*secundos ludos, ut Antias vult, M. Popilio Laenate IIII M. Valerio
Corvino cos*. Thus, if Lachmann was right, the second celebration,
according to Antias, was in 348 B.C. According to Antias and Livy,
says Censorinus,[3] the third celebration was in the consulship of
P. Claudius Pulcher [4] (249 B.C.), according to other authorities [5]
[? the *XVviri*] in the 518th year of the city [236]. About the
fourth, he warns us,[6] there are three opinions: Antias, Varro, and
Livy refer it to the 605th year [149 B.C.]; others, including a contemporary, Cassius Hemina, to the 608th [146]; the *XVviri*, who,
as Zosimus [7] tells us, investigated the question of the proper date
for the celebration which Augustus planned, to the 628th [126].
According to the *XVviri*, who adopted the alleged Etruscan view
that a *saeculum* was 110 years, the series was evidently 456, 346,
236,[8] and 126 B.C.

We must take account of the article, 'Saeculares ludi', which
Professor M. P. Nilsson contributed to *Paulys Real-Encyclopädie*.[9]

---

[1] xvii, 9.   [2] § 10.   [3] § 10.

[4] If Censorinus reported correctly the statement of Livy (evidently contained in xlix, one of the lost books), the text which he used must have
differed from that of the epitomizer. In the *Epitome* we read that a celebration—it is not called the third—had been held in the 502nd year of the city
(252 B.C.).

[5] After the mention of Claudius Pulcher and his colleague there is a lacuna
in the text.   [6] § 11.   [7] ii, 4, 2.

[8] In the *Fasti Capitolini* (*C.I.L.*, i², p. 29) the third celebration is referred
to 236.   [9] 1 A. 2, 1700–5.

He holds that Varro, whom he regards as the authority of Valerius Maximus, followed Antias in assigning the first celebration to 509 B.C., that Antias, who belonged to the Valerian *gens*, was more concerned to glorify it than to ascertain the truth, and that, despite the gap between that year and 348, he selected it as the most suitable starting-point for his series—509, 348, 249, 149—because it was the first year of the Republic and in it a famous Valerius was consul. Mommsen,[1] on the other hand, held that the date 509 was due to confusion between P. Valerius Poplicola, consul in that year, and L. Valerius Poplicola, consul in 449. The date, 449, which Eusebius adopted for the foundation of the festival, was devised, Nilsson suggests, by some one who wished to make it harmonize with the others in Antias's scheme. He may be right in preferring 146, the date which Censorinus ascribes to the contemporary writer, Heminas, to 149; but to estimate the credibility of Heminas is impossible. Nilsson's opinion, dogmatically expressed, that 249, to which Antias assigned the third celebration, was really the year of the first, appears to depend upon his conviction that Antias cared only to glorify his own *gens*. If it is true, the labour of Antias and of the great scholar, Varro, was labour lost. Anyhow it seems to me hopeless to attempt to fix the date of the institution of the festival.

WHEREABOUTS IN THE *CAMPUS MARTIUS* WAS TARENTUM?

The place called Tarentum, the scene of the nocturnal sacrifices in the celebration of the *ludi saeculares*, was in the Field of Mars;[2] but its precise limits are matter of controversy. If an altar, discovered in 1887 by the late Professor R. Lanciani,[3] was the *Ditis patris et Proserpinae ara* mentioned by Valerius Maximus,[4] Tarentum was in the most westerly part of the Field, enclosed by a bend of the Tiber, where it is placed in modern maps.[5] M. Pierre Boyancé[6] holds that this structure was not the altar with which Lanciani identified it, that Tarentum was further southward, and that it was a subterranean shrine: Dr. Ashby replies that there is no rock in the place indicated by Boyancé in which such a shrine

---

[1] *Op. cit.*, p. 182.

[2] Val. Max., ii, 4, 5; Censorinus, xvii, 8; Zosimus, ii, 3; Festus, ed. Müller, pp. 350–1.   [3] *Ruins and Excavations of Anc. Rome*, 1897, p. 449.

[4] Cp. Censorinus, xvii, 8.

[5] S. B. Platner's *Topographical Dict. of Anc. Rome*, completed and revised by Th. Ashby, 1929, pp. 508–9.

[6] *Mélanges d'archéol. et d'hist.*, 1925, pp. 135–46.

could have been excavated, and that, if there were, it would have been liable to frequent inundations. Nevertheless Boyancé's opinion is supported by the original authorities, and his arguments are not negligible. Zosimus[1] says that the altar was 20 feet below the surface;[2] Verrius Flaccus[3] that it was concealed by earth (*terra occultaretur*) and, like the *mundus* (a pit, in which were deposited sacrificial offerings) on the Palatine, opened when a festival was held and afterwards closed.[4] Ovid,[5] describing the arrival of Evander with his mother, the prophetess Carmenta, at the place where Rome was to be founded, says that she pointed to Tarentum as the spot where they were to land, which suggests that it was close to the gate called Porta Carmentalis; Servius[6] that the Tiber in one part of its course was itself called Tarentum, because it wore away its banks, which implies that the altar was close to the river; Ovid[7] again that hard by the river were the shallows (*vada*) of Tarentum.

LICINUS

According to Dio,[8] Licinus was a Gaul, according to Probus (?),[9] a German. Was his alleged statement about December (see page 56) an incredibly bad joke, as Jullian thinks, and did Dio misunderstand the authority which he used for the story ? The matter is hardly worth discussing; but if any one feels curiosity, he may satisfy it by consulting Jullian's *Histoire de la Gaule* (iv, 83, n. 7) and the comment of H. Dessau (*Gesch. d. Kaiserzeit*, i, 186, n. 1), who thinks Jullian's explanation too ingenious to be acceptable.

CAESAR-WORSHIP IN 'THE PROVINCE' (*GALLIA NARBONENSIS*)

Camille Jullian,[10] remarking that a scholar named Krascheninnikoff[11] has attempted to prove that Caesar-worship in the Province was organized by Vespasian, replies that, since it is difficult to suppose that the council of Narbo [that is, of the Province] did not exist in the time of Augustus, or that it and the Province were without an imperial cult, he would suggest that Augustus authorized for the Province, as for Aquitania, Celtica, and Belgica, an

---

[1] ii, 3, 2.　　　　　　　　　　[2] Cp. Val. Max., ii, 4, 5.
[3] Festus, ed. W. M. Lindsay, pp. 144, 440, 478–9.
[4] Cp. Val. Max., ii, 4, 5.　　　　　　[5] *Fasti*, i, 497–510.
[6] *ad Aen.*, viii, 63.　　　[7] *Fasti*, i, 501.　　　[8] liv, 21, 3.
[9] *Schol.* on Juvenal, i, 109.　　　　[10] *Hist. de la Gaule*, iv, 426, n. 5.
[11] *Philol.*, liii, 1894, pp. 147–68, 187–9. Cp. Rushforth, *Lat. Hist. Inscr.*[2], 1930, p. xxv, No. 35.

altar and a priest (*un simple prêtre*) 'in his own name'; that the
temple at Narbo (see p. 63, n. 7 *supra*) was erected later; that
later still the priest was succeeded by a *flamen* (that is, a priest
whose service belonged exclusively to one deity—in this case
Augustus); and that, if the *lex Narbonis* [1] was Vespasian's, it
regulated the status of the *flamen*.

THE DATE OF THE DEDICATION OF THE ALTAR AT LUGUDUNUM

Toutain,[2] remarking that Suetonius [3] gives 10 B.C. as the date
of the dedication of the altar at Lugudunum, affirms that, being
an imperial secretary with access to records, he had every means
of knowing. But, he adds, Dio's notice [4] refers to 12 B.C., and in
every other case of which we know the facts provincials took the
initiative in instituting the worship of Rome and Augustus. What
Dio says, he observes, is not that Drusus invited Gallic notables
to found a cult of Rome and Augustus, but that he sent for them
on the pretext of the festival which was celebrated in Dio's time
round the altar of Augustus at Lugudunum. Claudius, Toutain
insists, in a speech recorded on a bronze tablet at Lyons,[5] refers to
the deeds of Drusus in 12 B.C., but says nothing about the institution of the cult of Rome and Augustus. Toutain concludes that it
dated from 10 B.C., and that what was celebrated in 12 was a festival, already established, of which the new cult took the place two
years later.

Dr. G. F. Hill,[6] referring to a coin which commemorated the
inauguration of the altar, has expressed agreement with Toutain's
view: Dessau [7] thinks it hardly probable; I have not the slightest
doubt that it was wrong. Though Suetonius apparently refers the
dedication to 10 B.C., his words, *Claudius natus est Iullo Antonio
Fabio Africano conss. Kal. Aug. Luguduni e o i p s o d i e q u o
p r i m u m a r a i b i A u g u s t o dedicata est*, may only mean
that Claudius was born in the same month and on the same
day of the month in which the altar was dedicated; and if
he meant that the altar was dedicated in 10 B.C., it must not be
forgotten that he sometimes blundered grossly, for instance, in the
passage [8] in which he confounded the Dalmatian Bato with the

---

[1] *C.I.L.*, xii, 6038 (Rushforth, *op. cit.*, p. 44).
[2] *Soc. des Antiquaires de France*, Centénaire, 1904, pp. 456–60.
[3] *Claud.*, 2, 1.   [4] liv, 32, 1.   [5] Dessau, *Inscr. Lat.*, 212.
[6] *Historical Roman Coins*, p. 150.
[7] *Gesch. d. röm. Kaiserzeit*, i, 416, n. 2.   [8] *Tib.*, 20. See p. 122, n. 5.

Pannonian of the same name. If Dio is right, the festival of 12 B.C. was held in connexion with the altar of Rome and Augustus, and 'the festival already established' was earlier. The *Epitome*[1] of Livy, being an epitome, omits to mention Drusus in connexion with the dedication, but clearly implies that the dedication was in 12 B.C.[2] Finally, those who have read the speech of Claudius will agree that there was not the slightest reason why he should mention the institution of the cult. I am glad to find that Rushforth[3] accepts the date 12 B.C.

THE CAMPAIGNS OF DRUSUS IN 12–11 B.C.

Dio[4] relates that in 12 B.C. Drusus, after attacking the Sugambri while they were crossing the Rhine to invade Gaul, crossed it himself, invaded the country of the Usipetes, ravaged the Sugambrian territory, then sailed down the river to the North Sea and, crossing 'the lake' (evidently Zuyder Zee), invaded the country of the Chauci. His ships, Dio adds, were left aground by the ebb tide, but he was rescued by the Frisians, whose friendship he had gained. [Bor-chum.] Strabo[5] says that Drusus seized the island Burchanis, opposite the Frisian coast, and that in a naval battle on the Ems he defeated the Bructeri, who inhabited the country north of the Lippe. This would seem to have occurred in 12 B.C., the only year in which a naval expedition of Drusus is recorded.

Next year Drusus, according to Dio,[6] again crossed the Rhine, subdued the Usipetes, bridged the Lippe, marched through the Sugambrian territory into that of the Cherusci as far as the Weser, which shortage of supplies prevented him from crossing, and, returning, built a fort at the confluence of the Lippe with a tributary called the Eliso[7] and another on the Rhine in the country of the Chatti.

Florus[8] says that Drusus, on assuming command in Germany, subdued the Usipetes, and then marched through the country of the Tencteri and the Catthi (*sic*); Orosius[9] says much the same. Both, it will be noticed, are silent about the naval expedition.

Ferrero[10] concludes that 'it seems likely that the facts reported by Dio for . . . 11 are those which Orosius and Florus relate as having taken place at the beginning of the war with the sole difference that Dio speaks of the Sigambri (*sic*) in place of the

---

[1] 139.

[2] Ferrero (*Greatness and Decline*, &c., v, 194, n. *) seems to forget this.

[3] *Lat. Hist. Inscr.*[2], p. 48.   [4] liv, 32, 2–3.   [5] vii, 1, 3.

[6] liv, 33, 1–4.   [7] See pp. 78–9, 164.   [8] ii, 30, 23.

[9] vi, 21, 15.   [10] *Greatness and Decline*, &c., v, 194, n. †.

Tencteri—an easy confusion . . . Orosius and Florus apparently begin the story of the . . . campaign in . . . 11 and omit the events of . . . 12. . . . Dio's account of the battles which Drusus fought . . . before the naval expedition . . . is lacking in accuracy, and its vagueness induces us to suppose that he was confusing this and the next year'.

I have used Ferrero's own words, omitting none that affect his argument. His conclusion seems to me inconclusive. Dio's narrative is extremely laconic; but Ferrero offers no evidence to show that it is inaccurate, and I am unable to detect its alleged vagueness or to see how, even if it is vague, it justifies the supposition that Dio confused the events of 12 with those of 11. Evidently Florus and Orosius omitted the events of 12 either from ignorance or because they did not think it necessary for epitomizers to describe the expedition that secured the coast of the North Sea even though it prepared the way for the subjugation of the interior.

In a later note,[1] Ferrero says with self-evident truth that since Drusus bridged the Lippe to attack the Sugambri, who lived south of it, he must have been marching up the right bank, and that, if he had gone up-stream with the fleet, the bridge would not have been required. 'This,' he continues, 'lends force to the supposition [apparently based upon the statement of Strabo] that Drusus left . . . troops on the Ems in the preceding year [12 B.C.], and that these then went up-stream to join the troops which were following the valley of the Lippe.' Proceeding to remark that it seems unlikely to 'the majority of historians' that Drusus could have reached the country of the Bructeri in 12, he says that if Drusus did leave troops on the Ems, the naval battle may have been fought in 11. Finally he concludes that, if the Lippe was not navigable, we can understand the situation. 'As the valley of the Lippe possessed no adequate route, it was impossible to send too large a force along it; part of the army went by water . . . the river Ems.'

Now Mommsen,[2] wiser than 'the majority of historians', saw nothing improbable in the view that Drusus reached the country of the Bructeri in 12. Nor do I. Unless Dio made a gross blunder when he said that Drusus fought the naval battle in the year before the consulship of Q. Aelius and P. Fabius, it was fought in 12. The valley of the Lippe did posses an adequate route (see Mommsen's map (v) and page 172, *infra*), and even if part of the army went by water, that does not prove that the naval battle was fought in 11. Is it likely that troops would have been left on the

[1] *Ib.*, 201, n. *.   [2] *Röm. Gesch.*, v, 25 (Eng. tr., i, 28).

Ems if it had not been already fought and won? Our historical materials leave much to be desired; but let us avoid patching them by guess-work.

THE MOTIVES OF TIBERIUS FOR RETIRING TO RHODES

Velleius Paterculus, who served under Tiberius and warmly admired him,[1] tells us[2] that he left Rome for fear the splendour of his own renown might mar the opening career of his youthful stepsons,[3] but that at the time of his departure he dissembled his motive. One may venture to differ from a modern historian,[4] who, remarking that [according to Suetonius[5]] Augustus himself urged Tiberius to remain [evidently after Tiberius declined the offer of Armenia], and that he therefore 'could have had no scruples', stigmatizes the explanation given by Velleius as 'obviously false'. Tiberius may well have feared that his relations with his stepsons and their grandfather might become unpleasant if, by remaining, he should appear to be standing in their way.

Tacitus,[6] observing that Julia (the daughter of Augustus and the mother of Gaius and Lucius Caesar) looked down upon Tiberius as by birth her inferior, affirms that this was one of the reasons for his retirement—a statement which seems hardly credible—and adds that letters inveighing against him and addressed by her to her father, were believed to have been composed by Tiberius Gracchus, who was one of her lovers.[7] If the belief was based upon something more than idle gossip, the letters, the dates of which are unknown, could have had nothing to do with the retirement of Tiberius, who, after he declined the offer of Armenia, was urged by Augustus to remain in Rome.

Suetonius,[8] after remarking that the motive of Tiberius may have been either disgust with his wife,[9] whom (as the emperor's daughter) he dared neither accuse [of adultery] nor divorce, or 'to keep up his prestige by absence and even to increase it in case his country should ever need him', states that he asked for leave of absence on the plea that he needed rest, and that he would not listen either to his mother's entreaties or to his stepfather's complaint, made in the Senate, that he was himself being left in the lurch. The statement may be accepted; the conjectural explana-

---

[1] ii, 104, 3; 107. [2] 99, 2.

[3] Substantially this seems to be what Dio says when he tells us (lv, 9, 5) that Tiberius feared their anger, since they felt that they had been slighted.

[4] Ferrero (*Greatness and Decline*, &c., v, 245, n. †).

[5] *Tib.*, 10, 2. [6] *Ann.*, i, 53, 2. [7] Vell., ii, 100, 5.

[8] *Tib.*, 10. [9] Dio (lv, 9, 7) mentions gossip to the same effect.

tions of motive are obviously worthless: Tiberius with his Roman sense of public duty would never have allowed his wife's conduct to drive him into retirement. Incidentally Suetonius,[1] confirming the statement of Velleius, makes a valuable contribution to the discussion: Tiberius, he relates, on the expiration, five years after his departure, of his tribunician power, avowed that his sole motive had been to avoid the suspicion of rivalry with the two young Caesars.

Dio[2] begins by saying that Tiberius was sent to Rhodes on the pretext that he 'needed education' (ὡς καὶ παιδεύσεώς τινος δεόμενος); afterwards, noticing the story that he could no longer endure his wife, relates that some people said that he was offended at not having been himself, like the two boys, designated as a Caesar, and others that he was banished by his grandfather on the [alleged] ground that he was plotting against them; and finally, contradicting his own absurd opening statement, assures us that it, the story that he was displeased by the decrees passed in their favour, and many other guesses, which he does not particularize, were disproved not only by his subsequent actions, but also by his having opened his will before his departure and read it to his mother and his stepfather.

LEX IUNIA OR LEX IUNIA NORBANA?

Was the law which enacted that slaves, irregularly manumitted, were not to be admitted to Roman citizenship, but only to 'Junian Latinity', known as the *lex Iunia* or as the *lex Iunia Norbana?* In other words, was it enacted in 17 B.C., when C. Junius Silanus was a consul, or in A.D. 19, when the consuls were M. Junius Silanus and L. Norbanus Balbus? The question, which has exercised the ingenuity of many scholars, requires an answer, because in the latter case the law is irrelevant to the subject of this book. Willems[3] decided peremptorily, for the later date, which, he remarked, was [then] universally admitted; Mommsen,[4] Professor W. W. Buckland,[5] Mr. R. H. Barrow,[6] and Mr. A. M. Duff[7] for the earlier.

Mr. Duff remarks that 'the . . . designation *Iunia Norbana* is found only once, in . . . Justinian'[8] and that 'there the text is doubtful'. If, he says, the text is right, *Norbana* 'is an arbitrary

---

[1] *Tib.*, 11, 5. Cp. 10.   [2] lv, 9, 5–8.
[3] *Droit public rom.*², 1884, p. 412, n. 6.
[4] Cited by Buckland. See the next note.
[5] *The Roman Law of Slavery*, 1908, p. 534.
[6] *Slavery in the Roman Empire*, 1928, p. 185, n. 1.
[7] *Freedmen in the Early Roman Empire*, 1928, pp. 210–4.
[8] *Inst.*, i, 5, 3.

addition by one of Justinian's jurists, who wanted to distinguish this act from others of the name *Iunia*.' According to Gaius,[1] he adds, 'the *lex Aelia Sentia* [A.D. 4] gave citizenship in some circumstances to certain freedmen with Latin rights; the *lex Iunia* created . . . Latinity for freedmen;[2] thus the *lex Aelia Sentia* presupposes the *lex Iunia*'. Augustus, he says in conclusion, 'was not likely to leave untouched a state of things whereby *manumissio minus iusta* [irregular manumission] was continually filling society with persons who were *de iure* bond and *de facto* free; his attack on imprudent emancipation has . . . more force if it is preceded by the *lex Iunia*, for in that he could not have touched informal manumission unless he had first legalized it'.

An exhaustive discussion of the question is to be found in *Paulys Real-Encyclopädie*.[3] The writer, Steinwerter, noticing the argument (which in substance has been adopted by Mr. Duff), that the double name, *Iunia Norbana*, was due to a wish to bring the law into symmetrical relation with the *lex Aelia Sentia*,[4] replies that Theophilus would not have written it without MS. authority. That the classical writers (he means Gaius and Ulpian) omitted the name *Norbana* is not, he says, surprising, since they sometimes called the *lex Iunia Velleia* (simply) *Iunia* and the *lex Papia Poppaea* (simply) *Papia*. The *lex Aelia Sentia* did not, he insists, directly alter the status of slaves who were practically free, but added a new group to such freedmen by enacting that slaves under the age of 30 who had been irregularly manumitted should not receive the citizenship. This, he believes, was the situation which the *lex Iunia Norbana* found existing . The most important innovation which it made was that it *legally* freed such slaves, granting them, however, not citizenship, but only Latin rights. To the objection [adopted by Mr. Duff] that the *lex Iunia, quae Latinum genus introduxit*, must be older than the *lex Aelia Sentia*, for otherwise *Latini Aeliani* would have been spoken of, not *Latini Iuniani*, and it would not have been said that the status of *Latini* was due to the *lex Iunia*, and to the further objection that Augustus was not sympathetic towards freedmen, and, therefore, that the *lex Iunia* must have been passed before his reign, Steinwerter replies that while the classical writers often speak of *Latini* in commenting on the *lex Aelia Sentia* they never do so in a way that authorizes the assumption that the text of that law mentioned *Latini*: nay, *ideoque Latinus fit* (Ulpian, i, 12) and *Latini facti* (Gaius, i, 29, 31) are interpolations. More weighty, he observes, is the objection

---

[1] i, 29.   [2] *Frag. Dos.*, 12: *Lex Iunia quae Latinum genus introduxit.*
[3] xii, 910–4.   [4] Is it not more likely that it was due to an oversight ?

that Gaius, when he writes of marriage as recognized by the *lex Aelia Sentia*, always calls the freedman under 30 years old *Latinus*, and that such a freedman must necessarily have been a *Latinus* when the *lex Aelia Sentia* was enacted, for a man legally in the condition of a slave (*morans in libertate*) had no *matrimonium*. But, he insists, one may reply that it results from Gaius, i, 30 (*per legem Aeliam et Iuniam conubium inter eos dari*) compared with i, 29 (*ex lege Aelia Sentia uxorem ducere*) and Ulpian, iii, 3 (*lege Iunia cautum est*) that the *lex Iunia*, which from its position in the second place is manifestly to be regarded as the later [? [1]], simply took over the regulations of the *lex Aelia* about the exclusion from marriage of young freedmen, and therefore that Gaius was justified in writing of the *matrimonium* of a *Latinus e lege Aelia Sentia*. There is no ground here, he maintains, for assuming that the *lex Aelia* itself spoke of *Latini*. The words in Gaius, i, 29, *minores xxx annorum manumissi* [*et Latini facti*], *si uxores duxerint vel cives Romanas vel Latinas coloniarias v e l eiusdem condicionis et ipsi essent*, are significant: while the law avoids calling the young freedwoman *Latina*, it adopts the phrase *uxor eiusdem condicionis et ipsi* [sc. *minores xxx annorum manumissi*] *essent*. Thus, he concludes, it is clear that *Latini facti* was an interpolation made by Gaius.

To the objection, already noticed, that the assignment of the *lex Iunia* to A.D. 19 is inconsistent with the character, unsympathetic towards freedmen, of the Augustan and Tiberian legislation, Steinwerter replies that one must get rid of the notion that the introduction of Junian Latinity signified a special favour to freedmen. This view, he says, is mistaken, for the position of *Latini Iuniani* was anything but favourable. Salvianus in the fifth century wrote of 'the yoke and the bond of Latin freedom' (*iugum et vinculum Latinae libertatis*), which masters imposed upon slaves whom they deemed unworthy of the citizenship. So also Justinian.[2] Steinwerter concludes by giving his own view of the sequence of the three relevant laws. In 2 B.C. the *lex Fufia Caninia* limited the number of freedmen; in A.D. 4 followed the *lex Aelia*; two years later, in consequence of scarcity of food, *peregrini*, many slaves, and gladiators, were sent away from Rome.[3] Among the slaves were certainly those irregularly manumitted: if Latin freedmen had then existed, the authorities—No, I must interpolate, not

---

[1] Mr. Duff (*op. cit.*, p. 212) thinks it 'quite possible' that Gaius 'begins with the law . . . nearer in time to his own age', namely, as he holds, the *lex Aelia*.   [2] *Cod.*, vii, 6, 1; 11.

[3] Suet., *Aug.*, 42, 3 (who observes that foreign physicians and teachers were allowed to remain); Dio, lv, 26, 1.

Suetonius, nor Dio—would have taken care to mention them between *peregrini* and *servi*. Augustus in his will adjured his successor to be chary in granting citizenship.[1] A few years later came the *lex Iulia Norbana*.

I reply by stating the view which I formed when I began to study the question, and have never found reason to abandon. Far from conferring a special favour upon freedmen, the Junian law was the first that restricted their rights. In 44 B.C. freedmen, even if they had been irregularly manumitted, were Roman citizens: the Junian law made those who had been irregularly manumitted *Latini*, the Aelian-Sentian was more restrictive still. Mr. Duff's final argument seems to me wellnigh conclusive.

['I'm not at all sure', says a correspondent, 'that the curious conjunction of consuls in 25 and 24 B.C.[2] hasn't something to do with that troublesome Norbanus in the Institutes.'[3]]

ALISO

Where Aliso was situated, there is not, after all that has been written on the question, sufficient evidence to decide with certainty. The only ancient writers who mentioned the name were Velleius,[4] Tacitus,[5] and perhaps Ptolemy;[6] but Dio[7] may seem to have referred to it when he said that Drusus, after his campaign against the Sugambri, 'constructed a fort to coerce them, close to the confluence of the Lippe and the Elison'. The question of its geographical position is closely connected with that of the Varian disaster, which shall be discussed in the next article. Velleius relates that, immediately after the disaster, Aliso was blockaded by German troops—evidently those who had destroyed the army of Varus; Tacitus that Germanicus (in A.D. 16) fortified the whole country between Aliso and the Rhine. Karl Nipperdey pointed out that the fort on the Lippe (*castellum flumini Lupiae adpositum*) which Tacitus had already mentioned in the same paragraph (§ 5), was not Aliso; for if it had been, he would naturally have named it in mentioning it for the first time.

Mommsen[8] affirms that the fort mentioned by Dio was undoubtedly Aliso, and that the camp near the source of the Lippe

---

[1] Dio, lvi, 33, 3. Cp. p. 142.
[2] In 25 Augustus's colleague was M. Junius Silanus; in 24 C. Norbanus Flaccus.
[3] See pp. 107 and 161.   [4] ii, 120, 2.   [5] *Ann.*, ii, 7, 5.
[6] *Geogr.*, ed. C. Müller (1883), ii, 11, 14. Ptolemy speaks of Ἀλεισόν, for which one should perhaps read Ἀλεισών or Ἀλισών.
[7] liv, 33, 4.   [8] *Röm. Gesch.*, v, 31, n. 1 (Eng. tr., i, 34, n. 2).

(*ad caput Lupiae*),[1] in which Tiberius had established his winter quarters in A.D. 4, was probably the same. The upper Lippe, he says, has only one noteworthy affluent, the Alme; and close to the confluence is a town called Elsen, on the site of which he locates Aliso, remarking that some weight may be assigned to the likeness between the names. Observing that L. Schmidt places the fort at the confluence of the Liese with the Lippe, near Lippstadt, he objects that this view implies that it was different from the camp *ad caput Lupiae*.

Camille Jullian [2] thinks that Aliso was on the site of Haltern, which is close to the north bank of the lower Lippe, some 27 miles from the nearest point of the Rhine. This view and that of Emil Sadée,[3] who would look for the place between Haltern and the Rhine, perhaps near Dorsten, seem hardly consistent with the statement of Tacitus, for the distance between Haltern and the Rhine is too short.[4]

Edmund Meyer,[5] remarking that Aliso must have been distinct from the *castellum flumini Lupiae adpositum*, decided for Hamm, on the south bank of the Lippe, nearer to the Rhine than to Elsen. This conjecture had been already made, for it is noticed by C. Müller,[6] who points out that Hamm is close to the confluence of the Lippe with the Ahse, which, he says, was formerly called the Alse. Very likely; but is it not rash to assume that Aliso was close to the Alse? The reason that Meyer gave for his decision is, however, worthy of consideration: Drusus, he says, must have placed his fort at a point where it would protect the frontier on the Rhine from raids made through any of the passes in the Teutoburger Wald, and this could only have been done on the middle Lippe.

It seems to me that Mommsen was too confident in affirming that the fort which Dio described was 'undoubtedly Aliso'. If he was wrong, one had better abandon the search, unless some unexpected archaeological discovery should indicate the site.

[1] Vell., ii, 105, 3. *Lupiae*, a correction, made by Lipsius, of *Iuliae*, is certainly what Velleius wrote.   [2] *Hist. de la Gaule*, iv, 110, n. 2.

[3] *Bonner Jahrb.*, cxxx, 1923, pp. 302–9.

[4] Cp. L. Schmidt's remarks in *Korrespondenzblatt d. rom.-german. Komm. d. deutsch. archäol. Inst.*, x, 1926, pp. 113–4. I find that von Domaszewski (*Westd. Zeitschr.*, xxi, 1902, p. 205), who identified the fort at Haltern with the *castellum Lupiae flumini adpositum*, made the same objection.

[5] *Untersuch. über die Schlacht im Teutoburger Wald*, Berlin, 1893, pp. 201–4.

[6] Cp. n. 6 on the preceding page. I find that F. Knoke (*Kriegszüge d. Germanicus*, 1887–97, pp. 317–8) had also decided for Hamm (or rather, to speak more exactly, for Nieubrügge, about a mile from it); but in his second edition (p. 315) he changed his mind and argued enthusiastically for Oberaden.

THE SITE OF THE VARIAN DISASTER

The summer camp, from which Varus started, was in the territory of the Cherusci, on or near the western bank of the Weser;[1]
the tract on which his three legions were annihilated was near Aliso
(the site of which, as I have shown,[2] has not been, perhaps cannot
be, certainly identified), for immediately after the disaster that
fort was blockaded by his assailants.[3] It appears from the narratives of Strabo[4] and Dio[5] that the assailants were the Cherusci and
their dependants, who dwelt between the Weser and the Elbe; from
those of Velleius[6] and Florus[7] that the scene of the disaster was
wooded and marshy, from that of Dio[8] that the woods were pathless—in other words that Varus was not marching on a military
road—and that his object was to suppress a revolt which had been
organized in order to lure him away from his camp; that before the
attack began his troops were making roads and bridges (perhaps
causeways) across places otherwise impassable; that at the end of
the first day's march they encamped on a 'wooded mountain' (ἐν
ὄρει ὑλώδει); that next day, after advancing over open ground,
they plunged again into woods, where, finding themselves in a
narrow pass (στενοχωρίᾳ), they suffered their heaviest losses in
endeavouring to repel attack; and that the final catastrophe took
place on the third day.[9] Velleius[10] relates that Vala Numonius, one
of Varus's officers, forsook his comrades and attempted with the
cavalry, which he commanded, to reach the Rhine. From Tacitus[11]
we learn that in A.D. 15, six years after the disaster, Germanicus

---

[1] Dio, lvi, 18, 5. Cp. p. 117. [2] See pp. 164–5.
[3] Vell., ii, 120, 2.   [4] vii, 1, 4.   [5] lvi, 18, 5.
[6] ii, 119, 2.   [7] ii, 30, 36.   [8] lvi, 19, 3–5; 20–1.
[9] *Ib.*, 21, 2–3. The text of § 2 is corrupt. After relating (§ 1) that on the
second day of the march the troops reached open country and (§ 3) on setting
out thence (ἐντεῦθεν δὲ ἄραντες), plunged again into the woods, Dio continues,
according to the MS., τότε γὰρ 'τῇ τε' ἡμέραι πορευομένοις σφίσιν ἐγένετο,
καὶ αὐτοῖς ὑετός τε αὖθις λάβρος καὶ ἄνεμος μέγας προσπεσών, &c. The words
τότε . . . ἡμέραι obviously need emendation. Dindorf's, τετάρτη τε ἡμέρα,
has been adopted in the latest edition known to me—that of Melber (1928),
who considered that ἄραντες implied the beginning of a third day, and that
the dawn described by the words ἡμέρα πορευομένοις ἐγένετο was that of a
fourth. As I do not think that ἄραντες necessarily means more than 'setting
out', I am inclined to prefer τρίτη, an earlier emendation, to τετάρτη, for I
agree with P. von Rohden (*Paulys Real-Ency.*, ii, 1193) that Dio's narrative,
combined with that of Tacitus, which I shall presently examine, shows that
the third day was the last. Cp. p. 172, n. 1. [I have omitted to notice a later
attempt to amend the text (F. Knoke, *Kriegszüge d. Germanicus²*, 1922,
p. 76), for it seems to me useless.]
[10] ii, 119, 4.   [11] *Ann.*, i, 60; 61.

'devastated the country, between the Ems and the Lippe, not far
from the Teutoburgian forest (*Teutoburgiensis saltus*), in which the
corpses of men who had perished in the legions of Varus were said
to be lying unburied'. Germanicus, he adds, anxious that the last
rites should be duly performed, sent Caecina to explore the recesses
of the forest and to construct bridges and causeways over marshy
land. Caecina discovered 'Varus's first camp' (*prima Vari castra*),
which, Tacitus explains, had evidently been constructed by three
legions; 'further on', he continues, 'the half-completed rampart
[evidently of a camp made on the second day] . . . indicated where
the crippled remnant (*accisae reliquiae*) had made a stand . . . survivors of the disaster . . . told how the legates had fallen here, how
the standards of the legions had been captured there', &c.

Hermann Dessau [1] tells us that early in the sixteenth century
Philip Melancthon originated the view that the Lippischer Wald,
now called the Teutoburger Wald, is identical with the *Teutoburgiensis saltus*. Two centuries later, he continues, Justus Möser
placed the scene of the disaster in the neighbourhood of Osnabrück [2]
—more correctly, for in the so-called Teutoburger Wald the
marshes (*paludes*) in which, according to the best authority,
Varus's legions were destroyed, and to which Germanicus [3] drew
attention, are not to be found, and how could Varus have allowed
himself to be entrapped on or apart from the shortest line between
the Weser and the Lippe in a region which from the time of Drusus
Romans had often trodden? The question of the marshes shall
be examined presently: [4] to those who have gauged the military
ineptitude of Varus and his amazing credulity the answer to the
other is so obvious that I will not waste time by making it. Dessau
concluded, quite truly, that not one of the investigators who preceded him had reached a convincing result, but added that the
opinion of Mommsen deserved the most attention. We shall see.
Meanwhile let us consider the views of Sir Edward Creasy, the
author of *The Fifteen Decisive Battles of the World*, which, between
its publication in 1851 and 1883, was reprinted thirty times.

Creasy begins his narrative [5] with the statement that Varus, in
order to quell the prearranged revolt, 'marched eastward [evi-
dently from the summer camp, which he does not mention, but
seems to place 'near the centre of Westphalia'] . . . parallel to the
course of the Lippe'—a view which may astonish the reader who,
knowing that the summer camp was westward of the Weser, finds
that he places the scene of the disaster near Detmold. 'For some

---

[1] *Gesch. d. Kaiserzeit*, i, 444–5.
[2] Cp. Orelli's edition (1859) of the *Annals* of Tacitus, p. 51.
[3] Tac., *Ann.*, i, 61, 2.   [4] See p. 173.   [5] Pp. 119–22.

distance', he continues, 'his route lay along a level plain; but on
arriving at the tract between the upper part of that stream and the
sources of the Ems, the country assumes a very different character,'
which he proceeds to describe from information furnished by his
friend, Mr. Henry Pearson, and a German scholar, Dr. Plate. The
tract, he assures us, is 'intersected by deep and narrow valleys,
which in some places form small plains, surrounded by steep
mountains and rocks, and only accessible by narrow defiles. All
the valleys are traversed by rapid streams . . . forests [chiefly
oak] . . . cover the hills . . . both men and horses would move with
ease in the forests if the ground were not broken by gulleys, or
rendered impracticable by fallen trees . . . the names of several
localities on and near that spot seem to indicate that a great battle
had once been fought there . . . [for example] "der Winnefeld"
(the field of victory), "die Knockenbahn" (the bone-lane), "der
Mordkessel" (the kettle of slaughter).' Describing the second day's
march, Creasy says, 'After some little time,' during which the
column had been marching under 'heavy torrents of rain', 'the
van approached a ridge of high woody ground . . . between the
modern villages of Driburg and Bielefeld'. Here Creasy apparently
anticipated the view of Edmund Meyer (to be noticed presently),
who located the disaster between the Bielefelder pass and Lippspring.

Mommsen's opinion is to be gathered from a foot-note in the
concluding volume of his *History* [1] and from a treatise,[2] specially
devoted to the question, which was published in the same year,
1885.

In the foot-note he says, referring to the passage which I have
quoted from the *Annals* of Tacitus, 'as Germanicus, coming from
the Ems, lays waste the territory between the Ems and the Lippe.
that is, the region of Münster, and not far from it lies the *Teutoburgiensis saltus*, where Varus's army perished, it is most natural
to understand this description, which does not suit the flat
Münster region, of the range bounding the Münster region on the
north-east, the Osning; but it may also be deemed applicable to
the Wiehen range, somewhat further north, parallel with the
Osning, and stretching from Minden to the source of the Hunte . . .
the summer camp [which, as we have seen, was not far west of the
Weser] . . . was, in accordance with the position of Aliso [as
Mommsen holds, at Elsen[3]] near Paderborn, and with the con-

[1] *Röm. Gesch.*, v, 43, n. 1 (Eng. tr., i, 47, n. 1).
[2] *D. Örtlichkeit d. Varusschlacht*, reprinted from *Sitzungsber. d. K. preuss. Akad. d. Wiss.*, 1885, pp. 63–92, and again in Mommsen's *Gesammelte Schriften* iv. 200–46. [3] See p. 165.

nexions . . . between this and the Weser . . . probably somewhere near Minden. The direction of the march may have been any other except the nearest way to Aliso,[1] and the catastrophe consequently did not occur on the military line of communication between Minden and Paderborn [2] . . . Varus may have marched from Minden somewhat in the direction of Osnabrück, then after the attack have attempted to reach Paderborn, and have met with his end in one of those two ranges of hills'—the Osning and the Wiehen. Mommsen goes on to say that 'there have been found in the district of Venne at the source of the Hunte a . . . large number of Roman gold, silver, and copper coins, such as circulated in the time of Augustus, while later coins hardly occur there at all. . . . The coins thus found cannot belong to one store . . . on account of their scattered occurrence and of the difference of metals, nor to a seat of traffic on account of their proximity as regards time; they look quite like the leavings of a great extirpated army, and the accounts . . . as to the battle fought by Varus may be reconciled with this locality.'

Now for Mommsen's special treatise. Besides much that is contained in the foot-note, it includes other matter. The march, he says, was directed from the summer towards the winter camp, that is, towards the Rhine; for it was made in the autumn by the entire army. It was not made by the direct route, but was deflected to deal with a distant enemy [the tribes who took part in the revolt mentioned by Dio]. The statement of Tacitus, that the country devastated by Germanicus between the Ems and the Lippe was not far from the region in which the corpses of Varus and his legions were lying unburied, shows that the scene of the disaster was north of the Lippe and east of the Ems, and that the said region—the *Teutoburgiensis saltus*—was either the Osning or the Wiehen range. By *prima Vari castra* Tacitus evidently means the first camp reached by Germanicus on his march from the Ems: it follows that the camp was nearer the Ems than was the locality of the disaster, and that Varus changed his direction when the German attack began. But, one asks oneself, what induced Mommsen to abandon the view which he regarded as the 'most natural'—that the description given by Tacitus referred to the Osning range? Simply the coins which he described in his footnote, and of which he had more to say in his treatise. They were found in the vicinity of Barenau,[3] north of Osnabrück in the pass between Venne and Engber; and, as those in the best state of

---

[1] Because (so Mommsen obviously means) the original object of the march was simply to quell a local revolt.

[2] Cp. p. 168.   [3] *Die Örtlichkeit.*, &c., p. 46.

preservation were Augustan, and gold coins of the early Empire are rare in Germany, he inferred that they were lost by the troops of Varus, destroyed on the moor of Venne, which is east of the Ems, just north of the Wiehen range, and about midway between the Ems and Minden. Thus he decided that the *Teutoburgiensis saltus* was the Wiehen range, extending from the Margareta-Clus to Bramsche, on the western bank of the Haase.

Criticism was soon directed against the great scholar. Edmund Meyer[1] insists that the coins could not have been left at Barenau by the legions of Varus: on this question, he observes, the opinion of the best authorities is decisive. E. Ritterling,[2] remarking on the predominance of copper coins in a Roman camp of the early Imperial period, near Hofheim on Mount Taunus (where only 12 *denarii* and *quinarii* were found among about 700) and on other Roman sites, thinks it in the highest degree unlikely that those of Barenau, almost exclusively silver and gold, had any connexion with the disaster. F. Knoke[3] objects that the distance from Bramsche to Barenau is only 14 kilometres (less than 9 miles), and that the space for marching and encamping would have been too small. Besides, he adds,[4] since most of the corpses found by Germanicus were unburied, they must have been despoiled, and, if the final catastrophe had occurred on the moor of Venne, the bones would have sunk. The coins do not show that an entire army was destroyed, for, according to Mommsen himself, they belonged to individual fugitives. Knoke[5] believes that the [alleged] battle-field of Barenau was that of the principal combat in A.D. 15,[6] and, arguing that Varus marched westward from his summer camp up the valley of the Else in order to cross the Osning range concludes that the disaster occurred in the pass of Iburg, south of Osnabrück, which he identifies with the 'narrow place' ($\sigma\tau\epsilon\nu o\chi\omega\rho\iota a$) mentioned by Dio.[7] He thinks that Tacitus in the passage which I have quoted points to a place not far from the Ems, and that Numonius Vala might have attempted to reach the Rhine from the pass, but that from Barenau the attempt would have been hopeless.

Meyer[8] gives reasons for rejecting Knoke's view. He holds that Iburg is too remote from the 'furthest territories of the Bructeri'

[1] *Untersuch. über die Schlacht im Teutoburger Wald*, Berlin, 1893, p. 208, n. 4.

[2] *Ann. d. Vereins f. Nassauische Altertumskunde*, xl, 1912, p. 113, n. 140.

[3] *Kriegszüge d. Germanicus*[2], p. 199.   [4] *Ib.*, pp. 205, 207.

[5] *Ib.*, pp. 198–9, 208 (193–4, 207 of the first edition).

[6] Tac., *Ann.*, i, 63, 1–4.   [7] lvi, 21, 2.

[8] *Op. cit.*, pp. 210–14.

(*ultimos Bructerorum*[1]), to which Germanicus marched when he was
about to ravage the country between the Ems and the Lippe.
Knoke[2] had conjectured that the Bructeran territory did not
extend further eastward than a line extending between Lippstadt
and Iburg: Meyer considered this improbable, for he held that the
Teutoburger Wald was a natural boundary and that the territory
in question must have extended as far as the limit between forest
and inhabited land. Now it is manifestly impossible to define
tribal areas as exactly or as approximately in Germany as in
Gaul;[3] but Meyer's view seems to me reasonable. In a second
edition[4] Knoke, while he somewhat modified his view of the
eastern boundary of the Bructeri, adhered to the opinion that it
extended towards Iburg and not as far as the Osning range.[5]
Meyer,[6] to whom it seems clear that Tacitus, like Dio (so he says),
believed that Varus, after leaving the summer camp, made only
one, holds that by *prima Vari castra* Tacitus meant the former,
from which Varus started. This view seems to Miss Margaret
Alford (so she writes to me) 'to make nonsense'. But, she adds,
'perhaps it is not necessary in order that Tacitus may agree with
Dio. Might not the *accisae reliquiae* [the bones and fragments of
corpses which, according to the same passage in Tacitus, Caecina
found near *prima Vari castra*] have made their poor semblance of
a camp after the point at which Dio leaves off ?' This seems to me
more than unlikely. Dio evidently told the whole story so far as
he could ascertain it and thought necessary, and after the final
catastrophe, with the record of which his narrative ends, the survivors would surely have tried to escape instead of wasting time
in trying to make a camp. In another letter Miss Alford writes,
'Meyer holds that Dio and Tacitus both refer to two camps only,
of which one is the summer camp, and the other was built in the
evening after the start. This seems to me clearly wrong: if *prima
Vari castra* were the summer camp, there would be no point in the
contrast between it and the other.' Just what I had been thinking.
I regard it as certain that Tacitus meant by *prima Vari castra* the
camp which, as Dio says, was constructed on the evening of the
first day's march,[7] and I can only suppose that Dio omitted,

[1] Tac., *Ann.*, i, 60, 5.   [2] Pp. 57, 88 of the first edition.
[3] See *Caesar's Conquest of Gaul*², pp. 344–81 or my edition of the *Commentaries*, 1914, pp. 403–4.   [4] Pp. 66–7.
[5] Knoke also insisted in his second edition (pp. 121–4) that the *ultimi Bructeri* were not those whom Germanicus reached last, but those furthest from Rome. This opinion does not affect Meyer's criticism.
[6] *Op. cit.*, pp. 135–6, 160.
[7] This was the view of P. von Rohden (*Paulys Real-Ency.*, ii, 1192) as well as of Mommsen.

perhaps thought it needless, to mention that another was half constructed after the second.[1]

Meyer begins his own attempt to solve the problem by endeavouring to ascertain where was the summer camp, what were the tribes against which Varus was persuaded by Arminius to march, and by what route he set out to subdue them. If he can do these things, it should be comparatively easy to indicate, at least approximately, the scene of the disaster. Two roads, he explains, from Vetera (near Xanten, opposite the mouth of the Lippe), which was presumably his starting-point, extended along the river, one on each bank, joining apparently at Ringboke or Neuhaus: from the junction two very old commercial roads [2] ran to the Weser, one by Horn and south of Blomberg to Hameln, the other through the Dören gorge. The latter, he remarks, need not be considered; for if it had been the one to which Varus turned after he was attacked,[3] he would have reached it on his westward march, and would have been saved. This statement, unsupported, is a mere assertion. Since, Meyer continues, he turned to the road that passed Horn, the summer camp must have been in the region of Blomberg or Barntrup, which are about 3 miles apart, north of the road.[4] The main point, Meyer says later,[5] is that Varus in his

---

[1] This, I find, was implied by von Rohden (*op. cit.*, 1193). [Miss Alford has asked me a question which I had asked myself in vain—what Mommsen (*Röm. Gesch.*, v, 41, n. 1 [Eng tr., i, 45, n. 1]) meant when he alluded to the description by Tacitus of the three bivouacs. After carefully searching the *Annals* I could only find the well-known description (i, 61, 3) of two. It has been suggested, however, that Tacitus, when he spoke of the 'half-completed rampart' (see p. 167), may have meant that there were later camps, similarly incomplete. 'It is not natural', says the author of this suggestion, 'to understand thus for a reader who does not know the facts, but to those for whom Tacitus wrote the facts would be known or accessible'. The suggestion does not seem to me helpful.]

[2] *Op. cit.*, pp. 222–3. The proof which Meyer adduces of their antiquity—only valid, I would say, if the word 'antiquity' is used loosely—is that both are still frequently called 'Hellwege, i.e. Heerwege' (military roads).

[3] Knoke is his second edition (p. 201) says that there is no indication in our sources that Varus changed his direction. If 'no indication' means 'no direct evidence', this is true.

[4] P. 225; Meyer (*ib.*) says that Generalmajor Wolf (*That d. Arminius*, p. 55) identifies a rectangle at Barntrup, measuring 500 × 300 metres, with the camp constructed by Varus, who, he supposes, had stated at Rinteln, on the evening of the first day's fighting. If it does represent a Roman camp—a question which, Meyer suggests, might be decided by local investigation—Meyer would identify it rather with the summer camp. Rinteln is fully 14 miles in a straight line almost due north of Barntrup, a distance which could not have been covered under such conditions in one day. Jullian (*Hist. de la Gaule* iv, 121, n. 5) thinks that to attempt to locate the camp is hopeless.

[5] P. 229.

march towards the Weser used the road from the source of the
Lippe to Hameln, and must have established his summer camp at
no great distance from it, right or left. From the camp he must
have moved westward or north-westward towards Lemgo, about
10 miles from Blomberg and Barntrup, and have continued on the
same road after he was attacked in order to reach another that
may be supposed to have run southward from Lemgo. Why, the
reader may ask, must he have moved westward or north-westward
from the summer camp? Because, Meyer [1] argues, the rebellious
clans, against which he was persuaded to march, did not belong to
the Cherusci, whom Arminius had represented as loyal, nor to the
Chatti, who had never been subdued, but to the Chauci [2] and the
Bructeri. It does not seem to follow, however, that the objective
of Varus was Lemgo. According to a map published in 1790,
Meyer tells us, [3] the road from Blomberg to Lemgo answers so far to
Dio's description that it crosses several watercourses and extends
along the slope of mountains: indeed it may have been higher than
now if the valley was marshy. [4] The road from Barntrup by Gross-
marpen and Donop answers in some degree to Dio's [5] description,
ἀνώμαλος (uneven); still more the road from Barntrup to Donop.
Meyer [6] conjectures that Varus, after he was attacked—whether
on the first or the second day Meyer feels unable to decide—
changed his westerly or north-westerly direction in order to reach
the road, east or south-east of the place of the first attack, by
which he had marched to the summer camp. He remarks that the
two [or rather three [7]] days' march can hardly, owing to bad
weather, difficult ground, persistent attacks, and the encumbrance
of camp-followers, women, children, and (on the first day) wagons,
have covered more than 2 German (about 10 English) miles. The
scene of the disaster, he concludes, [8] as Mommsen was inclined
to do before he took account of the coins, was in the Osning range
in the region of Detmold in the tract rightly (he thinks) called
Teutoburger Wald—probably in that portion (the Lippischer
Wald) which adjoins on the north-west the part called Egge, between the Bielefelder pass and Lippspring. From the statement

[1] Pp. 190–1.
[2] Dio, lxi, 8, 1. Meyer (p. 191, n. 1) remarks that Χαύκους should be read
here.   [3] Pp. 200, n. 2, 226.
[4] Meyer (pp. 216–17) thinks it needless to search for a site with marshes
(paludes); for, he insists, Velleius and Florus, who mention them, are
rhetorical writers, and the mere fact that Germany was regarded as a land
of forests and marshes would account for their statements. Hardly, I think,
for Velleius's: he knew Germany by experience.
[5] lvi, 20. 1.   [6] Pp. 218–9.
[7] See pp. 166–7, 171–2, supra.   [8] Pp. 197–8, 200, 206.

of Tacitus, that Germanicus ravaged all the land between
the Ems and the Lippe, he infers, naturally enough, that he
marched between them as far as there was anything to be ravaged.
How far? The plain called Die Senne, south of the Lippischer
Wald and south-west of Detmold, is now, he tells us,[1] largely
drained and inhabited: in the time of Germanicus it must have
been marshy. The south-eastern part of the Osning range, where
a monument erected to Arminius may be seen, is the only one, he
remarks,[2] where the defiles described by Dio [3] are to be found.

   Let us come to a decision. Since reasons, which seem to me
sufficient, have been given for rejecting the views of Mommsen and
Knoke, while every site for which argument can be adduced has
been examined, I can only conclude that Meyer's, which coincides
with that of Creasy (except that the latter absurdly brought Varus
to the scene from the west) is substantially right; for, though his
arguments are not always cogent, he was wise, I feel sure, in
adhering to Mommsen's earlier view. But, even if it is impossible
to illustrate the story by a map which may be accepted with confidence—to attempt this on the evidence of Tacitus and Dio is
weary work to any one accustomed to the narrative of Caesar [4]—
we know that the Varian disaster occurred within a very small
area, which can be positively determined; and, apart from topo-
graphy, all that can be learned from it is known.

THE DATE OF THE VARIAN DISASTER

   The army of Varus was destroyed in A.D. 9.[5] Any attempt to
ascertain the month must depend on the supposition, which
Mommsen, rightly, as we shall see, treats as a fact, that Varus
originally intended to march from the summer to the winter camp,
on the statement of Velleius [6] that on the fifth day after the end of
the Pannonian war dispatches announcing the disaster were
received, and upon the interpretation of an entry in the *Fasti
Antiates* under August 3—*Tiberius Augustus in Illyrico vicit*. The
question is whether the entry refers to the capture of Andetrium
(A.D. 9), to the surrender of the Pannonian Bato's troops (A.D. 8),
or to some other event.[7] Otto Hirschfeld [8] argues that the victory
of Tiberius was that which led to the surrender of Bato's troops,
and therefore cannot be used for dating the Varian disaster. This

---

[1] P. 200.   [2] P. 206.   [3] lvi, 20, 1.
[4] I have therefore not attempted on my map to indicate lines of march.
[5] Cp. Mommsen, *Röm. Gesch.*, v, 43, n. 1 (Eng. tr., i, 47, n. 1).
[6] ii, 117, 1.   [7] See pp. 113–5.
[8] *Hermes*, xxv, 1890, pp. 358–62=*Kl. Schr.*, 1913, pp. 394–7.

was the judgement that suggested itself to me when I first approached the discussion of the question: the surrender of the Pannonian troops in A.D. 8 virtually decided the result of the war; therefore, I thought, the *Fasti* must have referred to that year. Hirschfeld fortifies his argument by observing that the capture of Andetrium did not immediately lead to the complete subjugation even of Dalmatia, and that, if it had been referred to in the *Fasti*, Velleius, the whole-hearted admirer of Tiberius, would have celebrated the event in his narrative. Both Velleius [1] and Dio,[2] he adds, emphasize the importance of the surrender; Dio [3] goes on to say that by the end of 8 the subjugation of the Pannonians, except some marauders, was complete; and the mere fact that the success in that year was reported to Augustus by Germanicus [4] proves its paramount importance. It must, however, be remembered that after the surrender of the Pannonian troops the Dalmatian Bato continued to fight until after the capture of Andetrium, and that the triumph of Tiberius, although it was postponed—in fact until October, A.D. 11 [5]—was decreed after that event and in consequence of the termination of the war.[6] Mommsen,[7] commenting on the entry in the *Fasti*, observes that in Illyricum both Dalmatia and Pannonia were then included, and goes on to say that he formerly [8] referred the entry to the capture of Andetrium, but now agrees with Hirschfeld. Edmund Meyer,[9] writing before the publication of Mommsen's commentary, expressed agreement with his earlier view, but rejected the inference which he drew from it— that, since only five days elapsed between the arrangement to celebrate the Illyrian victory and the arrival in Rome of the news of the disaster, and since the celebration did not immediately follow the victory, the disaster must have occurred in September or October, which conclusion, Mommsen added, 'accords with the circumstance that the last march of Varus was evidently the [intended] march back from the summer to the winter camp'. Meyer, remarking that we do not know from what point Velleius reckons the fifth day, nor how long the news of the disaster took to arrive, concluded (evidently disregarding the postponement of the celebration of Tiberius's victory) that the defeat of Varus occurred in the last days of July or the first days of August. No wonder that

---

[1] ii, 114, 4.   [2] lv, 34, 4.   [3] § 7.
[4] Dio, lvi, 17, 1. Note the words καὶ τότε.
[5] See p. 122.   [6] Suet., *Tib.*, 17, 1.
[7] *C.I.L.*, i², p. 323.
[8] *Röm. Gesch.*, v, 43, n. 1 (Eng. tr., i, 47, n. 1).
[9] *Untersuch. über die Schlacht im Teutoburger Wald*, Berlin, 1893, pp. 6–55.

he differs from C. Zangemeister,[1] who, reckoning that the news travelled at the rate of 200 Roman (about 183 English) miles a day, concludes that *via* Xanten it reached Tiberius, who, he supposes, was at Salonae, in 6 or 7 days, and therefore that the disaster occurred on August 1 or 2. An average of 200 miles a day would have been too fast.[2] The question relating to the *Fasti* may be left open, for the reader will presently see that, as regards the date, Mommsen was substantially right.

It may be admitted that, even if Varus intended, before he heard of the local revolt, to march from the summer to the winter camp, the disaster must have occurred before the beginning of August, unless Mommsen was right in reckoning the five days to which Velleius referred, not from the Illyrian victory, but from the arrangement to celebrate it.[3] Now, although Varus doubtless intended to march in due course to the winter camp, there is no direct evidence that he purposed to do so after quelling the revolt. But conclusive evidence there is. If he had not intended to march then to some other camp, he would not have allowed women and children to accompany the column;[4] and the fact that he did shows that the camp to which he intended to go was to be occupied for a long time—in other words, that it was the permanent camp on the Rhine, to which, as Mommsen said, he would naturally have moved in the early autumn. Moreover, what Dio[5] relates about the heavy rains, the violent winds, and the sodden ground that impeded the column suggests that the weather was autumnal;[6] and I therefore conclude that, whatever Velleius may have meant, the disaster occurred about the time of the equinox or in the following month. I say deliberately, 'whatever Velleius may have meant'. If he meant precisely what he said, the 'five days' immediately followed the Illyrian victory. But it would be unsafe to argue that a writer of his stamp did mean exactly what he seems to mean: Mommsen may have interpreted his meaning correctly: anyhow the evidence of Dio is conclusive.

[1] *Westdeutsche Zeitschr. f. Gesch. u. Kunst*, vi, 1887, pp. 239–42. The reader will see that Zangemeister, like Meyer, assumed that the *Fasti* referred to the capture of Andetrium.

[2] See p. 80.

[3] Mommsen evidently had in mind the statement of Dio (lvi, 18, 1) that the Senate's decree for celebrating the victory (*ib.*, 17) had hardly been passed when 'terrible news from the province of Germany prevented them from holding the festival'.

[4] Dio, lvi, 20, 2.

[5] lvi, 20, 3; 21, 3.

[6] I find that this remark was anticipated by P. von Rohden (*Paulys Real-Ency.*, ii, 1194).

IN WHAT RELATION DID AUGUSTUS STAND TO THE TREASURY?

Whether the *fiscus*, properly so called—the imperial treasury, as distinguished from the old State treasury (*aerarium Saturni*[1]) —existed before the reign of Claudius, is doubtful;[2] but, self-evidently, certain moneys, whether they were deposited in one central chest or not, were then treated as belonging to public purposes. Otto Hirschfeld,[3] who holds that the *fiscus* or, let us say, the sum of these moneys, was in no sense the private property of the Emperor, urges that Augustus, by leaving a general statement of the condition of the empire, including particulars of the money in the State treasury and in the *fisci*, to be read after his death,[4] showed that he regarded the matter as one about which the public had a right to be informed. Mattingly,[5] replies, unanswerably, that he 'showed his sense of a moral, not of a legal, obligation'. Again, replying to the same scholar, who adduces the statement of Tacitus,[6] that Pallas, the financial minister (*a rationibus*) of Claudius, had stipulated that, on retirement, he should not be called to account for his administration, as a conclusive proof of his own view, Mattingly remarks that the State could otherwise have required him to give account 'just as the Emperor himself might certainly have been called to give account had he ever retired'. I wonder that he did not appeal to the authority of Dio,[7] who says that Augustus 'controlled the funds' (τῶν χρημάτων κυριεύων), adding that 'nominally he had separated those of the public from his own, but in fact he regularly expended the former also as he thought fit' (λόγῳ μὲν γὰρ τὰ δημόσια ἀπὸ τῶν ἐκείνου ἀπεκέκριτο, ἔργῳ δὲ καὶ ταῦτα πρὸς τὴν γνώμην αὐτοῦ ἀνηλίσκετο). Mattingly[8] is substantially right in saying that 'From the strictly legal point of view the "fiscus" was the property of the Emperor'; but the word 'property' is, I think, liable to be misunderstood. So long as the Emperor remained such, he could not be called to account for his administration.

Before refuting Hirschfeld, Mattingly adduces arguments one of which seems to me superfluous, if not weak. He points to 'the

---

[1] See *The Roman Republic*, iii, 44 and *The Architect of the Roman Empire* (44–27 B.C.), p. 183.

[2] H. Mattingly, *The Imperial Civil Service*, &c., 1910, p. 14. Suetonius, however (*Aug.*, 101, 4), uses the plural, *fiscis*.

[3] *Kaiserl. Verwaltungsbeamten*, pp. 5–13.

[4] Suet., *Aug.*, 101, 4. Cp. Pelham, *Outlines of Rom. Hist.*, 1895, p. 385.

[5] P. 25.

[6] *Ann.*, xiii, 14.

[7] liii, 16, 1.

[8] *Op. cit.*, p. 16.

analogy of the general, who acquired a right of private ownership over the "manubiae"'[1] [money obtained from the sale of booty], but was morally bound to use it 'for public purposes'.[2] Is not the analogy, if it exists, negligible? Did Augustus trouble himself about it? Caesar used *manubiae* largely for what he doubtless regarded as a public purpose—to gain victory over Pompey; but the fortunes which he and his staff amassed were not spent only in this way, and we all know how Lucullus and Crassus used their prize-money.[3] Mattingly affirms[4] that Augustus 'mentions no other sources for his liberalities than the "manubiae" and his own "patrimonium"'[5] (which, as he truly remarks,[6] was regarded under the Julio-Claudian dynasty as 'the family property of the reigning house'), to which I may add what Augustus[7] called 'my own money' (*pecunia mea*). Again, Mattingly[8] emphasizes the statement of Seneca,[9] that all moneys, *fiscus* as well as *patrimonium*, are under the control of the Emperor (*Caesar omnia habet, fiscus eius privata tantum ac sua, et universa in imperio eius sunt, in patrimonio propria*), and holds that 'there is no reason for limiting the application of this passage to the unconstitutional government of [Seneca's contemporary] Nero'. I agree; but Seneca is only repeating in his own way the similar statement, which I have already quoted,[10] of Cassius Dio. ['By the *fiscus*', Mr. Hugh Last asks, 'does one mean a central chest in which moneys were deposited, or a central financial office which co-ordinated the accounts of those items of revenue and expenditure over which the *princeps* had direct control? If, as I do, the latter, then the fact that Augustus could produce such figures as are implied in Suet. *Aug.*, 101, by itself is enough to show that Hirschfeld is wrong in denying the existence of a central *fiscus* before Claudius. . . . Here I agree completely with Mommsen. On the other hand it is difficult to follow Mommsen against Hirschfeld on the relation of the *princeps* to the *fiscus*, and here I believe Mattingly to have backed a loser . . . the arguments attributed to Mattingly about (i) *manubiae* and (ii) Seneca, *de beneficiis*, vii, 6, 3 are really Mommsen's (*Droit public*, v, 290–6).'[11] Mattingly, I may add, refers to Mommsen.]

---

[1] *Op. cit.*, p. 23.   [2] *Ib.*, p. 16.
[3] See *The Roman Republic*, i, 195, 198, 200; ii, 160.
[4] *Op. cit.*, p. 24.
[5] *Mon. Ancyr.*, iii, 8–9, 39, 42; iv, 21, 24.
[6] P. 22.   [7] *Mon. Ancyr.*, iii, 34–5.
[8] P. 24.   [9] *De benef.*, vii, 6, 3.
[10] See p. 177.
[11] Mr. Last cited this translation, not having access to the German text.

WERE THERE KNIGHTS, SO CALLED BY COURTESY, UNDER AUGUSTUS, AS IN THE REPUBLIC?

Mommsen,[1] whose opinion has been supported by A. Stein,[2] holds that there were no knights under the Empire except those properly so called—the *equites equo publico*, or 'Roman knights'— in other words, that the non-military men of business whose property was not less than 400,000 sesterces were no longer recognized as knights.[3] Mattingly,[4] citing Dio, lvi, 42, 3—οἵ τε ἱππεῖς, οἵ τε ἐκ τοῦ τέλους καὶ οἱ ἄλλοι (the knights, military and other), finds 'strong [I should say 'unanswerable'] evidence . . . that the old extended use of the term "ordo equester" . . . continued', and thinks it 'extremely unlikely that those knights who availed themselves of Augustus' permission to resign the "equus publicus" at the age of thirty-five, ceased thereby to be knights'. Besides referring to Pliny's *Naturalis historia*[5] and to an inscription,[6] which Mommsen struggled to explain away, he might have observed that the mere fact of Augustus's having restricted service on juries to knights and to an additional class whose pecuniary qualification was only one half of theirs[7] was not less decisive.

[1] *Röm. Staatsr.*, i, 480, 489.
[2] *D. röm. Ritterstand*, 1927. Cp. Pelham, *Essays*, p. 130, n. 6.
[3] Cp. p. 135.
[4] *Op. cit.*, pp. 57–8.
[5] xxxiii, 1 (7), 29.
[6] G. Wilmanns, *Exempla*, &c., 2097 (=Dessau, *Inscr. Lat.* 6630).
[7] See p. 136.

ADDENDA

PAGE 86 ' . . . the subjection of the Pannonians . . . known.' Was the Sextus Appuleius mentioned in this passage the one referred to by Dio, liv, 30, 4?

PAGES 93–4. Since Professor Anderson's valuable article, 'Augustan edicts from Cyrene', to which I referred in these pages, appeared, he has published in the same periodical (*J.R.S.*, xix, 219–24) a review of 'Die Augustus-Inschrift auf dem Marktplatz von Kyrene' (by J. Stroux and L. Wenger). Remarking that the fourth edict (ll. 65–6) recognizes the governor's competence to decide criminal cases either by his own authority or by trial by jury, and that the decision rested with him, he observes that Stroux and Wenger take the same view in opposition to von Premerstein, who holds that the two methods were not alternatives. 'It would appear, then', he concludes, 'that . . . Augustus recognized and maintained the governor's judicial competence in criminal cases, and this competence is so definitely taken for granted that there is good reason for doubting Mommsen's denial of *Statthalterliches Strafrecht*' (a governor's criminal jurisdiction) 'under the Republic'.

'In *J.R.S.*' (xvii. 45) says Anderson, 'I took the view that the new procedure [under the fifth edict] is established for the trial of less serious cases . . . Von Premerstein took the same view (pp. 479, 516) . . . Stroux argues—and I think he is right—that the new procedure is an alternative to the old, and that the choice . . . lay in the hands of the prosecutors. . . . The new procedure is an illustration of the manner in which Augustus sought to put the relation of the provinces to the imperial government and its representatives on a new basis. But the humane trend of his policy was counteracted by the developments which took place under his successor. . . So long as there was no other tribunal to hear charges of extortion, except the *quaestio*—and he takes the view expressed in *J.R.S.* . . . p. 45, that there was none in 4 B.C.—the new procedure had a chance of developing; but as soon as the Senate became a court for hearing charges of *repetundae*, it was doomed to extinction. . . . A.D. 15 was . . . the turning-point. After that the mild procedure initiated by Augustus was displaced by a rigorous administration of criminal justice, exercised by senatorial *cognitio*.'

PAGE 120 (with which cp. 128). It might be inferred from a statement of Dio (lvi, 23, 4) that the *Germani corporis custodes*, mentioned by Suetonius (*Calig.* 58, 3. Cp. *Aug.* 49, 1), who formed a part of Augustus's bodyguard, were included in the Praetorian guards. He speaks of them as serving ἐν τῷ δορυφορικῷ (in the corps of guards). In the three passages (lii, 24, 3; liv, 25, 6; lv, 10, 10) in which he had before mentioned the δορυφόροι he evidently identified them with the Praetorians: if in lvi, 23 his meaning was different, he was guilty of obscurity. Kenne, however (*Paulys Real-Ency.*, iv, 1900–3), Cagnat (Daremberg and Saglio, *Dict. des ant. grecques et rom.*, ii, 789), and Jullian (*ib.*, 1549) hold that the two bodies were different; and Jullian remarks that the epitaphs of the *custodes* (Dessau, *Inscr. Lat.*, 1721–3, 1725–30) show that they were slaves. Reading Dessau's note (1723), I find that the epitaphs which he prints were those of freedmen and slaves; and Cagnat rightly says that among the *custodes* were both. As their special duty was to guard the person of the Emperor, and as some of them were slaves, they certainly differed from the Praetorian guards, commonly so called; but, unless the authority of Dio is to be ignored, they were popularly regarded as belonging to the corps. I am rather inclined to think that Augusus, who, as is well known, changed the character of the *praetoriae cohortes*, while he retained the name, did not feel it necessary to define the relation of his *corporis custodes* to them, and that Dio may have conformed to popular usage in counting them as part of the corps.

PAGE 122. Mr. Hugh Last suggests that Dr. Hill (now Director of the British Museum), with whom Stuart Jones (*Companion to Roman Hist.*, 1912, p. 424) agrees, may have been wrong in thinking that the Gemma Augustea depicts the triumph of Tiberius. This view, he says, 'involves seeing Germanicus in the figure in the upper register, which looks like a boy of about 12, whereas Germanicus was really in the middle twenties. There is something', he adds, 'in the suggestion that the boy is Gaius Caesar, and the occasion the triumph [in 8 B.C.] after the German war, though this does not fit in so well with Suetonius's story [*Tib.*, 20] of Tiberius's descending from his chariot to do homage to Augustus.' I would suggest that the artist may neither have known nor troubled himself about the age of Germanicus. Stuart Jones says, 'beside the car stands Germanicus, in cuirass and paludamentum', &c. The *paludamentum* was a military cloak worn by a general or a staff officer; in 8 B.C. Gaius Caesar was neither.

INDEX

INDEX OF MODERN COMMENTATORS

[Authors are referred to when their views have been stated or discussed, but not when their works have been merely cited.]

192   INDEX OF MODERN COMMENTATORS

Möser, J., 167.
Müller, C., 165.

NILSSON, M. P., 50 n. 6, 153 n. 1,
154–5.
Nischer, E. von, 112 n. 2.

OWEN, S. G., 42 n. 7.

PARKER, H. M. D., 106 n. 3, 112 n. 2,
128 n. 11.
Pelham, H. F., 29 n. 4, 30 n. 1, 70, 75
n. 6, 149–50.
Premerstein, A. von, 54 n. 7, 90 n. 1,
180.

RAMSAY, A. M., 80 n. 4.
Ramsay, G. G., 58 n. 7, 140 n. 1.
Ramsay, W. M., 1, 54 n. 7, 89.
Ritterling, E., 145–6, 170.
Rohden, P. von. 117 n. 2, 166 n. 9,
172 n. 1, 176 n. 6.
Rolfe, J. C., 135 n. 4.

Rostovtzeff, M., 62, 110 n. 5, 127 n. 6,
146.
Rushforth, G. McN., 86 n. 5, 87 n. 5,
158.

SADÉE, E., 165.
Schmidt, L., 165.
Stein, A., 147, 179.
Steinwerter, 162–4.
Stroux, J., 180.

TOUTAIN, 157.

WARMINGTON, E. H., 23 n. 1.
Wenger, L., 180.
Willems, P., 161.
Willers, 65 n. 1.
Winkelsesser, C., 53 n. 7.
Wissowa, G., 122 n. 2.
Wolf, 172 n. 4.

ZANGEMEISTER, C., 176.

PRINTED IN GREAT BRITAIN AT THE UNIVERSITY PRESS, OXFORD
BY JOHN JOHNSON, PRINTER TO THE UNIVERSITY